On the

PEDAGOGY

of

SUFFERING

Studies in the
Postmodern Theory of Education

Shirley R. Steinberg
General Editor

Vol. 464

The Counterpoints series is part of the Peter Lang Education list.
Every volume is peer reviewed and meets
the highest quality standards for content and production.

PETER LANG
New York • Bern • Frankfurt • Berlin
Brussels • Vienna • Oxford • Warsaw

On the

PEDAGOGY

of

SUFFERING

Hermeneutic and Buddhist Meditations

DAVID W. JARDINE,
CHRISTOPHER GILHAM,
GRAHAM MCCAFFREY,
Editors

PETER LANG
New York • Bern • Frankfurt • Berlin
Brussels • Vienna • Oxford • Warsaw

Library of Congress Cataloging-in-Publication Data

On the pedagogy of suffering: hermeneutic and Buddhist meditations /
edited by David W. Jardine, Christopher Gilham, Graham McCaffrey.
pages cm. — (Counterpoints: studies in the postmodern theory of education; Vol. 464)
Includes bibliographical references and index.
1. Suffering. 2. Suffering—Study and teaching.
3. Education—Study and teaching. 4. Suffering—Religious aspects—Buddhism.
I. Jardine, David William, editor.
B105.S79O5   128'.4—dc23   2014027217
ISBN 978-1-4331-2525-6 (hardcover)
ISBN 978-1-4331-2524-9 (paperback)
ISBN 978-1-4539-1425-0 (e-book)
ISSN 1058-1634

Bibliographic information published by **Die Deutsche Nationalbibliothek**.
Die Deutsche Nationalbibliothek lists this publication in the "Deutsche
Nationalbibliografie"; detailed bibliographic data are available
on the Internet at http://dnb.d-nb.de/.

The paper in this book meets the guidelines for permanence and durability
of the Committee on Production Guidelines for Book Longevity
of the Council of Library Resources.

© 2015 Peter Lang Publishing, Inc., New York
29 Broadway, 18th floor, New York, NY 10006
www.peterlang.com

Printed in the United States of America

Table of Contents

"Just This Once": An Introduction to the Pedagogy of Suffering 1
  David W. Jardine, Graham McCaffrey, and Christopher Gilham

Chapter One: "You're Very Clever Young Man" 7
  David W. Jardine

Chapter Two: Idiot Compassion 19
  Graham McCaffrey

Chapter Three: From the "Science of Disease" to the "Understanding
  of Those Who Suffer": The Cultivation of an Interpretive
  Understanding of "Behaviour Problems" in Children 29
  Christopher Gilham

Chapter Four: A Pocket of Darkness 47
  Judson Innes

Chapter Five: First Fragment: Breaking the Gaze 49
  David W. Jardine, Graham McCaffrey, & Christopher Gilham

Chapter Six: Suffering Loves and Needs Company: Buddhist and
  Daoist Perspectives on the Counselor as Companion 53
  Avraham Cohen & Heesoon Bai

Chapter Seven: Codes 67
  W. John Williamson

Chapter Eight: Second Fragment: Thoughts on "Breaking the Gaze" 71
  Christopher Gilham, David Jardine, & Graham McCaffrey

Chapter Nine My Treasured Relation 75
  Jodi Latremouille

Chapter Ten: Some Introductory Words for Two Little Earth-Cousins 83
  David W. Jardine

Chapter Eleven: This Is Why We Read. This Is Why We Write 87
  David W. Jardine

Chapter Twelve: The Elision of Suffering in Mental Health Nursing 89
  Graham McCaffrey

Chapter Thirteen: Fragment Three: Bringing Suffering into the Path 99
  David W. Jardine, Graham McCaffrey & Christopher Gilham

Chapter Fourteen: A Black Blessing 101
  Alexandra Fidyk

Chapter Fifteen: Time 107
  Judson Innes

Chapter Sixteen: Quickening, Patience, Suffering 109
  David W. Jardine

Chapter Seventeen: Smart Ass Cripple 123
  W. John Williamson

Chapter Eighteen: The Comfort of Suffering 141
  Gilbert Drapeau

Chapter Nineteen: Fragment Four: "And Yet, and Yet" 145
  Christopher Gilham, David W. Jardine & Graham McCaffrey

Chapter Twenty: "Neither They nor Their Reward" 147
  Alan A. Block

Chapter Twenty-One: "Nobody Understood Why I Should Be Grieving" 157
  David W. Jardine

Chapter Twenty-Two: "God's Sufferings Teach God Nothing":
  Some Emails 167
  Alan A. Block & David W. Jardine

Chapter Twenty-Three: Compassion Loves Suffering: Notes on a
    Paper Never Written 171
    Christopher Gilham, David Jardine, & Graham McCaffrey

Chapter Twenty-Four: "Isn't All Oncology Hermeneutic?" 173
    Nancy J. Moules, David W. Jardine, Graham McCaffrey, &
    Christopher Brown

Chapter Twenty-Five: "They Are All with Me": Troubled Youth
    in Troubled Schools 183
    Allan Donsky

Chapter Twenty-Six: Happiness in Bricks 199
    Alexander C. Cook

Chapter Twenty-Seven: Suffering "Like This": Interpretation and the
    Pedagogical Disruption of the Dual System of Education 213
    Christopher Gilham

Chapter Twenty-Eight: Morning Thoughts on Application 227
    David W. Jardine

Chapter Twenty-Nine: In Praise of Radiant Beings 231
    David W. Jardine

Contributor Bios 251
References 255
Index.. 271

"Just This Once": An Introduction TO THE Pedagogy OF Suffering

DAVID W. JARDINE, GRAHAM McCAFFREY,
& CHRISTOPHER GILHAM

The *Descent into the Womb Sutra* states:

> Even though you have been born a human with such limitless suffering, you still have the best of situations. It is difficult to attain this even in ten million eons. Even when a deity dies, the other deities say, "May you have a happy rebirth." By happy rebirth they mean a human rebirth.

> Why would I waste this…good life? When I act as though it were insignificant, I am deceiving myself. What could be more foolish than this? Just this once I am free.

> . . . .

> Although we have sunk into the midst of cyclic existence
> An ocean of suffering with neither bottom nor shore
> We are not disenchanted; we are pleased and excited.
> We boast of happiness. This seems insane.
> (Tsong-kha-pa, 2000, pp. 121, 333)

> We ought to be like elephants in the noontime sun in summer, when they are tormented by heat and thirst and catch sight of a cool lake. They throw themselves into the water with the greatest pleasure and without a moment's hesitation. In just the same way, for the sake of ourselves and others, we should give ourselves joyfully to the practice. (Kunzang Pelden, 2007, p. 255)

Our cover illustration by Katy Orme was done in a wonderful kindergarten classroom. Each year without fail, the teacher selects a particular artist or period of an artist's work, or has a local artist visit the classroom, and this becomes the locale of intense observation, appreciation, and emulation. The children imitate, practice, and talk with each other about the place they have found themselves in. In this particular case, we find ourselves in Pablo Picasso's *Blue Period*. If you are going to venture yourself to this time and place and palette, let alone in the company of very young children, you need to be, well, good. Discussions were had about Picasso's loss of a dear friend, about sadness, about colors and their emotional effects, about how the distortion or elongation of the face helps betray difficult things where words fail and images rise up. The children were gently pushed up against the limitations of the colors available to them and were encouraged to talk about how this hemmed them in and kept them focused and seemed to open up possibilities while at once constricting them. All in all, tough wonderful work. It is a mild and lovely instance of coming to learn through letting oneself undergo the trials and tribulations of a venture beyond oneself and the locales of one's comfort, and to return from that venture changed. It is an instance of the difficult work of pedagogical judgment, where the suicide of Picasso's friend was held in abeyance—too much, it was decided, would overwhelm the venture altogether. That turning thus towards a measure of suffering and endurance and transformation can afford, paradoxically, a great pleasure, is the sweet spot of our considerations of the *pedagogy of suffering*.

Many of our colleagues have been quite adamant: "This seems insane." But then, as teachers (and, we are finding, beyond this to many of those in other professions, and to many in their most intimate lives), we recognize something of the urge to test oneself against the world, to cultivate and practice this tough measure again and again, even though one could just as easily not do so. "Why don't they just stop?" (Jardine, Clifford, & Friesen, 2008, p. 213). Because somehow, despite its lack of necessity and crass, "real-world" utility, the gift of practice, of study, of *deliberately* suffering the consequences of coming to understand, lures and allures because, in its very lack of necessity, attending to suffering portends a lessening of suffering and an upwelling of generosity, love, compassion, and joy that emerges both because of and in spite of suffering itself:

> It is always and necessarily unnecessary. It is excessive (Schrift, 1997, p. 7). It is an abundance (Hyde, 1983, p. 22) that does not diminish but increases in the giving away. It is a form of love because, "as in love, our satisfaction sets us at ease because we know that somehow its use at once assures its plenty" (p. 22). (Jardine, Clifford, & Friesen 2008, p. 211)

This text aims to understand and articulate how and why suffering *can be* pedagogical in character and how it is often key to authentic and meaningful acts of teaching and learning. This is an ancient idea from the Greek tragedies of Aeschylus (c. 525 BCE)—*pathei mathos*, or, "learning through suffering." In our understandable rush to ameliorate suffering at every turn, and to consider every instance of it as an error to be avoided at all costs, we explore how the pedagogy that can come from suffering becomes obscured, and that something vital to a rich and vibrant pedagogy can become lost. This collection threads through education, nursing, psychiatry, ecology, medicine; through scholarship and intimate breaths; and blends together affinities between hermeneutic conceptions of the cultivation of character, and Buddhist meditations on suffering and its locale in our lives.

A key element in contemporary hermeneutic theory of experience is that there is something unavoidably difficult, and transformative, in the act of becoming experienced in the ways of the world. This experience extends across the whole gamut of human life, from small, exhilarating interruptions of one's expectations (moments of inquiry, learning, engagement, investigation, questioning) to traumatic experiences of mortality, impermanence, and illness, to cultural and intercultural, personal and imaginal, histories of grief, conflict, and potential reconciliation. Hermeneutically understood, education is centered on a concept from the Humanist tradition: *Bildung*, a German term meaning "self-formation." It is a process of *becoming someone*, a process that is undergone, endured, or "suffered" in the act of coming to know about oneself and the world.

Key elements of Buddhist thought and practice are insights into the suffering and impermanence of life, and the practices of mindfulness, compassion, and right conduct that might make such suffering endurable. Buddhism also provides articulations of how the panicky retreat from such realities only increases suffering and its hold. Buddhism's understanding of suffering thus provides, in many of the chapters of our text, an elaboration of how suffering can be understood, endured, and utilized as a site for the cultivation of knowledge and wisdom.

We fully understand the fact that all of the professions represented in our text are fraught with both histories and contemporary instances of inflicting suffering, as Alice Miller (1989) horrifyingly put it, "for your own good." We understand how our venture must be met with caution and concern. We know, too, how the amelioration of unnecessary suffering is precisely the work of these disciplines. That is why we will proceed hermeneutically in these explorations, that is, by paying close attention to cases, events, and episodes that open up the nature, limits, dangers, and potentialities of a pedagogy of suffering. We are interested, therefore, in the contingent and difficult *practices* that emerge in our professions around this phenomenon and the comportment of caution and hesitancy that is necessary to such practices precisely *because of* the risk inherent in the phenomenon of suffering. It is through paying close attention to those instances of suffering as a *pedagogic* experience that we can propose ways of finding the optimal balance between the opposite dangers for practitioners of being overwhelmed by suffering, or of denying it through mechanical routines.

We would like to acknowledge our contributors' gifts and thank them for their work. We acknowledge, too, the following journals for their permission to reprint some of the chapters that follow:

CHAPTER 3: Gilham, C. M. (2012). From the "Science of Disease" to the "Understanding of Those Who Suffer": The Cultivation of an Interpretive Understanding of "Behaviour Problems" in Children. *Journal of Applied Hermeneutics*. Retrieved from http://jah.synergiesprairies.ca/jah/index.php/jah/article/view/33

CHAPTERS 4 and 15: Innes, J. (2014). A Pocket of Darkness, and Time. In Seidel, J., & Jardine, D. (2014). *Ecological Pedagogy, Buddhist Pedagogy, Hermeneutic Pedagogy: Experiments in a Curriculum for Miracles* (pp. 102, 109). New York, NY: Peter Lang.

CHAPTERS 5, 8, 13, and 19: Jardine, D., McCaffrey, G., & Gilham C. (2014). The pedagogy of suffering: Four fragments. *Paideusis*, *21*(2), 4–12.

CHAPTER 6: Cohen, A., & Bai, H. (2008). Suffering Loves and Needs Company: Buddhist and Daoist Perspectives on the Counselor as Companion. *Canadian Journal of Counselling/Revue Canadienne de Counseling*, 42(1), 45–56.

CHAPTER 7: Williamson, J. (2012). Codes. *Canadian Journal of Disability Studies*. Retrieved from http://cjds.uwaterloo.ca/index.php/cjds/article/view/47/50

CHAPTER 9: Latremouille, J. (2014). My Treasured Relation. *Journal of Applied Hermeneutics*. Retrieved from http://jah.journalhosting.ucalgary.ca/jah/index.php/jah/article/view/62

CHAPTER 10: Jardine, D. (2014). Some Introductory Words for Two Little Earth Cousins. *Journal of Applied Hermeneutics*. Retrieved from http://jah.journalhosting.ucalgary.ca/jah/index.php/jah/article/view/61

CHAPTER 11: Jardine, D. (2014). This Is Why We Read. This Is Why We Write. *Journal of Applied Hermeneutics*. Retrieved from http://jah.journalhosting.ucalgary.ca/jah/index.php/jah/article/view/64/pdf

CHAPTER 24: Moules, N. J., Jardine, D., McCaffrey, G., & Brown, C. (2013). Isn't All of Oncology Hermeneutic? *Journal of Applied Hermeneutics*. Retrieved from http://jah.synergiesprairies.ca/jah/index.php/jah/article/view/43

CHAPTER 27: Gilham, C. (n.d.). Suffering "*Like This*": The Pedagogical Disruption of Special Education. *Paideusis*.

CHAPTER 28: Jardine, D. (2013). Guest Editorial: Morning Thoughts on Application. *Journal of Applied Hermeneutics.* Retrieved from http://jah.syner giesprairies.ca/jah/index.php/jah/article/view/52

CHAPTER 29: Jardine, D. (2014). In Praise of Radiant Beings. In Seidel, J., & Jardine, D., *Ecological Pedagogy, Buddhist Pedagogy, Hermeneutic Pedagogy: Experiments in a Curriculum for Miracles* (pp. 153–169). New York, NY: Peter Lang.

CHAPTER ONE

"You're Very Clever Young Man"

DAVID W. JARDINE

PRELUDE I: AN INVOCATION FROM ST. JEROME

"I said in my alarm, 'Every man is a liar!' " (Psalm 116:11). The Hebrew text varies a little: "I said in my alarm 'Every man is a lie!' " for the meaning of the word, ZECAM, is lie. I shall please the Lord in the land of the living; but I know that, as far as my body is concerned, I am nothing. There is no truth in our substance, there is only shadow and in a certain sense a lie. As I reflect on human life…I do not find truth in this world. "Lie" is used here in the sense of a shadow, as it were, a phantom. (Saint Jerome, 1964, pp. 293–294, emphasis added)

PRELUDE II: TWO INVOCATIONS FROM TSONG-KHA-PA

Ignorance mistakenly superimposes upon things an essence that they do not have. It is constituted so as to block perception of their nature. It is a concealer. (Tsong-kha-pa, 2002, p. 208)

Unskilled persons whose eye of intelligence is obscured by the darkness of delusion conceive of an essence in things and then generate attachment and hostility with regard to them. (Tsong-kha-pa, 2000, p. 210)

WHAT TRUTH LIES IN THE PHENOMENOLOGICAL
ANCESTRY OF CONTEMPORARY HERMENEUTICS?

This chapter sketches some of my own journey to understand the emergence of the hermeneutics of Hans-Georg Gadamer (1900–2002) from the phenomenological legacies of his teacher, Edmund Husserl (1859–1938), and his older contemporary and teacher, Martin Heidegger (1889–1976). It is not a factual account but an imaginal one, since "what happened" can only be remembered through present circumstances.

As Gary Madison (1988) has pointed out, Edmund Husserl's work is pivotal. "Like many a pivotal thinker, Husserl is an ambiguous figure, and thus the beginning he inaugurated is ambiguous also" (p. xi). It was Husserl, the father of contemporary phenomenology, who broke through the longstanding crust of European philosophizing out into the experience of *the life-world*, the world as lived, lived-experience. It is Husserl's legacy that asks us to now speak of the lives and experiences of children and teachers in school, to speak of the "curriculum-as-lived" and not just "-as-planned" (Aoki, 2005). It was he who deemed the understanding and exploration into this—the land of shadows, one might say, the land of our living—as precisely that which would provide philosophy with a foundation for its work. The pivot, for Husserl and his followers, becomes one of *how* to understand and explore this life-world, and what my relation to that life-world is in such acts of understanding and exploration.

Deeply embedded in Edmund Husserl's work is an old Enlightenment idea that is wrapped up, in part, in an equally deep psychological sense of trauma regarding the experience of life and its ways. Consider this from Husserl's (1970) last great work, *The Crisis of European Science and Transcendental Phenomenology*:

> Can the world and human existence in it truthfully have a meaning if…history has nothing more to teach us than all the shapes of the spiritual world, all the conditions of life, ideals, norms upon which man relies, form and dissolve themselves like fleeting waves, that it always was and ever will be so, that again and again reason must turn into nonsense, and well-being into misery? Can we console ourselves with that? Can we live in this world, where historical occurrence is nothing but an unending concatenation of illusory progress and bitter disappointment? (p. 7)

In another remarkable document written in 1917 to a younger colleague, entitled "A Letter to Arnold Metzger," Husserl (1964) did not hesitate to express some of the missionary zeal that shaped the origins of his subsequent work:

I can only think that you have sensed some of the sustaining ethos through the laconic sobriety and strict concentration on the matters at hand in my writings. You must have sensed that this ethos is genuine, because my writings…are born out of a need, out of an immense psychological need, out of a complete collapse in which the only hope is an entirely new life, a desperate, unyielding resolution to begin from the beginning. The decisive influences, which drove me from mathematics to philosophy as my vocation may lie in overpowering religious experiences and complete transformations. Indeed the powerful effect of the New Testament on a 23-year-old [circa 1882] gave rise to an impetus to discover the way to God and to a true life through a rigorous philosophical inquiry. (p. 56)

And again:

All philosophy bequeathed to us by history proved a failure: marked everywhere by lack of clarity, immature vagueness and incompleteness. There was nothing I could take from it, no fragment one could retain as a solid beginning…boundless and worthless. (p. 56)

The very image of "starting anew" reiterates old Cartesian urges and, back from there, echoes that are far older than that. In the face of the upwelling of the life-world in all its variegation—in the face of *life itself*—there arises a desire for a solid, reliable beginning, a foundation, a fresh start, some foothold, something permanent. This desire resounds up through education as a call of "back to the basics." Not only does this reaffirm a thread, for example, in Dilthey's work ("the inner need to find something firm in the ceaseless change of sense impressions, desires, and feelings, something that enables one's life to be steady and unified" [cited in Gadamer, 1989, p. 238]). It casts our attention back, through St. Jerome's (1964, c. 347–420) meditations on Psalm 115, "There is no truth in our substance, there is only shadow and in a certain sense a lie. As I reflect on human life…I do not find truth in this world" (pp. 293–294).

"There is no truth in our substance." The life-world seems nothing but a lie and a fleeting one at that. Husserl's work delivers us back to the deliciousness and difficulty of living, but then reels and swoons at the sight of it. This is why some versions of phenomenology, at this very pivot point, fall towards the world and the immersion in experience, and many founder in the Romance, lament, and sentiment of it all, even to the ecological extent of praising "becoming animal" (Abram, 2011).

Husserl's work, however, goes in two directions at once. The first is recognition of the viability of the life-world's ways, and an effort to not be bedazzled by the logico-mathematical exactitudes of the natural sciences as if those exactitudes point to "the real world" and all else is mere shadow in its measure. One can read this passage in parallel to the work of students and teachers in the classroom:

> The trader in the market has his market truth. In the relationship in which it stands, is his truth not a good one, and the best that a trader can use? Is it a pseudo-truth, merely because the scientist, involved in a different relativity and judging with other aims and ideas, looks for other truths with which a great many more things can be done, but not the one thing that has to be done in a market? It is high time that people got over being dazzled by the ideals and regulative ideas and methods of the "exact" sciences as though the in-itself of such sciences were actually an absolute norm for objective being and for truth. (1969, p. 278)

Here, Husserl placed the operations of the natural sciences back into the life-world, as *one way among many* in which we make our way in the world. Here, too, he side-stepped the battles between the ways, for example, of the contingent and emergent practical knowledge of teaching and cultivating effective classroom practice (or being a good trader in the market), and the ways of the natural sciences, by saying that the error is found in attempting to make one the measure of the other. Instead, phenomenology is bent on elaborating how each has its own horizon of operation. Each operates relative to its own procedures, histories, modes of knowledge, practices, demands, and forms of evidence, expectations and the like. Each finds its "truth" within itself, not against natural science, as if it were an absolute measure and not merely one (albeit powerful and dominant) way we get along in the world (this would be akin to using Standardized Provincial Examination rank orderings as the measure of classroom practice). The natural sciences cannot, therefore, understand and explore the life-world as a whole (e.g., of the living practices of teaching and learning) without *rendering* that world into something amenable to its logico-mathematical methods (e.g., standardized tests), thus placing an exogenous demand upon those features of the life-world that have a life and a "method" of their own.

To be understood, the life-world of teaching, with all its contingencies and emergent ways, must be understood in its own terms. Hence Husserl's (1969a) repeated call: "to the things themselves."

But then comes the pivot. Husserl instigated a project full of all the rendering hubris of European Enlightenment Rationality: *to find permanence and substance in the land of shadows*, in the life-world.

His phenomenology becomes an "*eidetic phenomenology*" (Gadamer, 1989, p. 254):

Remember that the only alternative to such essentializing, for Husserl, was the pure chaotic flux of incident after incident, never stepping, with Heraclitus, in the same river twice. Identity or sheer difference. Fixed essence or mere nonsensical accident.

There is no comfort in the land of shadows, no noble truth to our suffering. All sense, there, is nonsense. All life is the suffering of one thing after another from which only eidetic fixity can save us.

In fact, Husserl railed against his beloved students, accusing them, in their explorations of finitude, facticity, and existential matters of morality, authenticity, fallenness, life and death, of "succumbing to skepticism, irrationalism and mysticism" (Husserl, 1970, p. 3). He declared that within the orbit of his "pure phenomenology" (p. 5) "occurs *all the problems of accidental factualness, of death, of fate*, of the possibility of a *'genuine' human life* demanded as meaningful in the particular case" (1970b, p. 176). All these "problems" can fall to the fix of essence. Phenomenology is thus formulated by Husserl as a final fulfillment of "humanity's imperishable demand for pure and absolute knowledge" (1965, pp. 72–73).

"Husserl had…argue[d] against Heidegger that the meaning of facticity is itself an *eidos*, and that it therefore belongs essentially to the eidetic sphere of 'universality of essence'" (Gadamer, 1989, p. 255).

The always-oncoming life of the life-world required that Husserl cast phenomenological explication as an "infinite task" (Husserl, 1970, p. 291) even though it remained aimed at fixity. Thus Husserl (1969), this laconically sober, converted Jew, in the lament in the 1931 "Author's Preface to the English Edition" of his *Ideas Towards a Pure Phenomenology*, fully recognized his fate in Mosaic terms:

> The author sees the infinite open country of the true philosophy, the "promised land" on which he himself will never set foot. This confidence may wake a smile, but let each see for himself whether it has not some ground in the fragments laid before him. Gladly would be the hope that those who come after will take up these first ventures, carry them steadily forward, yes, and improve also their great deficiencies and defects of incompleteness. (p. 29)

Germany, 1931, right at the cusp of Husserl's conversion to Christianity in 1879, coming to mean nothing. Concrete facticity: a change in beliefs (his conversion to Christianity) does not entail a change in the Jewish blood of one's birth.

Soon, Husserl himself and so many others would come to be treated as accidental to, and contaminations of, the essence of the German homeland.

A BRIEF PSEUDO-PSYCHOLOGICAL/BIOGRAPHICAL
SPECULATION

> "This apple-tree in bloom, in this garden, and so forth." In the phenomenologically
> pure experience, we find, as belonging to its essence indissolubly the perceived as such,
> and under such titles as "material thing," "plant," "tree," "blossoming," and so forth.
> The *inverted commas* are clearly significant; they express that change of signature.
> The *tree plain and simple*, the thing in nature…can burn away. But the meaning—the
> meaning of this perception, something that belongs to its essence—cannot burn away.
> (Husserl, 1969, pp. 260–261)

So *this* tree can perish—that one, there, that spruce tree plain and simple, the one
my son, decades ago, called, with no prompting or warning, his "life-tree," asking
his mother, then, "Which one is yours?"—but its essential perishability cannot
perish.

Perishability, in essence, is imperishable. Yes. Impermanence is the fixed and
permanent essence of our living. A Noble Truth. What a relief!

Losing a child during the Great War, as Husserl himself suffered, can overwhelm one's life, but the essential *meaning*, the meaning of "losing a child," can
be, *in essence*, "equally accessible to all." I can divest myself of the intimacies of my
life-blood connection to such an event.

Only without attachment can attachment be understood and experienced "in
truth."

Pivot.

Only then can the suffering that shadows the life-world become sufferable.
Only then can we gather together in the shadows.

Compassion for our common lot of living in and through the ambiguity of
this life-world, caught in this lie about truth, where we recognize that essentially
we have no fixed essence that will save us from the suffering of the world. We have
no perch outside of this fray.

That all life is suffering is a Noble Truth only when it is suffered. Martin
Heidegger's (1962) weird adage that our essence is our existence. We have no
"substance." We are shadow.

"COMING TO GRIEF"

"The notion of the life-world has a revolutionary power that explodes the framework of Husserl's transcendental thinking"(Gadamer, 1977, p. 196).

Among the greatest insights that Plato's account of Socrates affords us is that, contrary to the general opinion, it is more difficult to ask questions than to answer them. When the partners in the Socratic dialogue are unable to answer Socrates' awkward questions and try to turn the tables by assuming what they suppose is the preferable role of the questioner, they come to grief. (Gadamer, 1989, pp. 362–363)

Ah yes. Coming to grief. Somewhere around 1973 I was in the middle of my master's degree in philosophy at McMaster University in Hamilton, Ontario. I was taking a graduate course on the work of Martin Heidegger from my thesis supervisor, Gary Madison.

Professor Madison had been instrumental in inviting Hans-Georg Gadamer to teach at McMaster University in Hamilton, Ontario, in the fall semester for a few years running. The first English translation of *Truth and Method* was just about to be published (1975), so his name was still more known than his work. Gadamer had agreed to come to McMaster, in part, because of an important piece that Professor Madison had written defending Gadamer's work against a critique of it found in E. D. Hirsch's (1967) *Validity in Interpretation*. It was read by a student of Gadamer's and, at the latter's request, translated and published in German as "Eine Kritik an Hirschs Begriff der 'Richtigkeit'" (Madison, 1978). The English version later became the first chapter of Madison's (1988) book *The Hermeneutics of Postmodernity: Figures and Themes*.

The topic of my master's degree was *The Question of Phenomenological Immanence* (Jardine, 1976), a study of Edmund Husserl's phenomenology and how phenomenology was able to drag into itself any possible critique by deflecting any possible question or assertion regarding "X" into the phenomenological-noetic question of "*How* is 'X' experienced?" and the phenomenological-noematic question of "*What* is 'X' experienced to be?" Phenomenological immanence, as I then termed it, gobbles up in advance any "question of transcendence" (as I named my last MA thesis chapter) into an "immanent transcendence," a "transcendence-as-experienced," and therefore a transcendence available to phenomenological description and subsequent eidetic variation, because that transcendence now falls within the reflective immanence of pure phenomenological experience. Phenomenology thus pretends to eat up the very impermanence of that apple tree by saying that that impermanence is *itself* an essential characteristic that is not itself impermanent.

Gadamer visited Madison's class on Heidegger. And after a brief talk that has faded from memory, I took the bait.

Why isn't Heidegger's affirmation of the existential character of being human simply an essential characteristic of being human? Isn't finitude itself an essential way in which being human is experienced and therefore part of the Husserlian project?

Professor Gadamer's answer was short and sweet: "You're very clever, young man."

END PART

As you can imagine, I made an appointment to speak with Professor Gadamer at his convenience. He was very good at proving that patience is a virtue. Here was the pull that I could nearly glimpse but not quite, that understanding our lives in the life-world is not just the specialized task of the phenomenologist, nor is it always awaiting the phenomenologist to rescue it from its lack of clarity. Nor is experience especially oriented towards the foreclosures of essences. As I would read and reread years later in *Truth and Method* (Gadamer, 1989):

> The truth of experience always implies an orientation to new experience. "Being experienced" does not consist in the fact that someone already knows everything and knows better than anyone else. Rather, the experienced person proves to be, on the contrary, someone who…because of the many experiences he has had and the knowledge he has drawn from them, is particularly well equipped to have new experiences and to learn from them. Experience has its proper fulfillment not in definitive ["essential"] knowledge but in the openness to experience that is made possible by experience itself. (p. 355)

And then this: "experience is always to be acquired, and from it no one can be exempt. Experience is not something anyone can be spared. Every experience worthy of the name thwarts expectation" (p. 355).

Martin Heidegger (1962) used the term *care* to identify this fundamental lot of being human. As Gadamer spoke in his office, I scrawled notes inside the front cover of *Being and Time*. Then this, perhaps addressed to his beloved teacher, Edmund Husserl, for whom his affection was as clear as his bewilderment: "Care is non-objectifying. It is internal to Being-in-the-world—a process of inner clarification—rather than its domineering father."

The German term that Heidegger uses in *Being and Time* and that is translated as "care," is *Sorge*.

Sorge. It is the root of the English term "sorrow." Little wonder that Heidegger's student and colleague (Gadamer, 1989, p. 356) turned to Aeschylus' image of *pathei mathos*, learning through suffering.

"The genuine result of experience—as of all desire to know—is to know what is" (Gadamer, 1989, p. 357)—the suffering that is at the heart of coming to understand. The well-being of the world and our lives in it are premised on embracing this insight and taking on that suffering as one's calling. This is the pedagogy of suffering that lies in the land of shadows.

CHAPTER TWO

Idiot Compassion

GRAHAM McCAFFREY

Compassion, "suffering with," is bound to suffering and arises in response to suffering. If suffering is part of the human condition, an aspect of experience that calls for understanding and not only complaint, rejection, and avoidance, then compassion cannot be simply a countervailing fix for suffering. If suffering is at least in some aspects pedagogic through its intimate place in ecologies of human life, then compassion also has to be honoured without idealization, along with its aporias, shadows, and absences. Here I explore compassion from various directions, including Mahayana Buddhist archetypes of compassion and wisdom and my own experience as a mental health nurse. Compassion deserves attention—it is worthwhile, which means that it is important but signals that it is not necessarily straightforward. "In asking after worthwhileness, we are asked to find our measure in such things that awaken us and our interest" (Jardine, 2012, p. 176). Necessity instils the tragic into suffering, and it does the same for compassion. Suffering and compassion are bound together dialectically. Exploring compassion critically is not about diminishing compassion or looking for self-protective distance. It is pointing to a fuller appreciation of compassion in a world in which it is, and will go on being, misplaced, misguided, or simply missing. And by world, I include my own "body, speech and mind" (Ehrhard, 1991, p. 25), using an expression from Vajrayana and Zen traditions that prompts attention to how we are immersed in the world.

Trungpa's (2003) pungent, cautionary phrase "idiot compassion" (p. 236) stands as the guiding sign for the following. The phrase is not meant as an insult, but only as a corrective, to keep compassion in proportion, where it belongs with all our emotions, motives, and actions in the phantasmagoria of human consciousness. Compassion is an event, often wonderful when it manifests, but evanescent, complicated, and mercurial. Attempts to essentialize and idealize compassion risk losing sight of the event of compassion in favour of moral exhortation.

COMPASSION'S CONTEMPORARY FACE: COMPASSION WITHOUT HORIZONS

When a colleague and I reviewed the literature about compassion in nursing we found over 2,000 articles published within the past 10 years. The stimulus for much of this material was the debate that has been going on in the UK about appalling incidents of neglect in healthcare settings in the UK. One theme of public concern is that nurses are not as compassionate as they used to be. Is it because they have degrees now, and are "too posh to wash," or conversely because care aides are untrained and underpaid? Or is it that waves of healthcare reform have led to a quasi business environment in which people perform to outcome measures rather than people's needs? One feature of the literature, in defense of compassionate nursing, is to treat compassion as one, if not the, essential feature of nursing. In a book designed to encourage compassionate care, two nurse authors wrote, "Compassion is the essence of caring, and therefore the essence of nursing" (Chambers & Ryder, 2009, p. 2).

Compassion has become popular concern in recent years and not only in relation to nursing. *The Charter for Compassion* was launched in 2009, an online project to elicit commitment to compassionate action, based on principles found in all "religious ethical and spiritual traditions" (Charter for Compassion, 2009). Essentialism is one current in the language of the Charter, which declares itself as a document designed to "restore not only compassionate thinking but, more importantly, compassionate action to the center of religious, moral and political life" (Charter for Compassion, 2009). It is the project of a British ex-nun and religious scholar, Karen Armstrong, who collaborated with religious leaders from different faith traditions to produce "a document that transcends religious, ideological, and national differences" (2009). The text of the Charter itself begins with the assertion that "the principle of compassion lies at the heart of all religious, ethical and spiritual traditions" and goes on, "Compassion impels us to work tirelessly to alleviate the suffering of our fellow creatures" (2009). The Charter presents a smooth, glistening surface that eliminates shadows of human failing, weakness, and, for that matter, humour. The Charter, for all its multifaith ecumenism, comes announced by evangelic trumpets.

Tellingly, the authors of the Charter set out to "restore" compassion to its central place in religion and politics, and to transcend "religious, ideological, and national differences" (2009). Restoration begs the question of when in history did compassion hold the centre of human affairs? Armstrong (2011) suggested there is something about the contemporary world that is uniquely resistant to compassion since capitalism "goes out of its way to encourage us to put ourselves first" (p. 12) and positivist scientists insist that human beings "are programmed to pursue our own interests at whatever cost to our rivals" (p. 11). The idea that the constraints of society distort a human nature which, left to itself, would be creative and cooperative goes back at least to Rousseau, and behind it lies the archetype of a Golden Age.

Transcendence too is problematic. The text of the Charter begins, "The principle of compassion lies at the heart of all religious, ethical and spiritual traditions" (2009). Another call to essence, this time on the grand stage of history. In this case, the claim appears historically dubious at first glance. That compassion is a persistent thread in many religious, ethical, and spiritual traditions would be a more reliable way of putting it. Compassion is worth our attention for that reason; it is a feature of human life and culture that has resonance in most people's experience of relating to others. But is it the single heart of religion, as opposed to say salvation, or even at times sectarian self-righteousness? Even to concede it is a prominent feature of traditions, does it not exist within those traditions as part of an ecology, culturally, linguistically, and historically?

As for the science, Armstrong (2011) enthusiastically took up the fashionable metaphor from neuroscience of the evolution of the human brain, with an old "reptilian" brain driven by primitive appetites and reactions overlaid by a "new" reasoning, caring brain (pp. 13–14). She set up a Manichean conflict between the two brains and concluded that we must make a choice to work at compassion over obedience to primitive drives for food, sex, and fight or flight (p. 22). More transcendence.

The language of the new and the old, the one supplanting the other is reminiscent of the Old and New Testament. "Behold, the days come, saith the Lord, that I will make a new covenant with the house of Israel, and with the house of Judah" (Jeremiah, 31:31).

A yearning for harmony and benevolence freed from the base demands of the flesh, however, is more of a gnostic trope (Layton, 1987) than orthodox Christian. Compassion as moral imperative.

Compassion as inner battle between good and evil, new brain and old brain. Compassion as an independent force that "impels us" (Charter for Compassion, 2009).

Compassion as the distillate of distinct and various traditions.

Armstrong acknowledged that compassion is difficult to achieve, and requires work, but in the way that compassion is presented as a pristine, uncontaminated force the Charter movement takes on the aura of a new religion.

INTERLUDE

The risk of compassion imagined as an essence is that it becomes an ethical Esperanto, unarguable but bland, beyond the reach of contradiction and poetry, addressing everyone and no one. Compassion, like its travelling companion, suffering, calls for many modest truths in the hermeneutic light of *aletheia*, or unconcealment (Heidegger, 1962). In this sense of truth, compassion becomes manifest in an event of practice. Gadamer (2001) caught this sense of truths moving through life in an answer to an interviewer who asked him what had attracted him to phenomenology in the first place: "The answer is simple. I went to Husserl's seminar, and when people spoke in a high-sounding manner he said: 'Not always the big notes! Small change gentlemen!'" (p. 105).

AN EASY MISTAKE

In healthcare it is easy to mistake treatment for compassion, putting recipients of care in the position of consumers whose options are gratitude for correct treatment or anger and litigation against incorrect treatment. Individual encounters between flesh and blood lives are incidental to a structural transaction between provider and consumer, whereby values such as compassion are instantiated in abstract statements of mission and value. "Difficult" patients are ungrateful patients, and "noncompliant" patients an obstacle between the evidence-based fit of treatment and body.

I worked with a leukemia patient facing a long hospital admission for chemotherapy, a man in his forties, leather jacket, quick to anger, verbally abusive— "noncompliant" in healthcare parlance. I knew him in my role as a psychiatric liaison nurse, part of a team with psychiatrists called upon to assess patients in hospital for bodily sickness, who then present with a mental affliction too. The hematology doctors, polite and frustrated, asked repeatedly for our recommendations to make the man into a good patient, one who would stop his quixotic refusals of treatment, his shouting and abuse, his walking off the unit to smoke on a whim.

I used to see him outside at the bike racks where patients went to smoke. I would talk to him while I was locking up my bike in the morning. When we talked there he was usually more relaxed, where he had a few minutes respite from the regimented, lifesaving, chemical kindness of his treatment.

. . . .

The emperor of southern China asked the great master Bodhidharma, "What is the highest meaning of the holy truths?"

Bodhidharma said, "Empty, without holiness."

The emperor asked, "Who is facing me?"

Bodhidharma replied, "Don't know." (Cleary, 2002, p. 2)

. . . .

I worked with the nurse educator on the unit to come up with a care plan, which we then talked over with the patient, setting out clearly the requirements for successful treatment, and some ideas for how he could manage his frustration and fear more civilly. We started with trying to see his suffering, his having a possibly fatal illness, and the pain, discomfort, and uncertainty attendant upon the treatment. The deal is that both patient and clinicians know about this, and accept it as the necessary course of things. Our patient did not recognize the deal—beneath his anger was a fear, and habits formed long ago that immediately converted all anxiety, fear, vulnerability into the currency of anger (so frustrating for the unit staff who worked with him every day—sometimes I was struck by the mismatch between the patient's bombastic offensiveness and his actual powerlessness).

A male nurse on the unit, when I explained our work with the patient on the plan, was completely dismissive. The man was a jerk and that was all he needed to know.

. . . . .

If you perceive the existence of all things
In terms of their essence,
Then this perception of all things
Will be without the perception of causes and conditions.
(Nagarjuna, 1995, p. 69)

In Mahayana Buddhist ontology, phenomena arise both because they are formed by causes and conditions, and because of their intrinsic emptiness. Phenomena can be considered concretely, defined, categorized, and set to work, and they blur, blend, appear, and disappear. Compassion, though prominent in the Buddhist tradition, is, like all phenomena, regarded as without essence, empty, brought about by causes and conditions. Nagarjuna's insight of the two truths, of these states happening together, not one hiding behind the other, is tantalizingly difficult to grasp and downright ordinary. As a way of seeing a human phenomenon such as compassion, it confounds attempts to essentialize while holding to the tenacious fact of our own experience.

. . . .

This is a familiar attitude from working in mental health, that patients are "manipulative" and "behavioural," meaning that the person is entirely responsible for behavior that has fallen foul of nurses' disapproval; it is a curious expression, as if everything humans do is not behavioural. A tension that exists among nurses (among—it flows between individuals and within them, its course shifts constantly) is here in this case. On one side, the need of nurses—some nurses, some of the time—to judge and to hold themselves in the right; on the other side, the recognition of suffering and suffering-with, compassion. Thinking of how the second position looks from the first, I thought of the expression "To understand everything is to forgive everything." Looking for the source, an internet search gave me an attribution to Madame de Stael, but more likely a French proverb, on a site called, "Fake Buddha Quotes" (http://www.fakebuddhaquotes.com/to-understand-everything-is-to-forgive-everything/).

The name of the website is serendipitous, because the expression does sound as though it could be a Buddhist idea, of compassion as transparent understanding, as unconditional forgiveness. Actually, Buddhist thought has a phenomenological clarity that often gets overlooked in the modern, Western search for consoling novelty. Compassion is linked in the first place to suffering, as in the etymological suffering-with, but it also carries the recognition that they are linked forever. Compassion is the answer to suffering in the sense of a response, but not in the sense of a rescuing solution or essential practice.

. . . .

An association between nursing and compassion is not random or willful or superfluous; it is historically and ethically well-grounded, but it cannot be tidily explained by an appeal to essences. Double-sealing nursing into essentialist mandates of compassion and caring claims too much and too little at the same time. It is at once hubristic, as though nurses are supremely compassionate, and crushingly perfectionist in the face of an unlimited ideal. A simplistic formula of equating nursing with compassion makes rhetorical sense but fails at the first encounter with a nurse who is indifferent or preoccupied. The challenge is to keep compassion connected to the vicissitudes of suffering and to retrieve it from essentialism, while trying to make space for the practice of compassion. Compassion,

as a human emotional response, comes and goes. Essence implies a steady state, a dispo-
sition of compassion humming in the background. Are all nurses compassionate because
they are nurses, or are nurses when they are not being compassionate not nurses?

It would be a mistake to ask what then, if not compassion and caring, is the essence
of nursing identity? Identity itself is at issue, and whether the focus should not be on
practice. Davey (2006), in his commentary on Gadamer's hermeneutics wrote:

"Our nature is formed from emergent sets of practical responses to the demands of the
natural and social environment. For a creature without essence, the wisdom and insights
of inherited practice are vital" (p. 55).

. . . .

Does my offering of this particular story from practice, along with my "analysis" mean
I am the compassionate one in the story? On that particular day, perhaps. Was I compas-
sionate towards the frustration of the other nurse? No, I was annoyed. He had to work
with the patient every working day, which I did not.

. . . .

Arriving at a working understanding of why the leukemia patient is a pain is not
going to stop him being a pain; it will not mean that caring for him is not still
likely to be uncomfortable and unpleasant at times. The second link is between
compassion and wisdom: the bodhisattva of compassion, Avalokitesvara, with her
endless capacity to hear the cries of the afflicted, and the bodhisattva of wisdom,
Manjusri, who *cuts off delusion with a sword.*

. . . . .

Chögyam Trungpa (1991) introduced the idea of idiot compassion from a practice tra-
dition. His concern in this passage is not with the role, status, or identity of the person
trying to be compassionate but with the question of whether the action fits the occasion,
whether, in fact, some manifestations of compassion are too idealistic and ultimately id-
iotic.

> *But it is necessary and very important to avoid idiot compassion. If one handles fire wrongly,*
> *he gets burned; if one rides a horse badly, he gets thrown. There is a sense of earthly reality.*
> *Working with the world requires some kind of practical intelligence. We cannot just be "love-*
> *and-light" bodhisattvas. If we do not work intelligently with sentient beings, quite possible*
> *our help will become addictive rather than beneficial. (p. 91)*

Idiot compassion is a phrase that interrupts simple accounts of compassion as an
obvious good, a salve, a balm to pull out on demand. It takes on its meaning and value

in practice and in the moment, unforeseeable and evanescent. To be effective, as Trungpa pointed out, requires grounding in reality and the exercise of judgment.

Avoiding idiot compassion makes demands of the practitioner not only to feel but to judge, to make sense of each occasion of suffering and to respond appropriately.

"If man [sic] always encounters the good in the form of the particular practical situation in which he finds himself, the task of moral knowledge is to determine what the concrete situation asks of him" (Gadamer, 1989, p. 313).

Nursing is a particular form of social role. It is a good conduit for compassion, because of nurses' intentional exposure to others' obvious suffering, but the role itself is nonetheless ultimately empty of a fixed essence, and full, instead, of the dependent arising of circumstances that call for compassionate action.

. . . .

Having some understanding of the leukemia patient, achieved through talking with him as well as about him, does give the nurses the possibility of letting go of the expectation that he will stop being a pain.

. . . .

If living beings suffer adversity
And are oppressed by countless pains,
The power of the wonderful wisdom of the Cry Regarder
Will liberate them from the world's suffering.

Perfect in divine powers,
Practicing wisdom of skillful means everywhere,
Throughout the universe there is no place
Where he does not appear.
(Reeves, 2008, p. 378)

Avalokitesvara, the Cry Regarder, is the Bodhisattva of compassion in Mahayana Buddhist traditions, appearing as a male figure in India and Tibet, and as the female Guanyin or Kannon in China and Japan, respectively (Leighton, 2003). S/he embodies the Mahayana ideal of compassion as completely selfless, as a mark of the emptying out of ego, not in seclusion, but in the midst of the world of suffering and need. The gender shifting, whose historical origins are obscure (Williams, 2009), is nevertheless fittingly symbolic of Avalokitesvara's endlessly plural responses to suffering.

Mahayana imagery often has an ebullient, hyperbolic multiplicity, and one version of the Cry Regarder has a thousand arms and hands, with an eye in each of the palms. "These thousand hands and eyes represent Avalokitesvara's practice of skillful means, compassionately assisting beings by whatever methods would be effective, using whatever comes to hand as a tool" (Leighton, 2003, p. 172). For the ideal figure of the bodhisattva, there is a perfect fit between each instance of pain and its solace, need and provision, problem and solution, which is why in popular religion she is the most popular bodhisattva.

Another image in traditional iconography is the Eleven-Headed Avalokitesvara. One traditional account is that as she was carrying "suffering beings from out of the samsaric realms of birth and death…she looked back and beheld all the spaces in samsara being filled again by new beings, and her head split apart in grief" (p. 171). Even in an archetypal realm, compassion is painful.

. . . . .

Almost incidentally, the patient may become less dependent on holding on to anger as his only way of hearing himself speak. For that to happen he needs to feel he has been heard in his grief. And for that to happen, for the nurse to know compassion, he or she must also touch not only the patient's suffering but Avalokitesvara's grief at samsara forever emptying and filling with new beings.

Where is the contact with grief beneath carapaces of professional experience, judgments, and endless attention to one task after another? Interconnected among causes and conditions, where do the hidden currents of grief and compassion flow beneath healthcare institutions, breaking into the open, disappearing again?

For compassion not to become idiotic, it needs grief as its consort.

AFTERWORD: COMPASSION WALKING

Sake for the body, haiku for the heart;
Sake is the haiku of the body,
Haiku is the sake of the heart (Santoka, 2009, p. 30)

Santoka was a Zen priest and haiku poet active in the first half of the twentieth century. He spent years as an itinerant priest, walking the country, begging to survive, drinking sake and writing haiku. He was well aware of both his alcoholism and his close identification between life and writing poems.

Today, still alive;
I stretch out my feet (Santoka, 2009, p. 86)

Finally, another poem by Santoka—of suffering or compassion?

High noon—in the deep grass
The cry of a frog
Being swallowed by a snake (p. 100)

From the "Science of Disease" to the "Understanding of Those Who Suffer": The Cultivation of an Interpretive Understanding of "Behaviour Problems" in Children

CHRISTOPHER GILHAM

The concern with things which are not understood, the attempt to grasp the unpredictable character of the spiritual and mental life of human beings, is the task of the art of understanding which we call hermeneutics. (Gadamer, 1996, p. 165)

Hans-Georg Gadamer (1900–2002) described hermeneutics as an emancipatory and practical philosophy (1977, p. 17). As a former consultant for "Emotional and Behavioural Disabilities" (EBD) in a large urban public school board, I worked with school teams to support their work with "behaviour" students. While a Faculty of Education PhD candidate specializing in interpretive work, my understanding of "behaviour" students profoundly changed. This emancipatory transformation, at the risk of over-simplifying, was largely the result of understanding some of the history of the Special Education work in which I had been immersed.

In this paper, I attempt to unpack some of the history and current framing of this discourse in schools. Furthermore, I problematize this history as "iatrogenic" (1975, p. 14) and "counterproductive" (pp. 212–214) in the sense articulated by

Ivan Illich (1926–2002). Through this interruption, I hope to offer an emancipating or generous understanding of difficult students in classrooms.

A CENTRAL AND ILLUSTRATIVE ANECDOTE:
SAM OVERFLOWS THE FRAME AROUND HIM

The setting was a highly resourced classroom—8 students and 3 adults—for young children with a particular severe physical disability. The administrator called me to help support her team with a student who was having severe behavioural difficulties. Here is an important, telling segment from my observation notes:

> Teacher asks Sam to come up to the board:
> "Come on Sam. Come here and give it a try."
> Sam looks around at peers. Pauses. Squirms in seat. Flaps arms. Puts fingers in mouth.
> Sam gets up. Slowly moves to front by Teacher while looking at peers and adults.
> Teacher encourages. "It's OK Sam. I'll help you."
> Teacher asks Sam to point to the numbers and count from 1 to 10.
> *Note: peers just counted as a group by 10s to 100 and Sam did not.*
> Sam takes pointer. Teacher helps Sam hold pointer.
> Sam looks at teacher. Sam looks at peers. Sam looks around the room.
> Teacher helps Sam point to 1 and Teacher says "1"
> Sam says "1." Sam's pronunciation is very difficult to understand.
> This pattern moves along to "5" when Sam suddenly throws pointer down, stomps floor, cringes face.
> Teacher: "Sam, that's not OK. We don't throw things here in this classroom. You're upset. Let's go sit down."
> Student aide comes over, standing close to Sam.
> Student aide reaches with her hand to take Sam's hand.
> Sam pulls away and kicks student aide in the shin.
> Student aide grabs Sam by the arm, angry look on face and with Sam resisting, pulls Sam to his desk.
> Sam is screaming and resisting.
> Teacher is now asking other students to follow along with her as she counts by 10s to 100.
> Sam is screaming at his desk.

This pattern continued throughout the morning observation. Sam was angry over getting in line, snack-time, and getting dressed in his winter clothes for recess. He is a very complex little boy, full of frustration.

Consistently frustrated and angry children are not typical in this unique program. It is a program for a particular severe physical disability. The teachers and their administrator feel as if they are not able to help a child like Sam, which is the reason why they asked for my support. Because I have helped many teachers with students like Sam, the administrator also asked me to be part of a larger meeting aimed to help persuade the decision makers in the school board to reconsider the kinds of students who enter the program. Sam and some of his peers are students with severe EBD and might better be educated in a program for students with EBD, the school claimed. Sam and others like him needed different programs that could best fit their "primary needs."

This term "primary needs," common to us in education, reveals a part of what is at play in contemporary education. It hints at a logic structuring the possible ways we think about students. This logic encloses identity. The current frame around the students in Sam's class is determined by the main physical disability coding placed on them as "kinds" (Hacking, 1995, p. 110) of human beings. This limits the ways the school team perceives students and enables the belief that a student like Sam, who also presents with severe behaviours, cannot receive a just education in that specific program.

Put differently, a standardized slotting mechanism dependent on disability status, which is informed by psychiatry's technical categories of human abnormality, and its influence in focusing our gaze in particular ways on student behaviours within classrooms does not seem to serve justice to Sam and others like him. Students that are complex, which most often includes EBD, are beyond Special Education's "wanting and doing" (Gadamer, 1989, p. xxvi). Given this, questions of concern lie within understanding what's at play.

INTERWOVEN, HISTORICAL LOGICS

Unsettled then, overflowing the codification as it were, Sam's anecdote is an example of the "untiring power of experience" (Gadamer, 1977, p. 38). It portends a world much greater, more complex around it. Within the anecdote, there are strong threads of both older and modern "logics" woven together plurivocaly (Weinsheimer, 1991, p. 183). These "threads interweaving and criss-crossing" (Wittgenstein, 1968, p. 32) form the discourse of Special Education. There are other thicker strands intertwined with Special Education as well. Framing students with EBD (and other diagnoses and codes) could be seen as a response to these various historical traditions woven together.

Aristotle's Logic of A=A

The current point of essential power in Special Education in Alberta is coding. The severe EBD coding can only occur if a psychiatrist or registered psychologist diagnoses a student with a disability found in the American Psychological Association's Diagnostic and Statistical Manual (DSM). The DSM clearly states that diagnosis is independent of the rest of the world. As Laurence and McCallum (2009) noted, in the DSM-IV-TR:

> …whatever their original cause, disorders must be considered "a manifestation of a be-havioural, psychological, or biological dysfunction in the individual" and that neither deviant behaviour (e.g. political, religious, or sexual) nor conflicts that are primarily between the individual and the society are mental disorders unless the deviance or conflict is a symptom of a dysfunction in the individual. (p. x)

Key here is the structural logic within the definition. This logic isolates the individual. The disability is inscribed on the person as an inherent abnormality found in the self. The functioning self is "out of order," independently of the world.

Interpretive scholars have argued (Jardine, Clifford, & Friesen, 2008; Kearney, 2003, pp. xxi, 66) that the logic of an independent, self-identifying order can be read back at least to ancient Greece as part of Aristotle's (384 BC–322 BC) logic in his work *Metaphysics*. Aristotle's logic starts with a "first principle" which states: "It is impossible for the same thing to belong and not belong simultaneously to the same thing in the same respect" (Aristotle, *Metaphysics. Book* IV 3 1005b19–20 in Gottlieb, 2011). This is known as the logic of non-contradiction. Such essential knowing could not contradict itself or be different than what we have claimed at the same time and space. For example, Sam's severe physical disability could not also be an EBD. If his primary way of being in the program was through an EBD diagnosis, he could not continue to be in the program designed for his particular severe physical disability. This is the logic of codification and is evidenced in the ways for which students are programmed:

Severe physical disability = program for severe physical disability
Severe EBD ≠ severe physical disability
Therefore, severe EBD ≠ program for severe physical disability
Consequently, severe EBD = program for severe EBD

If Sam were to stay in the program for the severe physical disability the administrator, teachers, and school board officials would need to break out of this applied logic of non-contradiction.

Sam's team and many of my peers in education would readily accept that Sam is more complex than the singularity of the codification and the program as described. Yet, a consistent practice in education is to claim that Sam needs something different than what can currently be provided for because educators are only prepared for the singular, primary codification or, more commonly, teachers in "regular" programming are only capable of working with mainly "regular" students. The inherited logic of A=A seems to profoundly limit educators' ability to see and practice outside a singular conceptualization of the student with Special Education status (or not).

Descartes' Isolated Knowing

Rene Descartes (1596–1650) inherited Aristotle's logic in his attempt to solidify the ground upon which humans could talk about knowing things with certainty. "Cogito ergo sum" was the result of his thought experiment: "I think, therefore I am" (Descartes, trans. 1988, p. 80) This "unshakable proof" for existence happened exclusively, according to this logic, in his mind at the exclusion of the world in which he was immersed (and thus the connection between his logic and the Aristotelian first principle).

Descartes then went back to his experiences of the world with his new certain causal foundation for knowing which allowed him to continue to follow the Aristotelian logic of a substance needing only itself to exist. This was a renewed interpretation of the non-contradictory principle through inner identity-making. Understanding the world was a matter of breaking the world down into its essential features. In the breaking down towards certainty, the world emerged as differentiated objects for study, separated from a diminishing whole.

Auguste Comte's Science, Logical Positivism, and Behaviourism

Comte (1798–1857) believed that science no longer concerned itself with first causes. His emphasis on concrete observations and logical analysis of those observations led to what was called Positivism (Gadamer, 1983, p. 6). According to Illich, Comte was also the first to take the then-expanding use of the term "norm" and apply it to medicine in the "…hope that once the laws relative to the normal state of the organism were known, it would be possible to engage in the study of comparative pathology" (1975, p. 165).

Another radical step was taken by a group of thinkers who believed that statements about the world were nonsensical if they could not directly point to the observed, experienced world in a logical, propositional fashion. This was known as the Correspondence Theory of Truth. Humanity's goal in the pursuit of truth is to simply describe everything as it is, via one singular universal and direct perception system of reality knowing.

Implicit in this system is the perceived direct literalness of human language: our speaking about the truth of things could never be speculative, poetic, metaphorical, "as" something (Davey, 2006; Weinsheimer, 1991, p. 129). Consequently, the aesthetic loses status as a bearer of truth and is relegated to an interpretation of subjectivity that seems powerless socially and communally. Gadamer called this denial of interpretation and historical influence in all human sense-making as the prejudice against prejudice of the Enlightenment period (Gadamer, 1989, pp. 271–273).

Positivism was also taken up in earnest by Ivan Pavlov (1849–1936) and especially B.F. Skinner (1904–1990) in their work on shaping behaviours through direct changes in the observable environment. Any notion of the inner working of the human being such as mental events and meaning-making were considered fictional (Phillips & Burbules, 2000, p. 9). Skinner's work was embraced by education in its attempt to shape students into particular kinds of human beings so that learning and an instrumental, productive society could ensue (Phelan, 1996).

> Positivist psychological theory of disruptive behaviour in school also embraces what is sometimes referred to as learning theory. Children's unacceptable behaviour is learned behaviour and needs to be identified, monitored and redirected. This represents the Skinnerian legacy in schools. Baseline data are gathered, students are regulated, their behaviour modified until elimination of the unwanted behaviour is achieved. (Slee, 1995, p. 96)

Hermeneutic philosopher, Paul Ricoeur (1913–2005), argued that behaviourism works as if human beings are technical, physical objects to manipulate. Through such methodology, the experimenter—an educator perhaps—assumes she/he knows all the variables of the object, and can, by changing such observable variables, extort the appropriate and hypothesized responses from the subject (Ricoeur, 2007, p. 188).

This Ancient-turned-Enlightened logic persists today in Special Education, despite the various research paradigms that emerged within what is generally known as the post-modern age (Sailor & Paul, 2004, pp. 37–45). As Kearney (2003) wrote: "Contemporary thinkers have made much of the fact that the Western metaphysical heritage, grounded in Greco-Roman thought, has generally discriminated against the Other in favour of the same, variously understood as Logos, Being, Substance, Reason or Ego" and "(m)ost ideas of identity, in short, have been constructed in relation to some notion of alterity" (p. 66).

AT PLAY IN EMOTIONAL-BEHAVIOURAL DISABILITIES TODAY

Simplified and Contradicting, Sometimes Paralyzing, Binaries

Sam's anecdote reveals this traditional enlightenment logic. Knowing students is a matter of non-contradiction or identity. Consequently, a fundamental binary logic of identity and difference sit as the magnetic-like forces upon which our understanding of students (and the world) either attracts to or repels. Kearney (2003) and Smith (2006) argued this logical binary has been inherited within the Western discourse of good and evil. Today, students with EBD are often seen as the monsters among us, on the margins within our schools, in jails and hospitals, too (see Chapters 16 and 31). This inherited understanding of difference is different from a logic of conviviality, kin (Jardine, 2012), and mutuality found in other cultures (Smith, 2006, pp. 35–58).

Today Special Education in Alberta insists on this logic of identity and difference. One is able or disabled, normal or abnormal. My observations of students in the unique program resulted in a contradiction within the inherited logic of equating objects with isolated essences or codes. Sam presented more complexly than a singular corresponding code would allow, as evidenced in the singular programming present in the classroom and the teachers' fears that they were not trained to teach students with severe behaviours (Jeary, Couture, & Alberta Teachers, 2009, p. 15). Something comprehensive in our understanding of students has been lost in the reification of a category like EBD via the logic of non-contradiction and the DSM's Skinnerian-like descriptive approach to constituting mental illness (Greenberg, 2010, pp. 238–252). Education's misbehaviour is also concealed in this focus on the disabled, isolated subject as object. Illich (1975) profoundly captured what might be taking place:

> In every society the classification of disease-the nosography-mirrors social organi- zation. The sickness that society produces is baptized by the doctor with names that bureaucrats cherish. "Learning disability," "hyperkinesis" (ADHD today), or "minimal brain function" explains to parents why their children do not learn, serving as an alibi for school's intolerance or incompetence. (p. 169)

As a result "the sick person is deprived of meaningful words for his anguish… his condition is interpreted according to a set of abstract rules in a language he cannot understand" (pp. 170–171) and what was once a rich vocabulary people were able to use to talk about and express their suffering is lost, concealed, and tak- en over by the "increasing dependence of socially acceptable speech on the special language of an elite profession" (p. 171). Gadamer (1996) described this technical knowing, yet limiting phenomenon, as the rational organization of science into a business-like model which has resulted in a general rule for the modern age: "the more rationally the organizational forms of life are shaped, the less is rational judgement exercised and trained among individuals" (p. 17).

The above speaks to the arrival of my current work as a strategist, as well; schools believe they have lost all their means to "control" students with EBD coding and call in the "expert" representing the discourse of Special Education to show them the strategy, the method, the best practice through which control can be had once again. In the process, the question of codification and slotting into further Special Education status emerges, almost inevitably as a result of the perceived inability to deal with the difficulties students present to us, as a result of inherited ways of categorizing the world into either "this" or "that." I can do "this with this," but not "that with that," it seems.

What the experience with Sam demands is

> …a redressing of the balance so as to arrive at a more ethical appreciation of otherness. Such an appreciation reminds us that the human stranger before us always escapes our egological schemas and defies our efforts to treat him/her as a scapegoated 'alien' or, at best, an alter ego. Openness to the Other beyond the same is called Justice. (Kearney, 2003, p. 67)

Moving, Accelerating, and Fragmenting Targets

> In the detection of sickness medicine does two things: it "discovers" new disorders, and it ascribes these disorders to concrete individuals. (Illich, 1975, p. 92)

Depending on time and place, who and what counts as an EBD student differs (Winzer, 2009, pp. 129–153). The logic driving the belief in an autonomous inherent disability within students also conceals the historically effected conditions under which students are seen as having this disability, by whatever names such inherent self-rooted behaviours have and will continue to be called over time.

> As special educators broke diffuse generic concepts into specific categories, the terms for categorical definitions of exactly who was behaviourally disordered constantly expanded, collapsed, and were reenvisioned. …In fact, the terminology used by the educational, legal, and correctional systems became so unclear and overlapping that a 1959 writer chided that "all of these categories, supposedly separate and distinct, represent a paragon of confusion since they may very well describe similar facts. (Clayton, 1959, in Winzer, 2009, p. 132)

As a result there has been a manifold, accelerating increase in codes. Neat little boxes for the autonomously independent and isolated disabilities have become the norm within the abnormal. There is a perpetual, non-stop attempt to categorize everything humans do deemed excessive, inappropriate, or abnormal. Normalcy increasingly disappears.

Illich argued (1975) that the modern medical profession was built upon a foundation of creating objective disease for the purpose of sustaining and enlarging the control and power of the medical bureaucracy. He took a much older and recognized medical phenomenon and applied it to the modern phenomenon I have been describing: "…an expanding proportion of the new burden of disease of the last fifteen years is itself the result of medical intervention in favor of people who are or might become sick. It is doctor-made, or iatrogenic" (p. 14) or, in other words, "all clinical conditions for which remedies, physicians, or hospitals are the pathogens, or 'sickening' agents" (p. 27).

Contemporary education—infused with educational psychology's power, and built upon an industrial model of schooling—is complicit as a "sickening" agent. Our society as iatrogenic (Illich, p. 88) resulting in an entire population as disabled: "At each stage of their lives people are age-specifically disabled" (p. 79).

"Just Plain Sick"

Gary Greenberg (2010) in *Manufacturing Depression* summarized the consequences of having an ever-increasing index cardlike codification of human life:

> We are just plain sick. Which means we can get better. We don't have to look back at the fire that rained down on us or outward to the inhumanity inflicted in the name of prosperity or forward to the certainty of our own suffering. We don't have to be stunned at the cruelty-or, for that matter, thrilled by the tragedy-of life on earth or worried that pursuing happiness the way we do is also pursuing destruction. We can be healed. We can get our minds to work the way they are supposed to. And then we can get back to business. (p. 314)

As Gadamer (1996) noted, this has become possible only in this technical age: "The intrinsic impossibility of simply making oneself an object to oneself emerges completely only with the objectifying methods of modern science" (p. 35). Allen Frances, once head of the now published DSM, is now adamantly opposed to the very idea of the DSM: "We're being overdosed and overmedicated. …We create a society of people who regard themselves as sick" (Wente, 2012). Some argue that in our hopes to preempt inappropriate behaviour we actually constitute more spaces through which we can marginalize children psychologically (Laurence & McCallum, 2009, p. 7).

Being "just plain sick" assumes that our modern medical institution conceals what Illich (1975) termed "the art of suffering" (p. 128), inherent to every traditional culture. Suffering, as a performative activity in traditional cultures, allowed humanity to engage with life fully.

> To be in good health means not only to be successful in coping with reality but also to enjoy the success; it means to be able to feel alive in pleasure and pain; it means to cherish but also to risk survival. … Each culture gives shape to a unique *Gestalt* of health and to a unique confirmation of attitudes towards pain, disease, impairment, and death, each of which designates a class of that human performance that has traditionally been called the art of suffering. (Illich, 1975, p. 128)

In the modern objectifying and levelling science of medicine, there is a "war against all suffering" which has "undermined the ability of individuals to face reality, to express their own values, and to accept inevitable and often irremediable pain and impairment, decline and death" (pp. 128–129). Once categorized or codified, the object that becomes of the human being must now be repaired, healed, or managed in order to get back onto the assembly line of modernity.

Psychiatry struggled to survive within this modern objectification of illness and concealment of suffering. It needed to be like modern medicine and thus the DSM was rewritten to allow for the confirmation of observable symptoms (Greenberg, 2010, pp. 238–252). This "new" DSM also has an early history attached to the emphasis on Positivism seen at the time of Comte through the work of Emil Kraepelin (1856–1926) (Young, 1995, pp. 95–96).

Diagnosing by symptoms as evidence of actual inherent illness or disease is the practice used today in school psychology, which is the necessary condition required for coding (Alberta, 2009). If an expert thinks a student meets the symptomology, validated by the reports of others around the student and forms of mental and behavioural measurement, then the student is diseased just as one might be diseased with cancer or diabetes. The goal in both diagnoses is to heal or manage such disease. Along with Greenberg and Illich, I suggest that life's difficulties, and the suffering that ensues is concealed by the push for dealing with these diseases and getting on with life, the life of production and consumption.

Shrinking "This," Expanding "That"

I argue we are part of a descending ladder of smaller divisions of classifications, a "typology of disasters" (Ricoeur, 2007, p. 196). This complex series of logics inherent in the approach to student (and adult) behaviour is an obstacle holding possibility for seeing and being otherwise chained to sickness. The idea that health is a balance (Gadamer, 1996, p. 19) of life within community is at stake here; any sign of suffering is often taken as disease, categorized and treated individually. Illich (1975) wrote over 35 years ago:

> Diagnosis always intensifies stress, defines incapacity, imposes inactivity, and focuses apprehension on non-recovery, and on one's dependence upon future medical findings, all of which amounts to a loss of autonomy for self-definition. It also isolates a person in a special role, separates him from the normal and healthy, and requires submission to the authority of specialized personnel. Once a society organizes for a preventive disease-hunt, it gives epidemic proportions to diagnosis. The ultimate triumph of therapeutic culture turns the independence of the average healthy person into an intolerable form of deviance. (p. 96)

At risk is our ability to see difference in others outside of the binary of a shrinking "this" and an ever-expanding "that." The norm retracts in the face of an ever-increasing abnormality.

> …as networks of governmental intelligibility grow more rigorous, and ever-increasing numbers of categories of difference are created and deployed…and as new norms of conduct are fashioned and enforced, we should perhaps be concerned that this occurrence is likely to happen with ever greater frequency. It seems somewhat inevitable that tolerance for difference will decrease as the parameters of the normal are more and more tightly drawn and policed, and the consequence may be that more and more children find themselves placed outside the mainstream door. (Tait, 2010, p. 91)

Rights as Choice and Defense

Alberta's education system is a high-pressure consumer-culture of educational choice: "Forced to act as 'citizen consumers' (Taylor and Woollard, 2003), parents shop for the most promising educational opportunities for their children, and the schools try to attract the top students with enrichment programmes" (Graham & Jahnukainen, 2011, p. 230). Families are swept up into this, hoping for further specialization (another form of fragmentation) for the personalized benefit of their children in the hopes they will be successful. Along with this, comes an attitude to preserve or defend the norm for children. It is extremely common in my work for both parents and teachers to claim that students with EBD should not be in regular classrooms because it is unfair to the other children, to have to suffer *that* child. There are times when the safety of children is at risk so the claims are warranted. There are many times though when this is not the case.

Entrenched in this culture of choice and defence are localized notions of the norm: the belief that particular schools are meant for particular kinds of learning, therefore particular kinds of students, especially when "students who constitute a threat to the school in terms of reputation (academic or otherwise) are poorly viewed, which creates hierarchies of student value and innumerable incentives to shift undesirable students elsewhere" (Ball, Gillborn, & Youdell, 2000, in Graham & Jahnukainen, 2011, p. 268).

In many charter and private schools, coded students are often screened out. In the public system, I have been witness to school administrators not accepting students with EBD codes into their schools because those students did not live in the school's designated communities. Yet, there were many students attending these same schools from outside the designated community who did not have an EBD code. The A=A logic finds itself abundant in this market-driven consumer culture of choice and defence and also, at the same time, abundantly selective.

Some argue this neo-liberal, market-driven social imaginary has dismantled a civil society human connection in preference to competitive individualism (Slee, 2011, p. 38; Smith, 2006). High stakes testing and accountability measures provide parents with what is considered rightful knowledge to choose the best education for their children. Choice and competition as "approaches to social policy pit 'different conceptions of rights against one another' as individual competition for public goods works in direct contrast to 'the idea that a universally accessible public education system ought to exist which is available to any [persons] regardless… of economic means'" (Davidson-Harden & Majhanovich, 2004, p. 270, in Graham & Jahnukainen, 2011, p. 280). At risk now in Alberta is a further decline in the idea of a plural school community, in the very idea of "public" education.

This individualism is oddly reversed and exacerbated in Special Education when the categories of EBD garner much attention through public sites. Everyone seems to be able to make a claim about who may or may not have a disability (Greenberg, 2010, p. 251). I constantly deflected teacher and administrator suggestions that their students have ADHD or anxiety, for example. As Laurence and McCallum (2009) wrote, "They (disability categories) are disseminated through a range of sites, including the mass media, so that although they may have begun as a norm implanted from above, they can be repossessed as a demand that citizens, consumers, survivors make of authorities in the name of their rights, their autonomy, their freedom" (p. xiii).

Furthermore, Illich (1975) argued that the above phenomenon is a sign of a "morbid society" where:

> …the belief prevails that defined and diagnosed ill-health is infinitely preferable to any other form of negative label or to no label at all. It is better than criminal or

political deviance, better than laziness, better than self-chosen absence from work… social life becomes a giving and receiving of therapy: medical, psychiatric, pedagogic, or geriatric. Claiming access to treatment becomes a political duty, and medical certification a powerful device for social control. (p. 123)

Coding's In-Efficiency Movement

The industrial production line model in education, a manifestation of the A=A logic, works tirelessly to meet the requirements for its own funding in Special Education. Teams of school psychologists work almost exclusively on social-emotional and cognitive assessments so that school administrators can attach coding status to students which results in increased funding for the school and supports for the students now codified. A part of that funding provided by the codes also pays for the psychologists to do the work needed to acquire the funding. The very system created to support students has resulted in its own army of expert mental measurers who could be directly supporting students in need but instead must spend their time producing psychological assessments to meet the criteria for coding (Janzen & Carter, 2001).

> Special Education funding in Alberta would better serve students who are diagnosed with emotional and/or behavioural disabilities if there was a base level of funding provided that was not attached to coding. Schools would not have to engage in extensive, time-consuming coding processes in order to access needed resources. It is highly detrimental to meeting students' needs to have the funding system leading the pedagogical decision-making, labelling students inappropriately and watering down the real meaning of 'severe disability' or 'severe behavioural disturbance', which has (and still is in many other countries/regions) been relatively rare and associated directly with mental illnesses (Cole, Visser, and Daniels 2001). (Wishart & Jahnukainen, 2010, pp. 186–187)

The government's own contracted research pointed this phenomenon out, as well (Graham & Jahnukainen, 2011).

The Norm: Misleading Logic and Exclusion

The self-fulfilling logic of A=A manifests in Special Education as the statistical norm. According to Ricoeur (2007), assumed within this tool and its creation of the norm is a conflated, misleading logic: the statistical norm is a universal constant, and this constant is separate from the valuative, ideal aspects of the norm in a given culture for example, happiness or success (pp. 189–190). The norm is ambiguous precisely because the tools of mental measurement like the standard bell curve are at once both contingent and expressions of value. Gadamer (1976) wrote: "One look at such fields of investigation as ethnology or history informs us that spaces and times produce highly different life-worlds in which highly different things pass as unquestioningly self-evident" (p. 189). In other words, the norm is relative to culture. "Normality is not an observation but a valuation. It contains not only a judgement about what is desirable, but an injunction as to a goal to be achieved. In so doing, the very notion of 'the normal' today awards power to scientific truth and expert authority" (Rose, 1989, p. 131 in Slee, 1985, p. 20).

Medical science (and Special Education) then carries within it these fixed assumptions, substituting social norms for statistical averages. "What is now normal is behaviour capable of satisfying the social criteria for life together with others" (Ricoeur, 2007, p. 192). In a society that sees the self as a rational, autonomous and freely choosing individual, anything outside of this social norm that requires assistance or control is seen as sickness. Hence, to be healed is to be like others, to act like others. Medicine then becomes an "obstacle to life" because "Life presents itself as an adventure in which we do not know what is a test or trial and what a failure. Life is always evaluated and this evaluation is always relative" (Ricoeur, 2007, p. 190). In the physical world, there is no place for illness (only natural laws like gravity) but in the biological world, the world of life, there is no absolute definition of disease. This is especially the case with EBDs which have changed over time and yet, psychiatry continues to "index card" mental health as sickness.

According to Ricoeur (2007), if one accepts that disease is not univocally understood, we are left with the idea that a human life that is abnormal or pathological is one that lives in a "shrunken milieu" (Kurt Goldstein—not referenced properly, in Ricoeur, 2007, p. 190). This is a claim about being in the world, not sickness. In Special Education, however, this idea of a shrunken milieu is often negatively read as sickness; therefore, being a student that requires severe and extensive support in his learning environment is to be a disabled student. This is because Special Education is founded upon a deficit discourse. The current discourse on pathology conceals the positive aspects of being a student who interacts with his world differently, in a "shrunken lifeworld" which as a form of existing or being in the world, deserves respect as a form of life with its own structure.

This is a very important move on Ricoeur's part. In the interpretive tradition, he attempted to renew our understanding of pathology. Pathos is "suffering" and logia is "to study" (Harper, 2012). Our modern understanding of pathology is the science or study of suffering, of diseases. Ricoeur re-appropriates "logia" as "logos."

Logos has not always been interpreted as an A=A analytical-type proposition for understanding the world, including human beings. Logos also can be read as "being" which is an ontological claim.

"Being," in this renewed ontological reading, wishes to respect Sam as a human life in the world, a world that both shapes and is shaped by Sam and others around him. "Being," in this interpretive sense, entails the understanding that thought does not precede language. Given this, language actually gives form to our understanding of the world. Language is therefore constitutive, and this action is not restrained within the mind of a reasoning being exclusively; nor is it free to be anything it wants. Both the world and those who use language interact. Being human is to be this being that is capable of codetermining being in the world through our full, conscious immersion in and as the world.

Ricoeur's renewal of pathology admits that human beings suffer, and we should study this suffering, but we should carefully consider how we study because in the "studying"—in the sense-making that takes place, like the use of the language of disability and coding—there are moral implications for human beings. These moral implications should help guide our constituting language actions. With great caution however, this does not mean that choosing our words carefully is all that needs to happen, either. The words we use—the language available to us—is deeply impacted by the traditions around us. It is not as if, in simply changing names of EBDs, we get around the deeper logic at play in what might normally be called ordinary language use. On the contrary, seeing the world differently requires seeing how it is that we are currently seeing and once this begins, new possibilities for understanding the world emerge, which is, at once, new ways to talk about others, like Sam.

In short, Ricoeur (2007) and Gadamer (1996) have led me to this understanding: Pathology as "the study of the being of those who suffer" is very different from "the science of disease."

Sadly though, in the anecdote, a student like Sam cannot be seen as co-existing in a relationship with the world that is smaller or more dependent than the ways of being of other, differing students, or other forms of life, despite all of our dependencies in and on the world. It is no surprise that asking Sam to count to ten—an impossible task for him at this time—would cause him intense frustration. The connection here to our understanding of teaching and learning is paramount. Codification within the norm displaces the understanding that humans are different and interact with the world in different ways by identifying this difference as disability or disorder. Whose disorder, I ask? Today, codification results in exclusion, the "social stigma par excellence" where "inferiority and depreciation are thus socially normed" (Ricoeur, 2007, p. 192).

COUNTERPRODUCTIVITY AND EMANCIPATION

"The most primordial mode in which the past is present is not remembering, but forgetting." (Gadamer, 1976, p. 203)

In the entrenched historical logics of knowledge and what has become Special Education for students with EBD, limits are reached and exceeded between the current dominant ways of knowing students, and how students actually live in classrooms. Another way of describing what I have attempted to explicate thus far is through Illich's (1975) notion of "counterproductivity": "It exists whenever the use of an institution paradoxically takes away from society those things the institution was designed to provide" (pp. 212–213). In our industrial society, he wrote that people want "to be taught, moved, treated, or guided rather than to learn, to heal, and to find their own way" (p. 214), and "When perception of personal needs is the result of professional diagnosis, dependence turns into painful disability" (p. 219).

The anecdote with Sam is a particular site of heated contestation around this phenomenon. I suggest Sam's anecdote is a practical, real summons to those of us in education to question that which has been, and continues to be, accepted, and perhaps taken for granted as the only fixed ways of seeing and being with students. How much of what we do in Special Education actually takes away from what we want education to do in the first place? A great deal, I have suggested.

Seeing what is going on around us as effects of our lived history is a way of engaging in emancipative action (Gadamer, 1976, p. 18). This is an act of historical consciousness-revealing, cultivating our ability to see what is or should be questionable (Gadamer, 1976, p. 13). This is also known as a "hermeneutic consciousness" which:

…finds its paradigmatic realization in the interpreter's awareness that the words and concepts he employs are historically conditioned and that they prejudice his interpretation. For this reason, he does not automatically accept their validity or assume their eternal verity; rather he inquires into their origin and history. (Weinsheimer, 1991, p. 229)

Despite experience's overturning actions, it is easy to fall back into the given of current ways of knowing the world because they are our traditions or pre-judgements.

Although our prejudices structure our ways of knowing, they do not restrict us from knowing differently. Gadamer (1976) argued that knowing these traditions as pre-judgements in our daily lives allows us to understand what is happening around us, and to be different (p. 9). Possibilities emerge once we notice *how* we have become, and are always on the way to becoming more than what we currently are. The challenge is to fuse the horizon of the past with the present, in anticipation of a different way of being tomorrow.

SHARED ESTEEM OR "OURSELVES AS OTHERS"

In modern society the "I" of our identity seems determined by a "complete self-transparency in the sense of a full presence of ourselves to ourselves" (Gadamer & Palmer, 2007, p. 239). I am what I see of myself as an independent, rationally acting and therefore free subject.

However, the "I" of self is a work of memory and narration within a life-world with others (Ricoeur, 2007, p. 196). One does not simply make oneself up even within the logic of A=A. Even Descartes' logic could not refute that his thinking took place somewhere, at some time, under some conditions. A part of this dialectical action between world and self requires one to make sense of loss, to mourn those things wanted but not gained, had but lost. Ricoeur (2007) called this the "double labor of memory and mourning that grafts together the sense of self-esteem" (p. 196). This self-recognition as a narrative capable of creating self-esteem is precisely at risk and "attacked in mental illness" (p. 196).

Following Ricoeur (2007), I want to hinge this notion of self-esteem more clearly onto the role of others in the world around us: "self-esteem does not re-duce to a simple relation of oneself to oneself alone. This feeling also includes, within itself, a claim to others. It includes an expectation of approbation coming from these others. In this sense, self-esteem is both a reflexive and a relational phenomenon, where the notion of dignity reunites the two faces of such recog-nition" (p. 196).

For students like Sam, the relationship between himself and the adults around him at school requires what Ricoeur (2007) called a *shared* or *supplementary esteem*. Again, this requires us to recognize the pathological as more than just negative: it is renewed or strengthened as a smaller, different lifeworld for Sam that is some-thing other than "a deficiency, a lack, a negative quality. It is another way of being in the world. It is in this sense that a patient has dignity, is an object of respect" (p. 197). This shared esteem assists "the other to become more resolutely other" and as a result "allows the other to put greater pressure on the adequacy of my self-understanding" (Davey, 2006, p. 249). This is to live in the world, with and for others with dignity, I suggest.

At this point, I finish with Ricoeur's challenge for those of us in the norm:

>...to discern in the handicapped individual those resources of conviviality, of sympathy, of living with and suffering that are bound expressly to the fact of being ill or handicapped. Yes, it is up to those who are well to welcome this proposition regarding the meaning of illness and to allow it to aid them in bearing their own precariousness, their own vulnerability, their own mortality. (Ricoeur, 2007, p. 197)

CHAPTER FOUR

A Pocket OF Darkness

JUDSON INNES

The comfort of timely darkness is banished
by artificial, unearthly glow.
On the extremes of the city the eternal, held off, awaits.

In the coulee a pocket of darkness.
Marbled pairs of reflected light,
briefly glow, then shimmer and fade out.
Alone now, they wind through tangles, relentless,
and re-emerge into one.
Call up to the creators; we are here, we are here.

What of those who occupy the spaces in between,
and linger along the precipice.
Outlines given vague shape by the fleeting;
ephemeral and haunting.
Await the familiar, an echo emerging from below.

CHAPTER FIVE

First Fragment: Breaking THE Gaze

DAVID W. JARDINE, GRAHAM McCAFFREY, &
CHRISTOPHER GILHAM

I

> To have an orientation to the world, however, means to keep oneself so free from what one
> encounters of the world that one can present it to oneself as it is. To rise above the pressure
> of what impinges on us from the world.
>
> HANS-GEORG GADAMER (1989, P. 444), FROM *TRUTH AND METHOD*

This is why hermeneutics is interested in "what happens to us over and above our
wanting and doing" (1989, p. xxviii), not merely what arises from the impingements of our wanting and doing or the wanting and doing of the world. It wants
to break this spell. For the world to present itself to us "as it is" means that what
we can know and experience of the world doesn't just rise up in relation to my
responses to it. Experience and knowledge need not be enslaved to the presumptions of constructivism where I can only make the world in my own image. With
practice, the world can start to "stand there," unlinked to my wanting and doing,
unlinked to my worry or fret.

The deepest stream of our deeply human, deeply animal responses to this
impingement is a sort of panicky retreat from a sense of threat. The deepest consequences of such impingements, so suggests Tsong-kha-pa (2002, p. 120), is
what he calls a "reifying view" wherein the thing that rises up in response to such

impingements becomes taken falsely to be a self-existent object and my responses to it start to kick in. In this cycle, another reification begins that seems to indicate that I, too, am a self-existent "myself" now caught in a death-throes battle with this "other." This (however contingently and occasionally understandable and war-rantable) double root response is the root of suffering itself because it presumes henceforth that there is some permanent object commensurate with our panic about our own frailty, and then sets off the futile pursuit of grasping at straws.

What "stands there," then, in hermeneutics? Not some permanent and self-existent object experienced by a permanent and self-existent self. "There is no truth in our substance" (from St. Jerome's [c. 347–420] commentary on the Psalms, 1964, p. 283). "The concept of substance is …inadequate for his-torical being and knowledge. [There is a] radical challenge to thought implicit in this inadequacy" (Gadamer 1989, p. 242). The radical challenge to thought entails breaking this duplicitous spell–"break[ing] open the *being* of the object" (p. 362, emphasis added) and therefore likewise breaking open the *being* of the one experiencing that object that stands there now broken open (breaking open our understanding and experience of what it means to be an object, what it means to be myself). Hermeneutic experience requires the long and difficult work of stepping out of this duplicity and coming upon "a hitherto concealed experience that transcends thinking from the position of subjectivity" (1989, p. 100) and therefore transcends experiencing things in our world as self-existent, self-contained, separate objects of such a self-existent, self-contained, separate subjectivity.

II

One of the key instances of our panicky retreat that conceals this "transcendent" experience is the fear that arises in an experience of one's own impermanence or the impermanence of the world. This experience of finitude (an experience that is central to hermeneutics) is a key cause of panic and retreat and retrenchment into feigned and delusional graspings at and subsequent attachments to a permanent self and a permanent world and all the vainglorious pursuits that then ensue. In the face of glimpsing the suffering of the world and ourselves—instead of experienc-ing the life-world "as it is"—we easily induce a whole new layer of delusion to pre-vent or conceal this realization, thus causing our suffering to become insufferable.

We then start looking for the cure of suffering within the very falsehoods and forgetfulness that keep it in place.

One common manifestation of this mechanism of delusional retreat is that of anger, one of my own terribly familiar consorts whose dance I've deviled far too often and easily.

So here is the tangle and another meager effort at untangling it all over again. (I need to remember that when Tsong-kha-pa states [2000, pp. 185–186] "the more you practice these things, the more accustomed your mind will become to them" this refers *both* to falling for this anger-cycle and to the work of breaking this spell; it refers equally, also, to cycles of pleasure and joy).

Anger entails being caught in the gaze of the very thing that is the object of anger. It is this persistent gaze that then codifies that object, strengthens it. It is strengthened by my anger, and condoned by all the furious attention I cede to it. It *feeds on* my attention to it. It seeks out my attention, lures it, and adores it, and the more I falsely reify it into something self-existing, the more its gravity (its draw and its seriousness) increases. The more *real* it appears and therefore the more legitimate appears my anger, now deemed a response to it. I might falsely believe that my negative attention towards it will dissipate its hold, but it does not. With my attention, it rises up, and then I rise up, again, to meet that rising.

I thus suffer it under a certain forgetting of my duplicity in its reality, and I blame it for my increasing arousal and anger at its existence. Thus my forgetting (*Lethe*) becomes lethal because I seek a relief to this suffering only *within* this complicity (hint: this is why Martin Heidegger deemed *aletheia* as a path to what is true). My desire to be the winner *in* and *of* this battle only deepens the trench.

Only by freeing myself from this cycle of mutual admiration (it really is admiration; I love my anger sometimes; it can make me feel alive and righteous) can I see it for what it *is*, and out from under the aroused distortions of my complicity in it, and the ways I've been "had" by this cycle. I can begin, however fleetingly and fraily and circumstantially, to feel compassion. I can begin to feel *its* suffering, not simply "my" suffering at its hands ("If only it would stop, I would stop!" Hah!).

Feeling compassion does not mean condoning what is occurring. That, too, attaches me to it (hint: this is why Edmund Husserl [1970] deemed that the phenomenological reduction did not entail an attitude of acceptance or an attitude of negation, but of a "suspension" of our relations to such matters. For Husserl, it was a [phenomenological] method. For his followers, it was a life-long practice, "a task that is never entirely finished" [Gadamer, 1989, p. 301]).

This never entirely finished task is the task of seeing it for what it *is*—a fleeting and impermanent flight of causes and conditions whose fleetingness and impermanence can now be interpreted and unraveled. It is now no longer a "game" we need to let "play" with us (for then it will surely outplay us), but an inheritance which we can now understand and begin to free ourselves from through such insight.

Through the ongoing effort of freeing ourselves from it, we free ourselves *for* it. We can now think and act out of love for this suffering. What changes is not that the world is now finally and fully "cured." What changes is our attachment to and investment in that incurable world, and our ability, for the sake of ourselves and others, to speak about such alluring attachment and the blindness and suffering that it causes.

CHAPTER SIX

Suffering Loves AND Needs Company: Buddhist AND Daoist Perspectives ON THE Counselor AS Companion

AVRAHAM COHEN & HEESOON BAI

Great Doubt, Great Awakening,
Little Doubt, Little Awakening,
No Doubt, No Awakening

ZEN SAYING (BATCHELOR, 2001, P. 29)

The word "suffer" is a variant of the Latin "*suffere;* to bear, undergo, endure, carry or put under," from sub "up, under" + ferre "to carry" (Online Etymology Dictionary, 2001). Note the physicalistic root of the word. A sufferer is one who is struggling, staggering, limping, maybe even collapsing, under the unbearable weight of a burden he or she is carrying. The importance of this physical image for us lies in its elicitation of a certain response from the witness, the counsellor. An ordinary response from us when we see someone staggering under the weight of a burden is to run to his aid, to lend a supportive hand, and even to take on some of the burden. All these and similar responses are solely focused on one thing and only one thing: a human being before you who is suffering. Not a disorder, a diagnostic category, a "case" of suffering, or some other label, but a person who is feeling pain and anguish in-the-moment. Never lose sight of the person (we lean towards the term 'person' in the service of emphasizing the personal nature of the encounter and deconstructing the idea of client or patient as an object upon whom the counsellor bestows treatments or "operates") who is carrying the suffering and see her (in the service of gender equality, we use the pronouns referencing gender randomly throughout our paper) as merely a cluster of symptoms, behaviors, and feelings. This is the fundamental principle for psychotherapy within the traditions of existentialism, humanistic psychology, and Eastern spiritual practices, from within which this paper is theoretically framed. By 'spiritual,' we mean specifically certain altered states of consciousness and a sense of connection characterized by a sense of non-duality between the perceiver and the perceived, subject and object. Such non-dual states can be achieved through practices in breath ('*spiritus*') work as in traditions of Buddhist and Daoist meditations, amongst others (Loy, 1999; Hahn, 2001; Thompson, 1998).

Let us be clear, your task is to see and connect with the person who stands before you (against the usual convention of academic writing, we chose to address the reader sometimes by the familiar 'you' in order to enact the I-Thou connection that we are thematizing in this paper, and to emphasize the significance of the other in the counselling relationship) in anguish and torment; to see *the person* who, however hard to find existentially, exists somewhere behind or within the pain that she is experiencing. Finding the person is difficult for two inter-related reasons: (a) The person's upset is so powerful it cloaks the individual like a dense fog and makes him invisible, and (b) The person's pain has such a strong effect on you that your capacity to see clearly is compromised. Your job is to see this suffering person with your full attention, which does not mean that you will ignore the pain, hers or your own. No, you will certainly be aware of the pain, but focusing on it is to focus on a symptom, which puts the *person*—her existential being—into the background.

The main point we will be making in this paper from various viewpoints, and particularly from Buddhist and Daoist perspectives, is that the underlying need of the suffering person is for ontological security (Laing, 1965) made possible by a two-fold connection: intra-subjective connection to self through integration of emotions, thoughts, and psycho-physical states; and inter-subjective connection to others, and which is initiated and modeled through the process of connection development with you. Both of these connections are invariably in a ruptured condition when a person suffers.

Our job is to find the way to the inter-subjective connection, and utilize this very process to facilitate the person coming back into a conscious connection with herself and with others. With this last comment, we completely endorse R. D. Laing's foundational insight into the therapeutic process: "Psychotherapy is an activity in which that aspect of the patient's being, his relatedness to others, is used for therapeutic ends" (Laing, 1965, p. 26). We base our approach to psychotherapy on the understanding, derived from Becker (1997), Laing, Loy (1996) and others, that suffering is about ontological insecurity based on disconnection from self and other, and a related felt sense of loss of meaning, purpose, and connection. The case that the relationship between counsellor and client is central to the process is not one that has to be made again here, but we will be looking a little more closely at both the psychologically based therapeutic practice, the underlying philosophy that illuminates practice, and the relationship between these two dimensions. This integration of practice and philosophy are the counsellor's meta-dimensions: "Meta-dimensions are the in-the-moment expressions of feelings and attitudes that are reflective of the most deeply held values and beliefs" (Cohen & Porath, 2007, p. 10). As well, we will present some stories from the counseling office based on experience and that are fictionalized to preserve confidentiality to illustrate our thesis.

MEETING THE PERSON: THE I, THE THOU, AND THE I-THOU

In this section, we explicate and illustrate the therapeutic orientation laid out in the previous section. How should a person who walks into a counselling office be met? Should they be met as a case of Anxiety Disorder, Clinical Depression, Borderline Personality Disorder, Post-Traumatic Stress Disorder, or a host of other possible disorders? Or should he or she be met as a person in a distressed state? What is the best way to understand these people and their experience, in terms of alleviating their suffering and helping them towards a felt sense of ontological security? How you proceed with a client depends on how you perceive the human being who is before you. Wittgenstein (1958) spoke of seeing-as, or perception as interpretation, teaching us that we do not just see things but we see things as *this* or *that*. As such, how we approach and treat the being in front of us all depends on how we see-as, frame, or interpret. Focusing on the problems that the client brings and diagnosing him with clinical labels frames the person and disposes the therapist to see him as a case, which creates an objectification of the person. That is, we separate the person from his suffering, ourselves from the person, and then we focus on the suffering as an object of our treatment. In Buber's (1970) terms, the person becomes an "it," an object. The irreducible and singular presence of a human being who stands before you is gone. The inter-subjectivity is also gone. This goes against a primary, and in our view, singularly valuable principle of existential psychotherapy based on the fundamental understanding that humans suffer when they experience twofold disconnections.

Instead of yet again theorizing and explaining further the approach we are taking, we shall illustrate it with an example of I-thou connection in practice:

A client comes to my (Cohen) office. He tells me that he has an addiction to pictures of young children. He says he has never done anything improper with a child and that his experiences are confined to viewing pictures on the internet. He feels shame and guilt. His wife knows about his predilection and is very worried about him and has strong concerns about who she is married to. This man would likely qualify for some kind of label that includes sexual addiction, perhaps pedophilia will come into the diagnosis as well. I hear a story about a man who works hard, is well liked, and is responsible in his life by most standards. I hear about a strict religious upbringing and a culture and family that emphasized that men do not show their emotions. He also describes being beaten for crying as a young boy. When he tells me this I notice a very slight shift in his tone, notice that he swallows a couple of times, and a bit of tightening around his eyes. Simultaneously, I feel a softening and sinking in my chest. I say, "Ah, I feel a pain and poignancy in my heart as you say this. I see an image of you as a small child, and I want to say to you, it's okay. It's okay. I will protect you." He looks at me. His eyes contract. His brow furrows. His mouth tightens. A single tear comes out of the corner of his left eye. Then he lurches forward a little and the floodgate opens. He cries and cries and then says, "Where were you when I was little?" We both know that he is both talking to me and to some guardian that did not exist. I work with him on his capacity to feel his emotions, to show them, to be vulnerable, and to allow others to get close. It comes out that his activities take place when his wife is not home. He is lonely when she is not there, but he hardly knows this because he has learned that he is not to feel or show emotion. Over time he feels his loneliness, shows his vulnerability to his wife (and himself), and begins to express his feelings. His interest in pictures of young children disappears. It turns out that his suffering was actually not about what he was doing, but about the loss of parental love (Schellenbaum, 1990) as a child and the energy it took in his adult life to suppress the emotions he had. He no longer has the need to see small children humiliated and abused because he is now connected with the abused child he was and does not have the false identification with the abuse perpetrator.

This story demonstrates the loss of connection to self and others. He has developed a strategy to cope. His behavior has been in the service of not feeling his pain related to his own childhood experience, his pain around being separate from himself, and his inability to cope with even short term separations from his wife, as they 'remind' him of his other separations, but the reminder is out of his awareness. By working with the lived experience of this person in a compassionate way the psychic numbing is thawed. What is the secret to this thawing moment?

1. The therapist's willingness to allow this person to feel his pain.
2. The person's willingness to allow himself to finally feel his pain.
3. The willingness of both of them to feel, speak, and be seen in their vulnerability. The therapeutic session is about two human beings meeting

authentically, openly, transparently. Let us now look at this possibility of open and honest encounter from a complementary perspective.

An idea that we believe is uncommon even in the counselling world about the development of personality structures and behaviors is that they are in the service of suppressing feeling and numbing psychological pain. Some such as Miller (2005), Schellenbaum (1990), and Reich, (1972) tell us that almost all personality and behavior is formed to provide the service of denying an inner reality that became too painful to endure a long time ago. From a process-oriented perspective (Mindell, 1982) these personality formations constitute limitations on a person's ability to be fully present and fully who he is. These formations are seen as having meaning and intent but also in a state of 'arrested becoming.' In process-oriented psychotherapy terms (Mindell, 2000), the suffering person is at an *edge*, which is simultaneously painful *and* a doorway into unrealized personal potential. It is just that the suffering person is not able to enter the doorway by himself. Too pained to enter the doorway, he unconsciously develops personality structures that are in the service of numbing pain. David Loy (2003), the Buddhist scholar, puts it thus: "the alternative to anesthesia is likely to be depression" (p. 51). His statement is drawn from Luc Sante, who writes, "The potent illusion that drugs provide is called upon when the more commonplace illusions fail, and especially when life appears as nothing more than the conduit between birth and death" (Loy, 2002, p. 179). Clients who come to us in a state of suffering, in fact, are suffering because they are caught between feeling and numbness. Their attempts to alleviate the pain are not working, and they are not able to fully feel the emotions that are affecting them. If they could, they would be able to complete the process that is lodged and immobilized within their psyche-soma. Hence the task of the counsellor is to join with them through companionship and help uncover the feelings that are caught within through compassion: a task that is surprisingly difficult for many counsellors, given the usual orientation of solution-focus and diagnosis.

In the next section, we turn to Buddhist philosophy/psychology to provide some illumination for this challenging task. The reason for our introducing the Buddhist resource is twofold:

1. Diversity and inclusion are the social principle of the contemporary multicultural and cross-cultural society we live in, and thus it is fitting that we look to traditions other than the modern West to bring in complementary approaches.
2. Buddhist and Daoist traditions are rich with resources particularly helpful to the task at hand, as we shall see.

SITTING IN THE MIDST OF FIRE WITH ANOTHER:
A BUDDHIST PERSPECTIVE

A cornerstone precept of Buddhism is compassion—the ability to feel the suffering of another being; in counselling terms, empathy. In Buddhism, four states of consciousness are held up as exemplary and known as "the four *brahma-viharas* ("heavenly abode" or modes of consciousness)—loving kindness [*metta*], sympathetic joy [*mudita*], compassion [*karuna*], and tranquility [*upekkha*]" (Bai, 1996, p. 1). These states of consciousness can be understood as 'being-for,' 'being with in suffering,' 'being with in joy,' and 'simply being,' respectively. Although all four states are interconnected and thus support each other, in this paper, we will focus on compassion (*karuna*) and tranquility (*upekkha*) for their specific relevance to the topic we treat. This ability to suffer with another person is difficult to gain when we are not open and receptive to the other person and her reality of experience because we are busy diagnosing her and thinking about how to solve her problems. For this reason, essential to the cultivation of compassion is the Buddhist 'mindfulness' (*sati*) practice that extends and augments the capacity to be receptive and attentive to the reality before you. Mindfulness practice, also known as Vipassana (insight) meditation, is a capacity-building practice where the ability to be fully present to and be with an experience exactly as it is developed. What prevents the ability to be fully present and fully attentive are all the conditioned mental-emotional-physical-behavioral habits that get built up and create an overlay that buries the authentic self (*bodhicitta* in Buddhist terminology, meaning enlightened heart-mind) of a person. The "goal" of mindfulness is enlightenment, where 'enlightenment' means, in psychological terms, seeing through the build-up of layers of protection and suffocation and into the pulsating and ever-changing 'fluid centre' (Schneider, 2004) that is our being.

It is difficult to be receptive to another's suffering when we are so affected and distressed by the story of suffering that we find ourselves recoiling from the reality of this suffering person and wanting to run away from him. In the current counselling literature, there is a lot of talk about helping professionals' burnout and vicarious trauma. Core to Buddhist training is strengthening of the witness consciousness and its ability to be tranquil (*upekkha*)—the capacity and ability to sit in the midst of raging fire, which life often is, and face *what is*. (In the next section, we will discuss *upekkha* more fully.) Also, if we are distracted because our mind is elsewhere, or bored with the story before us because we have heard the same story in some variation hundreds of times, again we are unable to feel with the sufferer.

The idea of caring, compassion, and equanimity as therapeutic resources is, of course, not restricted to the Buddhist tradition. Carl Rogers (1961), certainly not a Buddhist, has similar ideas and practices about the importance of the therapist's open, authentic, and receptive states of being. He speaks of the foundational conditions for learning in psychotherapy: (a) "The client is, first of all, up against a situation which he perceives as a serious and meaningful problem" (p. 281); (b) "[W]ithin the relationship he (the therapist) is exactly what he *is*—not a façade, or a role, or a pretense" (p. 282); (c) "It involves an acceptance of and a caring for the client as a *separate* person, with permission for him to have his own feelings and experiences, and to find his own meanings in them" (p. 283); and (d) "[T]he therapist is experiencing an accurate, empathic understanding of the client's world as seen from the inside" (p. 284). Rogers, in fact, demonstrates that you do not have to be officially a Buddhist to access and demonstrate holistic human qualities. These qualities transcend traditions and disciplines and are core, in our view, to being a whole human being.

A pertinent question for us to ask is how does a therapist develop compassion. It is too easily assumed that counsellors just have it, which, of course, is not the case. True: we all have the *capacity* for compassion. But the actual *ability* to generously practice or exercise compassion is underdeveloped and limited in most of us, notwithstanding the training that professional cousellors receive. We take the position that these human qualities cannot be trained for, unless we include personal inner work (Cohen, 2006, pp. 30–66), work that facilitates the emergence of the wholeness of the person, as part of the training. As mentioned earlier, our *compassion-ability* is quelled by personality structures that were set up as defense against wounding and pain. What is required to extend our compassion-ability is an on-going process of personal reflection highlighted by the practice of mindful attention that is being explored here.

A person suffers intensely when she perceives that there is no escape, or at least, the exit is not near enough. A person suffers even more intensely when she feels alone in her suffering. When the flesh is pressed into the fire, the flesh burns and the pain is excruciating. If only she could withdraw sufficiently to escape the agony! The person who suffers intensely has no ability to step aside from the burning pain of anguish, hatred, sorrow, and despair. For counsellors the task is to enter the space of the suffering person. The counsellor must join the sufferer in the fire. Your accompanying presence is potentially steadying, calming, and caring for the person in the midst of what seems like an unbearable pain, and your capacity to sit in the fire while it burns without losing your consciousness constitutes both accompaniment and modeling. The counsellor demonstrates that it is possible *to be* with the sufferer and her suffering. In other words, the counsellor models for the client a possibility of being with the person while the latter is in the grip of powerful emotional pain. The opposite, namely marginalizing the client, will occur if the counsellor has no capacity to be with strong feelings or avoids such experiences for his own reasons. The counsellor has to be able to generate a psychic zone of steadfastness and grounded safety for himself, which will offer the opportunity to move towards a more grounded possibility for the client.

This is where we find the Buddhist notion and practice of equanimity (*upekkha*), practiced in mindfulness meditation, most helpful. *Upekkha* is the energetic space (which we will discuss more in the next section) that enables a person to stay grounded in an energetically charged and secure space. Another way to describe this is the ability to stay centered in the midst of strong and swirling emotions. How to do this? There is no short or simple answer since this is not a matter of theoretical understanding. The requirement is practice and more practice of mindfulness, and this work is none other than the work of enlightenment as exemplified in Eastern traditions, which is a life-long learning and practice. In the way we understand and describe a counsellor's work it is, then, nothing other than the work of enlightenment. Theoretically speaking, there is nothing mystifying about enlightenment. Enlightenment is freedom from the conventional, everyday egoic, discursive consciousness that dualistically divides self from no-self, subject from object, and so on. Freedom from this habitual state of consciousness, which results in what is known as non-dual consciousness (Loy, 1999) is enlightenment. But the practice leading to enlightenment is arduous and rigorous. It was only after an original awakening (*bodhi* in Pali and *satori* in Japanese) that Siddhartha saw the world as it is and not as he thought it was or as he thought it *should* be. It was only after a journey of years of searching that he was able to finally 'give up' on the ego-mind's delusion to insist on seeing the world according to his thought-constructs. It was at that moment that he achieved enlightenment. This enlightenment work seems to be the ultimate model for counsellors. Counsellors have daily, indeed, moment-to-moment opportunities to sit in the midst of suffering as it enters our offices with our clients, and of course, as we all know, at times it enters our "office" within us. To the degree that we, the accompaniers, can sit in the midst of the raging fire of life, and engage in our process of becoming enlightened, to that degree can we provide service to the suffering persons who come to us for aid. And each and every time we can practice, however difficult, sitting with our clients in the midst of the pain that accompanies them as they enter our office, we potentially become a little more enlightened.

It can be hell to witness another's suffering. The counsellor, while listening to graphic accounts of suffering opens herself to experience all kinds of strong emotions. She must be willing to enter into the process of learning how to increasingly hold all those strong emotions without being thrown out of consciousness. In fact, the counsellor's capacity to actually feel his or her emotions is a major distinction between her and the sufferer who is partly feeling, partly fearing the feelings, or actively engaging in activities to numb the feelings. "I saw, too, that my willingness to crucify myself on dark impulses and emotions distinguishes me from the criminal, who merely acts on them" (Dallett, 1991, p. 11). For our purposes we substitute the word "sufferer" for the word "criminal." Frequently, the fear is that the feelings will just become increasingly more painful and never ever go away. Below we illustrate the challenge of sitting in the midst of the fire with a client, and how we can work with it. Please bear in mind that this example is presented for purposes of illustration and is not intended as a "method" for replication in a situation that might seem similar.

> A client whom I (Cohen) have seen a number of times comes into my office. She is an attractive, intelligent young woman with a childhood background of physical and sexual abuse and a history that includes two serious suicide attempts in the last five years. Our rapport has been tenuous but positive. She tells me about a number of incidents with a boyfriend that involve, by her report, his statements that he doesn't think he can take her mood swings anymore and his suggestion that he may terminate the relationship. She is deathly afraid of being alone and aside from him has no really substantial contacts with anyone. I listen attentively. She is certainly suffering. Her state does not allow for much sense of anything other than her fragility and her pain and fear. So, while I do feel compassionate, I am aware that she is not really even able to know this. She says, "I'm thinking about killing myself." I say, "I can understand that." This does not seem to be what she expected. She looks at me in a way that suggests that she actually heard my words. She says, "I feel that nothing will ever work out for me. I am miserable. I mess everything up. No one has ever loved me. No one ever will. I am not loveable. I am like a big open pit that sucks in anyone who comes near, chews them up, and swallows them. Who would want to be with someone like that? And, if someone did, they would surely have to be crazier than me? I think that I would be better off dead." She pauses and waits for my response. I imagine she expects me to say something like, "Oh, it's really not that bad. You are smart and pretty. I like you" and so on. In other words, dispute with her, and I consider this possibility, as, at the least, it might get her stirred up and angry with me that I am yet another person who really doesn't understand her experience and her misery. I also, entertain the possibility that she will meekly agree with me, still feel I don't understand, go away feeling very much alone, and possibly make a serious attempt to end her life. So, instead, after a reflective pause, I say, "I am having all kinds of thoughts and feelings, including arguing with you about your experience, but the truth is I really don't know what is right for you. Really, I don't know what is right for anyone. I do know that you have suffered a lot in your life on your own, that you have had to do most things by yourself and that you have felt lonely throughout your life. I am willing to walk down this road with you towards self-destruction. I don't feel you should have to go on such a difficult and painful journey alone. I will walk down the path towards suicide with you. I don't feel you should have to deal with this terrifying and ultimate decision all by yourself. If we

get to that point, I can't say what I will do. I know I am against you killing yourself, but I will walk with you as far as possible. I just really don't want you to have to be alone, yet again, in your life with such a terrifying possibility." There is a palpable silence. She seems dazed. Her eyes widened. She looks directly at me. She literally shakes herself and then says, "Wow, it seems so real when you say it." For the first time in the session she seems animated. Some colour comes into her cheeks. There is a change in the atmosphere of the room. She is crying again, but it is different than before. Something seems to be freed up. The conversation shifts to a more practical level, which is interspersed with tears and childhood memories of abuse, isolation, and feelings of being a strange "other," who was somehow unlike other children.

Enlightenment involves a developed capacity for full awareness in the moment and accepting reality as it actually is. The young woman in the above story is trapped in a world that does not coincide with her dreams and hopes. She wants to be with her boyfriend. She wants to have a happy life. She cannot see how this is possible. In fact, she cannot see how her life will ever be anything but suffering. She sees herself as not lovable and cannot imagine living life as she now experiences it. Her identity is frozen into a configuration that includes these strongly held, unquestioned, and seemingly unquestionable ideas that are seamlessly intertwined with a complex of emotions, body-states, and unconscious patterns and effects of personal history. The outcome is a reaction to a history of feeling unloved, which manifests in the present as a painful disparity between what is and what she longs for. Another way of putting this is that she did not experience a sufficient level of bonding and being loved. From a Buddhist standpoint, she needs to work on letting go of her conditioned image of herself that is unloved and unwanted, and start to build the inner and outer connections that will support the process of developing ontological security. However, the catch here is that in order to be able to let go of one's old and conditioned image of oneself, a person must have sufficient ontological security, and in order to have the latter, one has to be able to do the former! The therapist walks into this double-bind situation, holds the difficult space with mindful presence, and thus lends enough support to enable the client to re-build both ontological security and a letting go of the conditioned self-image. As she experiences an increasing connection to herself and to other significant people in her life, her sense of wholeness grows and she will feel more ontologically secure.

DAOIST PERSPECTIVE AND RESOURCES

In this section, we wish to bring a Daoist perspective to our inquiry into accompanying the sufferer. Daoism too has valuable resources for us, and they can be a supplement to the Buddhist resources we have been working with hitherto. The ancient and one of the most revered texts in Chinese culture, Dao-De-Ching, is full of messages about the master or sage who is in touch with the energy (*qi*) flow of all things. Qi literally means breath or air, and signifies energy that is manifest in all beings and phenomena. Daoism is, besides being a philosophy, a system of somaesthetic practices that enable us to access sources of energy and become energetically empowered. Inasmuch as we see counselling as a mental work, still it is tremendously energy-demanding work. Daoist practices, such as Tai Chi and Qi Gong (just to cite two well-known practices) both work with energy and energy flow. We see such practices as a valuable support to counselling. Space limits a deeper exploration of theory and practice of Daoist energy work, but there is currently a wealth of books, online and multimedia materials on the subject, all demonstrating that Qi work and Daoist philosophy are not esoteric. In contrast, however, there is a relative paucity of materials on applying Daoist work to counselling, which we begin to address herein.

What is the relevance of Daoist work to our discussions about accompanying the sufferer? Our succinct response is that Daoist practice and view of life help us approach and engage with counselling as an energetic work. Clients come to counselling with a felt sense of distress and disorder that pervades their being. Their energy is blocked in various ways and is accompanied by a feeling of disjunct with the world. The counsellor has to not only work with this blocked energy in the client but also empower herself and hold the energetic space for the client and herself to do the counselling work. From a Daoist perspective, the counsellor who is in touch with the Dao field of energy (qi) will represent a centering potential. The energetic presence of the counsellor—the very state and way of being that the counsellor brings to the encounter—has a positive potential to help the suffering person begin to feel her own flow and connection to the world as it is.

In the last story about the woman who was entertaining dark thoughts of ending her life, she was engulfed in a "death-trance." The term 'death-trance' refers to a state of non-feeling, an emotionally vacant state, or, more likely a state of partial feeling that is accompanied by both undifferentiated fear and numbness. From a Daoist frame of reference she is blocked in her connection to her own energy flow and to the energy flow of the world. Being caught in the painful trap of her inner and outer life, she looked towards an ultimate and irrevocable way out of her pain, ending her life. The Daoist psychotherapist's energetic presence can awaken the awareness of the suffering person and help her to unblock from her frozen state of being. In this particular instance, the energy of the client, frozen and contemplating self-annihilation, was joined with by the counsellor and this joining was crucial to the thawing experience. The counsellor's connection with the Dao-Field was extended to and hence inclusive of her and her experience.

From the Daoist perspective, the only relevant question in each situation is whether a person is in touch with the creative and potent Dao-field of energy or not. If a person is, then there is nothing to do, and if they are not, the task is to return to this connection to the field. The identified problem is a signal that in fact the person is out of touch with the Dao-field. The task of the Daoist counsellor is to create conditions where this awareness is catalyzed, available, and activated in his client. In non-Daoist terms, the counsellor's presence and innate ability to be connected to themselves and to connect to the client and what is actually happening at a level beyond this person's stuck state makes a crucial difference. In the simplest of terms, the counsellor becomes a reference point. This is not about technique, but rather a way of being.

In Daoism the idea of *wu-wei* (literally, 'no effort' or 'no work' in the sense of production) is central—the idea of non-doing. A psychotherapist in this state of non-doing is not passive. She is still, in the sense of being so potently and fully open that presence and attention do not waver. She is alert, energetically centered, and responsive and able to engage with whatever comes in the way that makes sense and takes account in-the-moment of self, other, and context. In this state of *wu-wei*, the need to do anything is not there. Her very *presence* is calming and nurturing for anyone in her presence. We believe that Daoist practice of in-the-moment stillness and meditative awareness and awakening is facilitative of the awakening that the suffering person is both struggling to find, perhaps without realizing this and, of his efforts to avoid feeling the pain. This latter may even be successful in the short term, but in the long term guarantees the return of his pain.

The Daoist counsellor works to connect the suffering person to his own latent and obscured potentials of self-healing, wellness, and wholeness. Chapter 17 from the Dao-de-ching tells us:

> A leader is best
> When people barely know that he exists,
> Not so good when people obey and acclaim him,
> Worst when they despise him.
> 'Fail to honour people,
> They fail to honour you;'
> But of a good leader, who talks little,
> When his work is done, his aim fulfilled,
> They will all say, 'We did this ourselves.' (Lao Tzu, 1972, p. 35)

Perhaps, as counsellors we can take something from this idea of *wu-wei*, silence, and doing nothing invasive while being fully present. If we accept these ways of being as having something significant to offer, then we are committed to practices that will take us towards our own individual and unique place of realization or enlightenment, and through this process we will increasingly become a more subtly charged companion for ourselves and for those who are suffering.

JOURNEY'S END

Human life is to be journeyed in company. Hermits and wilderness folks are no exceptions: they seek the better company of God, gods, spirits, and Nature. While suffering clients may not say that they are looking for company when they come to see us, they are certainly there because they are finding it difficult to go on in their life's journey without support and help. We counsellors are fellow travelers who lend a supporting arm to those staggering under the weight of their suffering. Do we need to be Buddhists or Daoist to be fellow travelers? For sure, the answer is, *Not at all*. Names and "isms" do not matter in the final analysis. What matters is how authentically we can meet and walk along with the suffering, struggling other. In our paper we have suggested that Buddhism and Daoism offer powerful resources that can help.

CHAPTER SEVEN

Codes

W. JOHN WILLIAMSON

CODES

My students have codes
Special education codes
Colds, viral, pathological, easy to catch
Codes, more serious in their grim munificence
They linger long beyond school

When our daughter was little
My wife and I spoke in code
For her own protection
From what was too intense, too incomprehensible
As most parents do
We've stopped now that she's older and can decipher our codes
Our cat didn't "go the farm", he died; she was old enough to know almost every-thing
Now she speaks in code with her friends
Their interference thwarts our interference
And we're the baffled ones

Maybe special education codes are meant to protect too
Euphemistically muting diagnoses

Problem is colleges don't speak these codes
If our students want the same accommodations there
They can't say they were *coded*
They have to learn to call themselves *disabled*
We call this self-advocacy

Some students with 54 codes
Have trouble with printed codes we take for granted
A computer programming code can be made to have machines read to them
Reading out loud like the ancients did
The first silent reader a witch
But now they say most readers read well silently
Except for some code 54s
Whose brains over-recruit for visual tasks
They see so damn well, even in 3 dimensions, that
When silently reading they lack synapses to hear the words in their… heads
Or so the research says
Code 42s have trouble with the code of conduct
And the code of conduct has trouble with them
Like musicians the conductor can't get to play in time
Like they don't conduct electricity or conduct it too much

A code 44, severely medically disabled, could have autism, troubles with social codes
Or leukemia, thousands of tiny gene coding errors we're only starting to crack

An IQ test has a coding task
Which means copying, which you're not supposed to do in school,
Except off the blackboard
Which is a sign of intelligence

From what I'm told (thanks mom)
If they had them back in the day
I would have had a code in school too
I was, apparently, so clumsy that I was tested and found wanting
In visual motor integration
The doctor called it mild brain damage
Then, as mom cried, he shrugged and said maybe I'd outgrow the worst
I do remember I couldn't write neatly, copy off the board, count little dots, play sports very well
These were valued codes in school and I wasn't very popular

But sometimes my mom recopied my stories for me and teachers read them to the class

And no one could believe it
And I got bigger, not much but enough
And I learned I was better at contact sports

With their own codes of violence

So it all sort of worked out but not before I got the feeling
That I was the only one in the room who didn't know the code
Which has never quite left me
But maybe feeling this way could be coded as normal
Would I have been better off if there were codes when I was a kid?
That's a code I'll never crack

Last year the Alberta government was going to get rid of codes
Action on Inclusion—the new black, the new sheriff in town, the latest thing,
The going concern in special education
Said codes, despite the good intentions,
Were too clinical, too medical, too negative and exclusionary
Codes' days were numbered
Suddenly, Action on Inclusion is dead
And the codes are back, with a vengeance, their cancellation cancelled,
Termination terminated, bells unrung
Codes unbroken

CHAPTER EIGHT

Second Fragment: Thoughts on "Breaking the Gaze"

CHRISTOPHER GILHAM, DAVID JARDINE, &
GRAHAM McCAFFREY

CG: *Monday, August 5, 2013, 9:14 am*: "The deepest stream of our deeply human, deeply animal responses to this impingement is a sort of panicky retreat from a sense of threat" *or* the face to face fight so common with the students I've worked with–who are also at once, the leukemia patient Graham wrote about (See Chapter 2).

Or is paralysis, too, a response?

I wonder if the root of suffering is necessarily a first and natural response that is, with practice, caught early on and seen for what it is. In other words, the initial response of impingement-suffering might be necessary for the cultivation of the ability to distance and see one within that cycle. Without this noticing practice the subsequent attachment to the cycle is unnecessary suffering but not the root of suffering.

Kearney's reference to interpretive work or hermeneutics as involving Joyce's two minds (Kearney, 2011) rings a bell here, and serves as another connection to this piece. Perhaps with practice we can almost instantly have two minds about situations and one of them is always initiated as an impingement or suffering... only once we catch what was thrown can we put language to it and world it in such a way that it is livable. Not sure if my distinction is distinct enough to be clear but this is, anyhow, how it seems to be for me. Perhaps a sign of my own need for ongoing practice. I always seem to suffer at least a twinge of single-mindedness (sometimes as the inner voice of "f%#& you!") but sometimes can catch myself and have that fuller mind or mindfulness or that reposing. Seems to me the paper does say this too…the breaking open is needed…if not, then one tries to evade suffering altogether and the logic of a search for cure through mindfulness is at play.

In other words, the initial impingement can be both necessary and sufficient condition for either further suffering or livability with suffering, if that makes sense.

"We then start looking for the cure of suffering within the very falsehoods and forgetfulness that keep it in place." The falsehood of behaviourist strategies (I really like Graham's take on this! The term is utterly over-determined) to ameliorate suffering is based on the reality of self-existence, that is, the problem is inherent to the child. No wonder, as you both pointed out, vituperation amplifies among some students and patients, as if to say to oneself and others "It's not me" or "It's not just me." And also, there are reasons for this anger, and they depend on the world and not just issuances from my own battered ego.

Your comment on practice as possibility for both repeating the cycle or getting out of it really hits home with my experiences. This reminds me of one student I had in my special education classroom who did pretty much everything to get us to respond to his anger in kind. We locked down the school and removed the rest of the kids from the classroom—he was a big fella—and he destroyed our classroom. We dodged a few desks and chairs, but he never came at me or the counselor in the room. We worked hard to keep our distance and stay calm and show compassion for his anger. He screamed and yelled and called us names. He was desperate for us to enter the cycle and feed it. Alas when we did not and he was exhausted, he collapsed and whimpered on the floor. The tough guy image he held for so long shattered because we broke the gaze for him, in that instance. He was so used to having his family and other people respond in kind that his suffering was reinforced and expected and actually sought after.

Some "brain people" would claim that the biochemistry of his brain was wired to seek those pathways and chemical feeds that arise from escalation, that the escalation cycle releases endorphins that are addictive and thus reinforce the ways people are.

But that is my other self from another time in special education.

CG: *Mon, August 5, 2013, 6:41 pm*: And then I'm reminded of the phenomenon at hand and how sometimes the different, "inner" forms of knowing conceal wisdoms derived from talking about and being with phenomenon. I feel the mix too but have come to believe that in education the inner forms or the psychology of behaviour or trauma, for example is reified so much that it becomes all there is and conceals the complex fabric of life together. It's so much easier to say "It's his brain doing it" and then the work becomes something else for someone different at the same time educators are asked to do that work, too. Like you wrote Graham, sometimes it's a copout. When it could be held differently. Again, the in-between of not claiming anything once and for all makes our work that much more difficult for the sensitivity it requires. Thanks for the replies. I truly find them very helpful!

DJ: *Monday, August 5, 2013, 8:29 pm*: Yep, Chris, I think this is exactly right. First of all, yes, yes, yes, "the inner voice of 'f%$# you'" sounds, gulp, *vaguely* familiar to me.

And that "big fella" you talked about—the anger, like, perhaps, the anger of Graham's leukemia patient—comes after and is built upon that "inner reification" and the anger intensifies and deepens that reification and masks it with ensuing arguments and fights over the "object" of the anger itself. "In education, the inner stuff…is reified"—this is really important, because if our students come to us already encased…my belief has always been that teaching is a gesture of trying to open this encasement. Not just "keeping ourselves open" to the world but also, as Mircea Eliade (1968, p. 139) put it, "keeping the world open." That is why yours and the counselor's "calm" becomes important, because if there is no open, free space in the world, there is no "where" for an encased life to open out into, so to speak.

In this regard, the "brain" stuff is as pernicious, potentially, as the OCD or ADHD labeling, which simply gives that inner reification a reality that is—again, to use Graham's term—*utterly over-determined. Then* we end up with arguments about whether it is the right over-determined term that further suppress that first gesture.

The first gesture, in Buddhist stuff, isn't the fight. It is the first retraction into some embattled sense of myself that "becomes all there is" and therefore needs to be fought for. Big fella might have felt that "there is no way out," which simply amplifies the delusion of self-existent encasement. That's why anger "itself" isn't the issue, exactly. This is why, in an oversimplified way, ignorance of our lot is placed as the second noble truth after the truth of suffering as the root afflictive cause of suffering. Not just any ignorance: ignorance of the emptiness of self that doesn't need the battle. Such battles simply mask something and makes the mask more and more masking—it "conceals the complex fabric of life together"…nice phrase.

This thing you noted about the collapse and exhaustion. These are really interesting words. Tsong-kha-pa talks about burning off one's afflictions, about, shall we say, "exhausting" them.

CHAPTER NINE

My Treasured Relation

JODI LATREMOUILLE

I have always wanted to write about my cousin Shelby, but whenever I try, the words just don't seem to do justice to my cousin who never grew up. I want to make him live again in this story. But mostly, I would just really like to not cry today.

Shelby was born to my aunt, with too much life ahead of her, and so he was raised by my silent-stoic, gentle grandfather, Dave, and Leona, the asthmatic, arthritic heart-young grandmother, with more love in her than those sick lungs could handle.

This little boy was never formally diagnosed, as he never got the opportunity to spend much time in school, but looking back now, I know that he did indeed have certain cognitive delays, which I did not, and still cannot, name. Nor do I want to. Socially constructed deficiencies are not lovable. To me, he was just Shelby, even though on that level beyond the one that we talk about, we all knew that he didn't function in quite the same way we all did.

Shelby was diagnosed with something, though. He was diagnosed with leukemia at the age of five. His childhood years were a blur for all of us.

Waiting and hoping,
trips to Vancouver through the Fraser Canyon—and later, over the Coquihalla,
stays at the Ronald McDonald house,
fundraising projects,
months in isolation units,

missed school,
missed life,
hours and hours stalking and thrashing in the shallow end of the backyard
pool:
daring us to venture near him.
A wheelchair-bound, abbreviated trip to Disneyland,
Make-A-Wish dream visits with Hulk Hogan and Trevor Linden,
Birthday pizzas delivered by none other than
Raphael the Teenage Mutant Ninja Turtle,
and a failed autologous bone marrow transplant.

We were told that Shelby was going to receive a "miracle cure," a treatment that my 11-year-old brain understood in the following terms: the doctors would take a massive needle that would suck the bone marrow from his spine, purge it of cancer cells with radiation, and return it back to his body with another massive needle, with the expectation that the healthy bone marrow would regenerate and grow, filling his spine with healthy bone marrow. My sister and I have always wondered if our matching needle phobias were inspired by bearing witness to our cousin's medical treatments.

I learned the language of platelets and prednisone
and blood counts and spinal taps and we-still-have-hope
and in/remission/out and chemo and things-are-not-looking good
and be-nicer-he's-sick and making time count.
No, wait a minute
Time counted us
by appointments
and remissions
and birthdays
and good days
bad days
and
one
more
day.
We counted everything
Except time.

I now understand this "miracle cure" autologous bone marrow transplant the way the doctors and all the adults in the room did, as what it was in those days, as more of a "last ditch experimental treatment." Shelby spent three months in complete isolation while the bone marrow was being purged of cancer cells. In order to visit him, we had to wash our hands to the elbow with stinging, sharp-smelling disinfectant soap, walk through the sliding door into the closet-sized "isolation chamber," wash our hands again for several minutes, don plastic shoe coverings, plastic clothing, and face masks, then enter through a second sliding door, careful, fearful, not to get too close. We could touch his hand, but hugs were out of the question. We just couldn't risk it. He was my alien-cousin, a lovable monster descended from another planet, participating in an experimental study, peering out from behind his oxygen mask. Then I would hear his muffled, cheerful gravelly voice, saying "Hi, Jode!" as if he were just my good old, familiar little earth-cousin. At age ten, he was much more subdued, resigned to the treatments, than he had been in the early years.

Six-year-old tornado.
"I am a DINOSAUR and I am going to SMASH YOU!"
Pierced.
"I am a LION and I am going to EAT YOU!"
Swearing.
"SHIT! I HATE YOU!"
Despising his cruel saviours.
"I am JAKE THE SNAKE and I am going to do a D.D.T. right on your HEAD!"
Restrained.
"I am going to ride my snowmobile all the way back to Merritt and you will never find me again!"

My sister and I spent many hours with Shelby through the years, his contracted playmates, and I think our company probably was one of the reasons my grandmother was able to maintain some semblance of sanity. He was a challenging kid to begin with, prone to temper tantrums and boiling-over fits of anger. And having to be stuck with needles, of varying diameters, on a daily basis, was, and still is, unfathomable to me. Anyone who had to go through all of that would, understandably, be just a little "on edge." My mother would send us over to Grandma's house every day after school until we became too busy with our extracurricular lives; in the later years we would squeeze in weekend sleepovers and pool parties when we could. The two girls would play Duck Hunter and Super Mario Brothers for hours and hours on end, while Shelby wrestled in the background with his stuffed animals and Teenage Mutant Ninja Turtle figurines, shouting out the play-by-play, occasionally jumping off the couch and squashing us flat-out under his roly-poly body, making us gasp under his weight, begging to be freed, to breathe again.

On the day of my 8th birthday party, all of my friends had come over to celebrate. Of course, Shelby was invited. It was a glorious spring day at the "Fox Farm," our 5-acre mountainside hobby farm, perfect for badminton on the lawn and hikes up the mountain to the magical forest. My father had installed a rope swing in the woods about 200 metres above the house. All of the kids were taking turns. One of the less experienced "city slickers" lost his grip and launched himself into space, then landed softly, unbelievably, gracefully, like a ski-jumper on the steep landing slope, sliding down the leaf-strewn mountainside straight into an anthill. One girl forgot the only safety rule (to launch yourself *away* from the tree in a circular trajectory), and flew straight out from the tree, then straight back in, smashing into the tree trunk. We watched her float in slow-motion horror, and then cringed in sympathy, shielding our eyes and turning away, wincing at the inevitable "thud." We turned back and peeled our hands from our eyes to watch her loosen her grip and slither listlessly off the rope into a weeping heap at the base of the tree. Only two casualties this time. Not bad.

Shelby was down at the house, as it was too difficult for him to hump all the way up the sidehill to the rope swing. I am pretty sure that what we did that day was my idea. One of us ran down to the house to grab a bottle of ketchup. We chose a "victim," smeared the ketchup on her, and started hollering. "Shelby, help! Tracy fell off the rope swing and she's bleeding!" I heard him, out of sight near the house, yelling, "What? Oh no! I'm coming, Jode!" And we were all snickering and jeering, until we saw him emerge over the hill, panting and crying, wheezing, tripping over sticks, stumbling up, knees dirty, nose running.

Distraught.

Our laughter froze instantly to silence. He had brought a tea towel. I didn't know what he thought he was going to do with that. I guess… I suppose… that was the funny part. It was just a joke.

For his 10th birthday, our family bought him a funny little voice-activated yellow plastic sunflower in a funny little plastic green pot that danced a herky-jerky hula, its funny little happy sunglassed face bobbing along to the Mini Pops singing their funny little-kid version of "karma chameleon."

That flower was cool, man. Totally rocked that song.

In order to get it into the room we had to unwrap and open up the package, then wipe down every single surface with the disinfectant, including the batteries. The nurses brought it in for him, as that day he was having a "bad immune system day." We smiled through the window as he tried it out, grinning from cheek to soft, chubby cheek. We could see him laughing through the glass, and in my head I could hear his hoarse, breathless chortle. My mom picked out that flower for him. I am sure she thought it would cheer him up. It did; she nailed it out of the park. He loved that flower. All the days of his life. Because you should never grow out of silly little things.

Shelby finally did make his escape.
We were called in to visit him in the hometown Merritt hospital.

I knew it was bad,
because any self-respecting version of Hope would have bundled him up in her
arms and magically swooped him all the way back up and over
the winter-blizzard highway
to Vancouver Children's Hospital.

Bloated, drained, cushioned by crisp white pillows
and our false cheerfulness.
Distracted by niceties and pain.
We, the kids, protected, excluded.
Unaware but still knowing.

Just a short visit.
Tired. Ready. Calm. Barely eleven years old.
Selfless. Raspy.
"Have fun skiing tomorrow, Jode."
Big, soft, squishy, forever hug.
We knew things were bad when we were allowed to hug him.

Wait, hold it, hold on, for him.
Cry in the backseat on the way home.
Look out the foggy window at the hazy, unending night.

Shelby died on a blowing-snow January night, at the age of 11. I was 12 years old.

I got my first menstrual period the day of the funeral. What a day for firsts. I wasn't particularly afraid or ashamed, as some young girls were back in the days before moms were supposed to be a girl's best friend and talk about, oh, about just absolutely everything! I had read about it in a book somewhere, and had some "samples" stashed in my bathroom cupboard. I was just, oh, just annoyed, awkward and lonely. I just wasn't ready to grow up, not just yet.

Shelby's neighbour
and best friend in the whole entire world,
a mature young woman-ish,
kind, gentle 12-year old
Robyn,
who didn't have to be his friend,
with two perfect, large fake front teeth
that got knocked out years ago in a biking accident
riding down "Suicide Hill" by our neighbourhood school,
who felt-penned a massive "Hulkamania!" poster for Shelby's best-day-ever
and who probably got her period (light-years) months before me,
and who I imagined would know
exactly how
to handle her newfound womanhood
gracefully,
(She didn't. She told me so years later.)
was beside herself after she returned from viewing his body.

His Vancouver Canucks jerseyed,
google-eyeballed Disneyland-Goofy capped,
painless body.

"That's the first time in his life that he has ever been alone."
She wanted to wait with him in that room until the service began.

Our great-aunt was asked to perform the eulogy, and my narrow little 12-year-old self was disappointed in the choice, expecting that she was just way too stuffy and stodgy to do my hilarious, ridiculous, lovely little cousin justice. My mom had written the eulogy—oh, it was just so perfect—and I didn't want it spoiled by someone who didn't know him just the way we did. I think back now and realize that my pin-curled aunt was probably the only one in the entire jam-packed room of 300 people who was tightly wound enough to hold it together for the entire speech.

And she re-called him to a "T".
A "D.D.T.," that is:

"I know that Shelby is up there in heaven,
riding his snowmobile
and doing D.D.T.'S on all the angels."

Shelby was the exception. To everything. He was the beautiful little monster who reflected back to us who we really were. We were rude, wild, loud, unfiltered, imaginative, hungry, hurting, scared-cruel dreamers.

That is what love does.
It makes us want to do justice.
Without justice we are merely co-existing.
Waiting for the reward.
Labelling.
Judging—and moving on.
I will never move on.
I want to make him live again.
My treasured teacher.
My relation.
Alien-cousin.
Brother.
Heart-swelling baby dinosaur.
Lion.
Hulk.

CHAPTER TEN

Some Introductory Words FOR Two Little Earth-Cousins

DAVID W. JARDINE

Out from behind his oxygen mask
As if he were just my good old, familiar little earth-cousin.

Cancer really is one of "those" words. Two days ago, an old friend, Fernando, died of it, and the funeral is this Thursday, January 23rd—lung cancer come down hard and fast, as it often does. And then there's me at 8-years-old and my mother, 1958, undergoing a radical mastectomy. Drawn living room curtains for weeks, a big wicker laundry basket full of neighbors' tiny presents, one to be opened each day, smells of soaps and lotions and other notions, meant to help stretch out time's lingering, I guess, and to show wee affections without words, without "that" word. Easy to recall how many had to disappear from view, unable to be present to such things.

Understandable in its own sad way. Makes my own skin lesions over the past couple of years seem quite silly in comparison, not only because they are less severe and the suffering is near nil (although hearing "that" word chills nevertheless), but because, at the level of our living and dying, cancer is always incomparable. It follows an old Gadamerian (1989, p. 39) adage: "the individual case ...is not exhausted by being a particular example of a universal law or concept." My doctor and I joked about how this could be some sort of long-in-arriving anniversary—maybe even the summer of 1958, too much sun swimming at the Second Tower with my brother and father in Burlington, and the great peels of skin afterwards. Funny how cancer takes its time sometimes, sometimes as fleet as the quick of life itself, and sometimes, well, as sheer chance would have it, my mother lived till 2002.

Of course, as Jodi Latremouille's wonderful, heartbreaking writing "My Treasured Relation" demonstrates, broad, universal concepts and images and ideas are always needed in the act of articulating one's experience. We always run the risk of using words that can be understood differently than we meant. This circumstance is in the very nature of writing and reading itself, and it is why the *mens auctoris* is not the lynchpin of hermeneutic work (Gadamer, 2007, p. 57). It is also why hermeneutic research is so bloody difficult. You have to be disciplined and rigorous and attentive to handle this circumstance gracefully and well. Remaining true to the intimacy of this "special case" (Gadamer, 1989, p. 39), dear Shelby, is an especially difficult form of research that requires generosity, patience, perseverance, discipline, stillness and wisdom (6 aspired to "perfections," [Sanskrit: *paramitas*; see Tsong-kha-pa, 2000, 2002, 2004]).

All clustered, of course, around impermanence. "We will have to hold firmly to the standpoint of finiteness" (Gadamer, 1989, p. 99), both in the topics we consider and in the expended breath of our consideration itself. Why? Because the topic of a hermeneutic study is finite as is our insight into it. "Future generations will understand differently" (p. 340) and therefore, the purpose of a hermeneutic inquiry is to "keep [the topic] open for the future" (p. 340).

We already know this. Cancer will never leave our consciousness. There are myriad ways of experiencing it, articulating it, investigating it, naming it, and these have cascaded down to us over time, admixed, sometimes battling each other, sometimes quelled, finally, in the soft presence of death. We can never say once and for all what needs to be said, and the worlds of swimming and breast cancer in 1958 have turned out to be something different than we could have imagined. "It would be a poor hermeneuticist who thought he could have, or had to have, the last word" (Gadamer, 1989a, p. 579).

In this sense, "My Treasured Relation" is hermeneutic in its best light. It is intent on remaining true to the "stubborn particularity" (Wallace, 1987) of the case while, at the same time, drawing us into the world of its orbit in which we, as readers, already live. And, at once, it casts us back on our own life in this troubled life-world—all this with an eye to both the opening this topic and "find[ing] that opening in each of us" (Wallace, 1987, p. 13), as readers, where we can experience our own "miraculous returns" (p. 13) to the lives we have already been leading. This complex and pitched spiral of effects that defines the rigorousness of hermeneutic inquiry has an axis. Its goal is to remain true to its object, and Jodi Latremouille's writing finds this sweet and aching spot. It seeks the address of this case, and that's what compels our attention and makes this compelling breakout beyond the confines of the case to something that feels universal. But this is no longer a slippery universal full of Romantic woozyness. It is a universal that has been, in the best senses, humiliated by the case. Life. Childhood. Illness. Relations. Suffering.

All these become disciplined and strengthened by the case itself. "It is truly an achievement of undemonstrable tact to hit the target and to discipline the application of the universal" (Gadamer, 1989, pp. 39–40). Without this discipline of application, phrases like "childhood leukemia" loses the function of "responding and summoning" (Gadamer, 1989, p. 458). It becomes a hard category of illness, and our responses to it become subjectivized into nothing but "moist gastric intimacy" (Sartre, 1970, p. 4).

These are the two extremes that hermeneutics avoids, and the two degradations that it can fall into when it fails.

Jodi Latremouille's work thus reminds us of a hermeneutic truth, that one must avoid the temptations of casting our eyes too high. And, as with another recent piece of writing (Latremouille, in press), her work reminds us, too, of another feature of hermeneutics:

> To be properly understood and articulated, … locales of intimacy don't lend themselves to forms of research that demand generalities or methodological anonymity as is proper to various social sciences. They demand a form of research that is proper to the object of its concern–an old Aristotelian idea, that knowledge must "remain something adapted to the object, a *mensuratio ad rem*" (Gadamer, 1989, p. 261). (Jardine, in press)

A good interpretation must be adapted to the object it is considering. Pediatric oncology can be understood as a medical condition and, understood as such it summons a certain way of writing/speaking/investigating that is proper to that object. But the cancer of a child is also understandable as a sphere of treasured relations filled with this child and no other. This is also what it is. In this case, precisely as in the case of medical research, good writing seeks its proper measure in this object of consideration. There is no battle here between types of research and all that worn-out piffle about qualitative and quantitative. One of these is not the "secret measure" (Gadamer, 1989, p. 112) of the other. Both forms of writing and research are "objective" in the sense that both seek to cleave properly to the object each is considering. Both seek to do justice to the thing and bring it to an illumination proper to it. Both therefore are "hermeneutic" in the sense that they both heed the demand of the *mensuratio ad rem*. Differently put, not only is all oncology hermeneutic (see Chapter XXX). Cancer, as it actually lives in the world (of families, of medicine, of nursing, of philosophy, of economics, of the tremors felt over diagnosis, of the bedsides, of the ways the word can find air in some settings of fear and trembling) is myriad in its being. It therefore requires myriad articulations in order to be properly understood in its fulsome being.

"Only in the multifariousness of such voices does it exist" (Gadamer, 1989, p. 284).

Hermeneutic work always involves the application of particular cases to the universals (concepts, images, hopes, desires, ideas, rules, laws, principles, themes, procedures, guidelines, expectations voiced and unvoiced, and so on) that have come to guide our lives, demanding of them that they listen to the difference that the case portends and don't turn away to heavenly, self-enclosed ideation (Jardine, 2013). But it involves another form of application. "Understanding always involves something like applying the text to be understood to the interpreter's present situation" (Gadamer, 1989, p. 308).

In reading this paper, I'm blessed with the meeting of these two earth cousins that make me remember that I, too, and however near or distant, am a third earth cousin in this fatal round.

Interpretive work is meant to be read interpretively. It is meant to be suffered. Read this and let yourself be third.

CHAPTER ELEVEN

This Is Why We Read
This Is Why We Write

DAVID W. JARDINE

Discussion bears fruit. The participants part from one another as changed beings. The individual perspectives with which they entered upon the discussion have been transformed, and so they have been transformed themselves. This, then, is a kind of progress—not the progress proper to research but rather a progress that always must be renewed in the effort of our living.

H.G. GADAMER (2007, P. 244) FROM *HERMENEUTICS AS A PRACTICAL PHILOSOPHY*

In response to reading Jodi Latremouille's "My Treasured Relation," Christine McIver, CEO and founder of Kids Cancer Care Foundation of Alberta who lost her son, Derek, to cancer, sent the following email to Dr. Nancy Moules, the editor of the *Journal of Applied Hermeneutics*:

> The piece by Jodi Latremouille. I read a lot of this stuff, so much it's in danger of becoming a blur. This is exceptional. I am going to share it with our staff if that is okay. She writes exactly how I think. In paragraphs full of description and illustration—and then words that hit the moment. I was surprised at the moment of Shelby's death, I was overcome again with the very same pain and sadness as when Derek died. This writing…it is SO good. Illustrates the journey perfectly. It needs to be seen.

There is, here, something deeply recognizable to those of us who work with the living and the dying and the dead, something that nebulously defines being part of a profession. It is something we need to admit to because its admission is a vehicle to its remedy—"a progress that always must be renewed in the effort of our living."

There is a certain ennui here, something like having experienced too much, having seemingly heard it all before, something like the exhaustion of efforts to name this pain, this suffering, and how language itself seems to start to wear thin and then wear on you over time, wear you out. This is the secret lot of nurses and teachers, of parents and doctors—perhaps a secret lot of being human itself. The effort of our living can lose its power to renew. We can become halt and the glow of language that once bound us together in commiseration can burn out, and us with it.

We lose our avail.

I'm reminded of this passage from David G. Smith:

> "Education is suffering from narration-sickness," says Paulo Freire. It speaks out of a story, which was once full of enthusiasm, but now shows itself incapable of a surprise ending. The nausea of narration-sickness comes from having heard enough, of hearing many variations on a theme but no new theme. (Smith, 1999, pp. 135–136)

Why do we write emails in response to reading Jodi Latremouille's work? Why am I compelled to write about earth cousins and now this little editorial?

This compulsion is part of why attention is given in *Truth and Method* (Gadamer, 1989, p. 60) to "[Immanuel] Kant's doctrine of the heightening of the feeling of life (*Lebensgefühl*)." Despite Gadamer's detailed caveats about this notion, it is one of the deep sources of hermeneutic work, percolating up through Husserl's ideas of lived experience and the life-world. Part of the orbit of hermeneutic research is to revive in writers and readers the possibilities of our commiseration. Hans-Georg Gadamer (1986, p. 59) called it the opening up of "free spaces" and learning, in consequence, how we might then shape our lives in light of such possibilities, forging, if you will, "new solidarities" (p. 59).

This, then, is the other clue I got from Christine's email about why we read, why we write, why this journal—the hit, the moment. This is the aesthesis of aesthetics, as James Hillman (2006, p. 36) noted, "which means at root a breathing in or taking in of the world, the gasp, "aha," the "uh" of the breath in wonder, shock, amazement, and aesthetic response." Hermeneutics lingers about the in-breath—" I was surprised at the moment …—where something hits us and wakes us up out of our melancholia over the wearying sameness of things. It is where our living can become spacious and open and full of possibility again, and we no longer feel locked into the often-panicky confines and immediacies of our circumstances.

This, too, is why some writing—Jodi's writing and, yes, even that email, in its own way—can be properly called beautiful, that is, precipitating of such aesthetic arrival even when it speaks of sad departure.

CHAPTER TWELVE

The Elision OF Suffering IN Mental Health Nursing

GRAHAM McCAFFREY

No, this is unease. It is a preeminent reality. (Wallis, 2007, p. 36)

On the surface, it seems unexceptionable to suggest that patients on mental health units are likely to be suffering somehow and that there are nursing activities that can help to relieve that suffering. Buddhist thought begins with the First Noble Truth that human existence is marked by suffering, and it unfolds from there in elaborations of this insight and of how best to respond. These two statements about suffering immediately suggest an affinity between nursing and Buddhism, and yet there are differences. Mental health nursing lives within taxonomies of mental disorders in which suffering is only a result of categorized symptoms, whereas Buddhism proposes that suffering is an inevitable consequence of the natural human inclination towards grasping. The space between these two horizons is the hermeneutic invitation to a critical questioning of the assumptions permeating practice on mental health units. In this chapter, I elaborate on these differences and use material from interviews with nurses to suggest that suffering is elided in mental health nursing, and that the Buddhist perspective offers a way of retrieving it for humane practice.

SUFFERING AS EPIPHENOMENON

Suffering in modern discourse about mental health is inferred rather than explicit. This may be because to talk of suffering is immediately to raise tricky questions about who is attributing suffering to whom or how much suffering requires professional help. There are people, for example, who live quietly with delusional beliefs, going about their ordinary business, who do not in their own minds suffer much at all, even though they can be said to be suffering a marked symptom of a mental disorder. A person in a manic state usually does not perceive him or herself to be suffering; quite the opposite, he or she feels magnificent. Those around the person are probably suffering more, aware of the difficulties that can ensue as a result of a bout of endless energy and wildly distorted judgment.

The picture is further complicated by the reality that the idea of mental illness is itself contested. It is worthwhile considering variant perspectives of mental illness before we can come to any conclusions about where suffering resides. *The Diagnostic and Statistical Manual of Mental Disorders*, Fifth edition (DSM V) (American Psychiatric Association, 2013) is the current version of the classification system of mental disorders that "is the most recognized and most thoroughly researched model available" (Munson, 2001, p. xix). The DSM focuses on classification by listing symptoms, which define disorders that can then be used to formulate a diagnosis that can be more or less agreed upon by any clinician conversant with the taxonomic system. In the introduction to the previous DSM IV (Text Revision) (American Psychiatric Association, 2000) there was a general statement about the understanding of mental disorder and why it matters.

> In DSM-IV each of the mental disorders is conceptualized as a clinically significant behavioral or psychological syndrome or pattern that occurs in an individual and that is associated with present distress (e.g., a painful symptom) or disability (i.e., impairment in one or more important areas of functioning) or with significantly increased risk of suffering, death, pain, disability, or an important loss of freedom. (p. xxi)

Suffering here is a part of the reason why the enterprise of classification and diagnosis is undertaken so as to be able to identify sources of human distress and treat them. The equivalent section of the DSM V has dispensed with the word suffering altogether.

There have been many critiques of the taxonomic approach. Within nursing, Barker (2009), for example, critiqued the DSM for being a manifestation of the "medicalization of problems of living" (p. 129) that narrows to a one-dimensional focus on people as sources of prescribed kinds of information and fosters separation and stigma. He also pointed out that the process of definition has become politicized. The two approaches are explained to some degree in Munson's (2001) differentiation between process and categorical models of mental illness. In the former type, mental illness is seen as "a result of a process of events that produce symptoms and difficulties" and in the latter "mental illness produces a set of symptoms that can be used to define and diagnose disorders" (p. 18). According to this basic distinction, Barker is a process man, and the DSM, with its numerous contributors, is a categorical work. The contrast between the individual author and the corporatist product neatly illustrates one of the differences between the two ways of seeing mental disorder. In the process view, it is the individual experience that matters and that constitutes the raw material for recovery. The categorical approach, in contrast, lends itself to generalized treatments, most notably pharmacological, fitted to diagnostic categories. The process perspective inclines towards a dynamic view of causation and change, whereas the categorical is more static and based on the supposedly objective observation of behavior and collection of information.

(There is a nice irony here that the DSM, for all its authoritative status, is an example of impermanence and historicism, itself subject to process and flow. It is now on its fifth edition since 1952, making it absurd to pretend this is anything like a description of objective reality rather than an instrumental lexicon for communicating about complex human phenomena.)

However, although the overarching Barker (Barker & Buchanan-Barker, 2005) label for mental disorders, borrowed from Thomas Szasz, of "problems of living" (p. 7), does the job of getting out from under existing psychiatric labeling, it is itself the seed of an as yet unwritten taxonomy. The idea of a problem of living still does not solve the earlier questions around who is suffering and how, and how best to respond? It is a problem of living when I mislay my keys, but probably not one requiring professional help.

SUFFERING: OCCASIONS AND ELISIONS

According to the *Canadian Oxford Dictionary*, to suffer is to "undergo pain, grief, damage, etc" (Barber, 1998, p. 1450). Suffering is always suffering from something, and to undergo carries intimations of descent, of the shadowy underworld of Orpheus and Eurydice. There is an intimacy to suffering because not only do the external causes differ, but also the manner of its undergoing. To say in a general way that someone suffers from a mental illness is only to name a point on a map. This place rather than another place, suffering from mental illness rather than, say heart disease, or from depression and not schizophrenia. The elaborations of the DSM zoom in as if Google Maps had surveyed the district of suffering called mental health. There is more detail, but it is still only a map. Maps, of course, have their uses in just this, finding the spot, working out directions. If the "problems of living" were a map, it would have less detail, but precisely in its weaker claim to represent the lie of the land, it would enjoin us to find out more, to get out and ask for directions of those who live there, to ask what it feels like, this suffering, how it arrived in one's life, how one might look for a road out.

In research conversations I conducted with nurses, suffering appeared more often than not tangentially, through the lens of symptoms and diagnoses. Hermeneutic mindfulness, however, is about bringing attention back to the obvious, that which seems already given. "Experience is initially always experience of negation: something is not what we supposed it to be" (Gadamer, 2004, p. 349). The fact of remembrance, that these instances remained in the mind of the nurses, even years later, reflects some form of contact. In some cases the nurse expressed still feeling troubled. This, I suggest, is an effect of the visceral face-to-face contact with the suffering other even if we do not have to name it as such.

> *I remember this one girl coming in and she was acutely psychotic and she—she was acutely psy—I remember her name—she was acutely psychotic for—and with us for a long time and she was under the belief—the delusion—that she was in love with the band Kiss and Gene Simmons.*

The awareness of suffering is less in the overt description—one mental health nurse talking to another, after all, note the self correction from "*belief*" to the more properly clinical "*delusion*"—than in the hesitations, repetitions, and memory of the girl's name. "*She was under the belief,*" burdened by it, undergoing it, in her own world, her own underworld. The nurse went on, in clinical mode, to wonder about the causes of the psychosis, but came back to the poignant question, "*why some people and not others?*" This question appears to follow from the categorical approach, to share in the implied belief in a notional realm of normality, outside of mental disorder. There is, however, a worry in the question that hints at a more unsettling thought, that there is an unpredictability and unknowability in the visitations of mental illness, an inherent instability in the borderline between suffering and being all right.

One nurse talked about how in her practice she drew together the information from the map and the inquiry. "*If someone said to me 'I'm hallucinating right now'—'Is that distressing to you?'—because maybe that's normal for them on a daily basis.*" Here she is trying to find out about suffering and not make the assumption that it is the same as the symptom. Looking at the transcript, I only noticed after many re-readings that there was a break, where we switched from this mode of generalized call and response around symptoms and behaviours to more personal content. At this point in the interview the nurse got some mascara in her eye, and there was a long pause while I went to look for a tissue. When we sat down again she said, "*Sorry I've forgotten the question.*" The question was whether she remembered working with a particular individual when the relationship she made with the patient had seemed helpful. She forgot the question, and I failed for a long time to notice the shift in the interview. The everyday elision, mostly unnoticed, is also part of our response to suffering.

She went on to answer the question by talking about a woman with whom she had worked for three months. She mentioned the woman's diagnosis, but also that over the years of contacts with psychiatrists, she had picked up a succession of different diagnoses. She recalled asking the patient to tell her about her life, which she presented as a succession of losses and failures with a persistent sense of terrible isolation.

> *She could recall tons of things, but all of them with a negative undertone as to why, you know, how she lost her daughter, how her marriage broke up, how she was living in this trailer.*

The nurse described a pattern of dependence, as though the woman had come to see the unit and the staff there as a place where her suffering could be held, and temporarily assuaged. She tried to honour this while helping her to seek a way beyond the same pattern.

> *But on the unit she was just so comfortable. And I remember asking her, "All this time we've had together, you have been able to recall all these incidences that have brought you to a negative place. Can you recall one incident that would or has brought you to a positive point?" She wasn't able really to pinpoint anything.*

What came next in the nurse's account was that the patient was discharged before she could continue to work with her around this question. There is a weight to the nurse's experience, having asked for the story of suffering, being then left with it, not knowing what happened next.

Another nurse, in responding to the same kind of question, raised this point of being left with suffering under uncertainty, and an unspoken question of whether the work he had done was effective, or even helpful.

> *eventually a psychiatrist decided that he could go home and he left one day and he had a two week supply of something, amitriptyline or whatever it was, an outpatient card in his hand and that was the last time I ever saw him.*

What if the worst had happened, "*he could have died a week later.*" The nurse described the way in which the patient, a young man of around 18, felt he had no way forward when he came to the unit.

> *He came in following a suicide attempt and was really quite ambivalent about the whole experience—he'd been through quite a lot of trials and tribulations and different stressors and he decided that he couldn't cope with it anymore.*

This crisis was related to being gay, having experienced years of bullying at school and rejection by his family. He had a profound sense of dislocation.

> *One of the things that consistently came up for him was this, this feeling of really being out on a limb, there was this strangeness about him, that he couldn't find a way he thought he would fit back into the world once he was discharged. …What he was seeking was an anchor, because he felt himself moving from the world.*

For the nurse, it was only through opening himself to the young man's suffering in this sense of being lost, by asking him about it, spending time with him, that he could work with him to help him begin to build a stronger, more alive identity. There is an offering of self, to go with the patient to her or his own underworld, but carrying the knowledge of a path back. This double movement of the acceptance of suffering, and its refusal through holding out a curiosity about the possibility of change, appeared when the participants were most involved in talking about a relationship with a particular patient. There is a risk in this; as in the myth, Orpheus has to travel to the underworld to rescue Eurydice, but there is no guarantee of success. There is the risk too, that the nurse must be changed in this willing proximity to suffering. To step into the (under)world of the patient is to invite suffering. Donna Orange (2011), in a hermeneutic account of psychotherapy, wrote that "understanding…is receptivity and suffering" (p. 23).

The closeness to another's suffering is difficult, and consequently it brings with it a countering resistance and self-protection that can take various forms. This other side of being in the presence of suffering also emerged through the interviews. One nurse used the expression "*nursing from the desk*" to describe a style of nursing that relied on observation of symptoms, literally keeping a distance from patients and their particular experience by watching them across the divide of the desk along the unit. Another nurse was sensitive to the way in which this kind of approach could be a reflection, and a reinforcement of an attitude of "*disrespect and discounting someone because they're a mental health patient.*" She was also able to see how this could come about under the continual demands of the nursing role.

If nurses start to get frustrated for whatever reason with just working eight hours with clients who are at the desk all the time or have continuous demands, or, you know, it can be very exhausting and you start to not treat people in general as well, so it's raising your voice at them, or "You have to take this medication," and I think it's more the approach and the way things are said.

The desk figures again, as a border that separates but also brings people face to face, which differentiates one place from another while paradoxically demonstrating their connection to each other.

Another nurse revealed this work along the borders of suffering, of exposure and self-protection, understanding and distancing, when she talked about using black humour with colleagues as a way of coping with the closeness to patients' distress.

I remember working nights with [a colleague] and we developed a game—and the game was—this is so awful—where I am, at a point in my life where, right now—sometimes when I think about how we practiced back then, I just cringe. So the game was, what would be the worst possible thing we could say to this [patient] at this time…and in some ways it showed an insight that we knew where this [patient] was at, that we would know the trigger.

Perhaps it was because the nurse was reflecting back to a much earlier time in her career that she felt able to bring this up at all. This theme of black humour is familiar to me from working in mental health and as the nurse noted herself, the game required an intimacy with the patients' distress and a sense of the responsibility that the nurses held for their vulnerability. It is reminiscent of the sense of vertigo that some people feel standing close to a cliff edge, a keen awareness of where one is and the nearness to something potentially disastrous. There is also, however, the element of immanent hostility in contemplating the worst one could say to a patient, which is perhaps what made the nurse cringe on looking back.

One response to these strategies of distancing is to address them as examples of stigmatizing people with mental illness. Only one of the participants actually used the word *stigma*, and her nursing practice was strongly influenced by time she had spent working with the Canadian Mental Health Association in the community. She commented on hearing nurses on her unit express *"this normative idea that, 'By now you should be better—good grief, it's been two weeks, like you should be over your depression.' So even—there's a stigma and these ideas about mental health within the staff, no question."* The literature on stigma in mental health certainly endorses this concern that it exists among professionals, and particularly those working in acute care who see people at the most extreme points of distress (Berry, Gerry, Hayward, & Chandler, 2010; Gouthro, 2009; Horsfall, Cleary, & Hunt, 2010).

I do not want to dismiss the discourse around stigma, and the importance of addressing adverse and limiting judgments about people with mental illness. I do, however, want to stay with the ambivalences that I have discussed above that are attendant upon the willed exposure to mental distress, and to sound a caution, from a standpoint of hermeneutic openness, about being too quick to stigmatize stigma. It is at this point that I want to undertake an interpretive look at the intertwined experiences of mental disorders and suffering using a perspective based on Buddhist thought.

SUFFERING: A BUDDHIST THOUGHT EXPERIMENT

The quotation that heads this chapter is a translation of a line from the Buddha's first discourse in which the Pali word *dukkha* is rendered as unease. Here is the same line in a version that uses the more commonly accepted English translation as suffering.

> Now this, monks, is the noble truth of suffering: birth is suffering, aging is suffering, illness is suffering, death is suffering; union with what is displeasing is suffering; separation from what is pleasing is suffering; not to get what one wants is suffering; in brief, the five aggregates[1] subject to clinging are suffering. (Bodhi, 2005, p. 76)

The first thing to notice is that suffering here is not a periodic occurrence of harmful events, but an inevitable feature of human life, stemming from the human inclination to cling to that which is in reality impermanent. This is why Wallis (2007) preferred the word unease, since it is easier to comprehend every day frustrations when things do not go the way we expect as uncomfortable rather than as suffering, which seems more extreme. When we start to think about mental illness, there is something to be said for this argument. As with the term problems of living, there is a risk of conflating differences to such an extent that intense distress can be ignored since, after all, we all suffer from problems of living. This is not the direction taken in the Buddhist tradition, however, since the concept of conditioned existence means that each person, at each moment, manifests the existential truth of suffering in a unique way. Thus it is possible to keep sight of the universality of suffering while still recognizing the unique circumstances of the individual.

The Buddhist conception of suffering has two parts, first, the existential givens of birth, illness, aging, and death, and then the way in which suffering stems from our attempts to resist these parts of life by grasping. "Grasping…gives birth to aversion and delusion, and from these three routes arise all the other unhealthy

states, such as jealousy, anxiety, hatred, addiction, possessiveness, and shameless-
ness" (Kornfield, 2008, pp. 242–243). This is very different to looking in on mental
illness from an implicit standpoint of non-suffering, observing how mental disorders can lead to suffering. The significance of the difference is in the implication
that professionals are also subject to suffering from grasping, aversion, and delusion. In the examples above, there could be clinging to the idea of getting through
a quiet, uncomplicated shift in nursing from the desk, aversion from the extremes
of psychosis in the black humour, or simply indifference to the patient who has already been on the unit for two weeks. The point is not, then, that we simply accept
these responses as only human, but that we can address them with a compassionate curiosity because they are human, rather than from a standpoint of judgment
as if we are free from grasping, aversion, and delusion. As mental health nurses,
our practice is the compassionate response to those suffering as a result of mental
disorders, but part of that practice becomes the recognition of our own moments
of fear and unwillingness, or for that matter the clinging of over-absorption in
certain stories.

Another direction of considering the Buddhist conception of suffering is to
imagine a taxonomy of mental disorder based on the three fundamental roots of
suffering. Disorders of grasping might include addictions, obsessiveness, and depression when it manifests as the inability to move on with losses. Disorders of
aversion might include anxiety, which is usually characterized by the powerful
need to avoid certain situations or thoughts. Thirdly, disorders of delusion could
include psychotic conditions, when there is a severe disconnect from commonly
shared realities. My main purpose in introducing this thought experiment is to
note how, in such a scheme, there is always going to be a spectrum that includes
all of us. Our desires for certain habitual ways of doing things, or comforts, might
fall short of a harmful obsession or addiction, but the basic structure is not hard to
see and not hard to identify with. Similarly, degrees of anxiety are part of normal
experience (which is where Wallis' "unease" [2007, p. 36] becomes the more appo-
site translation). Kornfield (2009), a Western Buddhist teacher and psychologist,
discussed delusion in this way in a work presenting a Buddhist psychology for a
contemporary Western audience. "At its extreme, delusion becomes outright psychosis. Our ordinary delusion can take us from the reality of the present into the
unreality of our thoughts and confused misperceptions" (p. 224). Thus we can still
distinguish extreme delusion as a potentially harmful symptom, but also recognize
that we are continually prone to the many distractions of ordinary delusion. This
notion of identification with elements of mental disorder is hardly new. There can
be few readers of the diagnostic criteria in the DSM who have not felt some lurch
of self-recognition on finding one symptom or another in its pages. One of the

nurses interviewed raised this point, commenting, "*I've done things in my life that I can see could appear—even to me—to be like borderline things—or histrionic, narcissistic—there's aspects of those in all of us.*"

Whereas the worldview represented by the DSM tends to encourage us not to want to find such identifications, the outlook of Buddhist baseline unease tells us to expect them. These two points of view have different implications for practice. The first is more likely to emphasize the otherness of those suffering from a mental disorder and the second is more likely to foster first empathy, then accountability for our own selves in our own responses. In this way, the complications that I have raised, both from the point of view of identifying suffering in the discourses of mental health/illness, and from the experiences of the participants, become places of practice in themselves. If our goal is to cultivate an awareness of our own reactions of grasping, aversion, and delusion in clinical settings, we can explore what ways of working and what institutional structures will best help us to pursue the goal. We also bring to awareness that practice is ongoing. The discourse around stigma, for example, often takes on a judgmental and projective aspect (Harrison & Gill, 2010), as if to name it and talk about it is to absolve oneself. The human inclusiveness of the Buddhist view of suffering offers an alternative to the satisfactions of righteous judgment, in compassionate explorations of our own particular entanglements with grasping, aversion, and delusion.

NOTE

1. The five aggregates in Buddhist thought are the "components which collectively constitute the human individual," namely, "form…feelings…perception…volitional factors [and] consciousness" (Keown, 2004, p. 270).

CHAPTER THIRTEEN

Fragment Three: Bringing Suffering INTO THE Path

DAVID W. JARDINE, GRAHAM McCAFFREY
& CHRISTOPHER GILHAM

You must accept [suffering] when [it] arise[s] because (1) if you do not do this, in addition to the basic suffering, you have the suffering of worry that is produced by your own thoughts, and then the suffering becomes very difficult for you to bear; (2) if you accept the suffering, you let the basic suffering be and do not stop it, but you never have the suffering of worry that creates discontentment when you focus on the basic suffering; and (3) since you are using a method to bring even basic sufferings into the path, you greatly lessen your suffering, so you can bear it. Therefore, it is very crucial that you generate the patience that accepts suffering.

TSONG-KHA-PA (2004, PP. 172–173)

This reminds me of an admixture that has been at the heart of our venture. This in particular: to "let the basic suffering be."

We want to "bring it into the path," that is, to use the Greco-European formulation, we want to see the good in it and not simply recoil away from its appearances. "As you continually experience …suffering …you must know how to bring it into the path. Otherwise …you either generate hostility or you become discouraged" (Tsong-kha-pa, 2004, p. 172).

When the First Noble Truth states that all life is suffering, accepting this truth and learning to be patient with its endless reappearance in our lives and the lives of our students, clients, patients, etc., prevents the arising of a sort of "secondary suffering" that is based on worrying about this "primary" or "basic" suffering, becoming frantic in relationship to it, complicating it with overlays of anxiety, anger, or resentment, as well as overlays of well-meaning sympathies, optimism, promises of cures or schemes of facilitation in its weakest senses (attempts to "make things facile/easy").

This idea of "let[ting] the basic suffering be" is an interestingly phenomenological move, similar to Martin Heidegger's (1963, p. 58) tortuous formulation: "'phenomenology' means …to let that which shows itself be seen from itself in the very way in which it shows itself from itself." He continues by asking "What is it that phenomenology is to 'let us see'?" (p. 59):

> Manifestly, it is something that proximally and for the most part does *not* show itself at all: it is something that lies *hidden* …but at the same time it is something that belongs to what thus shows itself. That which remains *hidden* in a egregious sense, or which relapses and gets *covered up* again, or which shows itself only '*in disguise*', is not just this entity or that, but rather the *Being* of entities. (p. 59)

To the extent that hermeneutics proceeds to identify this Being of entities with impermanence, dependent co-arising, historicity, finitude, and the enduring of experience (*Erfahrung*, which is linked by Gadamer [1989, p. 356] to *pathei mathos*), this passage is rich and full and useful for our purposes.

The recognition of basic suffering often relapses into hiddenness under regimes of cure. The basic difficulty in, for example, coming to learn to read, is masked or disguised by the promises of reading programs designed to make it easy, as if its basic suffering is not actually basic but just an error that can be eradicated through technical means. The basic suffering appears, but only "in disguise"—the guise is not seen through, and we become entranced by the guise and caught in the false promises of the various "cover ups."

CHAPTER FOURTEEN

A Black Blessing

ALEXANDRA FIDYK

> The dread and resistance which every natural human being experiences when it comes to delving too deeply into himself is, at bottom, the fear of the journey to Hades.
> ~ C. G. JUNG, *PSYCHOLOGY AND ALCHEMY*

> Right at the beginning you meet the dragon, the chthonic spirit, the devil or, as the alchemists called it, the blackness, the nigredo, and this encounter produces suffering.
> ~ C. G. JUNG, *C. G JUNG SPEAKING: INTERVIEWS AND ENCOUNTERS*

A pedagogy of suffering begins with black.

Descent into the underworld has been called many names: Black, no-thing-ness, the void, the abyss, land of the Mud Mothers, and, simply, hell. It has been accounted for in Goethe's *Faust*, Bunyan's *Pilgrim's Progress*, and T. S. Eliot's "The Wasteland." It has been described in the *Book of Job*; Melville's *Moby Dick*; the Japanese Izanami; the Greek Kore-Persephone myth; the fairy-tale maidens who go to Baba Yaga; and Perera's Sumerian story of Inanna and Ereshkigal, the Dark Goddess. The theme knows no boundaries. It is known throughout history and across cultures because it refers to an "innate, necessary psychic movement which must take place sooner or later when the conscious ego has exhausted the resources and energies of a given life attitude" (Edinger, 1975, p. 21). It plunges one's whole being into great doubt: Emotions are exhausted; intellect is taken to extremity. While the experience is feared, cultural practices, institutions, and belief systems that promote avoidance or denigration of this journey are dangerous. To deny its call is to miss the depth that beckons and the mystery that opens to a new movement.

Within depth psychology, with its mythological and alchemical roots, descent is known as *nigredo* because it is characterized by "blackening" and known experientially through darkness, despair, and depression. Jung used the Greek word *nekyia* to designate this journey into the land of the dead. A journey that is "no aimless or destructive fall into the abyss, but a meaningful *katabasis eis antron,* a descent into the cave of initiation and secret knowledge" (Jung, 1966/1978, para. 213; Hopper, 1989, p. 118). For Hillman (1979) this "disintegrative" method of depth is soul-making; it refers to the mythologems of Hades. Hades, the God of Depths, the God of Invisibles, the God of the Hidden Wealth or Riches of the Earth. He has much in common with Hermes. Indeed, they are the only gods who can tack between the underworld and the upper worlds. In this way they are both invaluable teachers. Of this journey, Heraclitus, perhaps the first depth psychologist, viewed soul as his *archon*—his first principle. He initiated the conjunction of *psyche, logos,* and *bathun* (depth): "You could not find the ends of the soul though you travelled every way, so deep is its logos" (Hillman, 1979, p. 25). Soul-like truth (in a Gadamerian sense) is a living event; it is ever-changing, expansive, and ripe with potentiality. As with any hermetic art, to uncover the "structure of things, [one] must go into their darkness" (p. 26). The method remains vital today: It is one of depth—the quality and dimension of psyche—not space and not accumulation. It seeks "to show the eventfulness of a topic…[by] keeping something open, in not thinking that something is known… [in] paying attention to what comes to meet" you (Moules, 2002, p. 11). Likewise, it implies that what is considered natural or visible is alone not adequate for soul. To enter the depths, to go ever inward and deeper is to enter the darkness—to meet the unseen, unexpected, and unknown. At one time or another, most people arrive here due to a prolonged and overwhelming period of sadness, illness, loss, trial, frustration, or failure. Heraclitus suggested that true equals deep, a viewpoint of soul, which sounds akin to "understand." He opened the way for a psychological hermeneutics, an archetypal hermeneutics, for to arrive at an understanding, one must look from below, from beneath; one must go into its depth. It is through the act of penetrating, "an insighting into depths that makes soul as it proceeds" (Hillman, 1979, p. 26). In the pursuit of hidden connections in a limitless dimension—"all things become soul" (p. 26). "By cosmic rule" all things compose and decompose; reveal and conceal; die and rise again (frg. 36; Heraclitus, 2001, p. 25).

Here we find Hermes—patron of alchemy, magic, and the hermetic arts. Artistic and artful, he marks the boundaries of our psychological frontiers and the territory in our psyche where the foreign and alien begin. The root of the term "alchemy," *khem*, refers to Egypt as the "land of black soil" or "black land" (Hillman, 1997, p. 45) and its *techne* can be traced through the "black art" of Egyptian embalming, jewelry making, and the dyeing of cloth (p. 45). Viewed as a symbolic art, alchemy has been used to illustrate the process of psychological development or individuation—a term used by Jung "to denote the process by which a person becomes a psychological 'in-dividual', that is, [a] separate, indivisible unity or 'whole'" (Spiegelman & Miyuki, 1994, p. 172). It is the lifelong process of becoming an individual, to be less identified with collective images and actions. For alchemists, this art of becoming unfolds through the conscious work of separation, transformation and integration. Their task was to bring about the unification of disparate parts—to achieve philosophical gold. In psychological terms, the task aims for the "restoration of the whole [person]" (Jung, 1966/1978, para. 213) and the "salvation of the cosmos" (Jung, 1977, p. 228). In pedagogical terms the task aims to evoke in learners a new way of understanding themselves and the lives they and others are living, to re-cognize spiritual and ecological interrelatedness.

While there are four variations of unification in alchemy—*nigredo, albedo, citrinitas,* and *rubedo*—nigredo is the initial process. It marks a descent into the unconscious *and* it signals an accomplishment. It is a condition of having been worked upon, as "charcoal is the result of fire acting on a naïve and natural condition of wood" (Hillman, 1997, p. 47). It is considered "the most negative and difficult operation" in the process (Marlan, 2005, p. 11). It is also one of the most numinous. It requires a dissolution; a stripping to the bone; a shattering—through the application of heat or the intensification of circumstances. Marlan described it thus: "The black sun, blackness, *putrefactio, mortification,* the *nigredo*, poisoning, torture, killing, decomposition, rotting, and death all form a web of interrelationships that describe a terrifying, if most often provisional, eclipse of consciousness or of our conscious standpoint" (p. 11). To endure such suffering seeks to transform the earthly nature within each of us—to release one's attachment to body, possessions, ideas, beauty, and loved ones. The lesson is to learn to let go. As long as one remains attached to or unconsciously identified with such things and their corresponding emotions (desire, pride, envy, or fear), one remains internally separated and divided (Fidyk, 2010, p. 8). Ultimately, it leads to the fading of the ego's light and a death—as portrayed by the black sun. In alchemy, "the loss of light renders the soul burnt out, dried up, and picked bare" (Marlan, 2005, p. 26). It is this place where one must enter to understand the *Sol niger* and the nigredo process. This wisdom echoes Buddhism's Four Noble Truths, beginning with the first premise: all life is suffering (Fidyk, 2013). Followed by the second, where one learns to release attachments. The difficulty in each perspective, however, is to survive this place and its forms of thievery.

Darkness is not a phenomenon welcomed by many. Historically, it has not been treated hospitably by psychiatry, medicine, counseling, or education. As such, it has remained in the unconscious and is viewed "primarily in its negative aspect," itself constituting a shadow—"something to integrate, to move through and beyond" (Marlan, 2005, p. 12)—its intrinsic importance bypassed. Jung (1963/1989) noted, however, that darkness "has its own peculiar intellect and its own logic which should be taken very seriously" (para. 345). While black dissolves meaning and the hope for meaning, indeed, destroys any philosophy, theory, or belief of anything else unfolding, it is absolutely necessary for a shift in the way one sees and so becomes. As Eliot (n.d.) aptly wrote, "wait without hope, for hope would be hope for the wrong thing;…[w]ait without thought, for you are not ready for thought." As such, black breaks paradigms (Hillman, 1997) and makes one keenly aware of one's own inadequacy in bringing required change. It severs ego's identification and separates the head and body: Black decapitates. Only then might the mind begin to recognize what the body *alone* feels for the mind is forced out of its abstractions and its "habitual concretisms" (p. 51). When all defenses and mental constructs have been dissolved, one eventually surrenders and discovers suffering as a valid part of life's process—a fact of the human condition. By extension, this knowing removes suffering from the "patriarchal-adversary-scapegoating perspective that blames someone or something and wants it removed, wants something actively done with it" (Perera, 1981, pp. 73–74).

*****

Suffering has a purpose: when it is transformed, it gives rise to insight, empathy, receptivity, and renewal. Unexpectedly, it may even teach one how to thrive, for its aim is greater wholeness. It teaches one to subordinate light—be it knowledge, attachment to colour consciousness, or the belief that phenomena can be understood (Hillman, 1997, p. 47). In this way, one also learns to receive, to read loss as an accomplishment, and to embrace deconstruction again and again. The journey to the underworld has also been known as a source of significant creativity and growth for having surrendered. As Jung and others experienced, "the artistic venture often begins with the symbol of the nekyia" (Hopper, 1989, p. 118). In learning to suffer through, healing occurs not only because meaning or image is found but also because the process of life is attended with an "empathetic presence and a mirroring that touches it wherever it is" (Perera, 1981, p. 74). This is where light seeps in, where creative energy breaks forth. As the alchemists knew, even when black turns blue, the depth of the former blackness does not disappear; blue renders darkness visible (Hillman, n.d., p. 37).

This is where I currently dwell. Gunmetal blue.

Sometimes the transition from darkness to light is an elongated curve through a series of other tints and tones, notably darker hues, "the blues of bruises, sobriety" and self-examination (Hillman, n.d., p. 1). This "blue transit between black and white is like that: Sadness which emerges from despair as it proceeds towards reflection" (pp. 1–2). Reflection here is not a concentrated act; rather, it is marked by embodied attention, an earthened presence, and an empathetic ear. While blue brings black along with it, there has been a silvering, and because of it a profound distinction. I am aware of a new attitude. Humility. Grounded and weighted—for having released to death deep within the Earth, in black humus, in what makes one humble, humane, human.

Although slight in movement, its meaning is tantamount, as black no longer binds me, like the stickiness of pitch or tar. Black pulverized my old thinking patterns (systems of thought central to an academic life), decapitated my will, dissolved visibility, and trapped psyche in the "inertia and extension of matter" (p. 2). True to the art, *mortificatio* is a time of symptoms.

After struggling for 10 years with chronic pain, tumors, infections, endless fatigue, and brain fog, the stress of another international relocation initiated collapse. Within weeks of starting fall term, I struggled to remember colleagues' names. Within a month, a 10-block drive to campus brought me to tears, as I could no longer coordinate mind, body, and vehicle. Within four months, short-term memory, subtle emotions, and cognitive acuity were gone. Then, a full decapitation of not only my will, but also my ability to read and write (via brain atrophy)—and with it, all capacity to care. Life as I knew it was done. As was I.

Diagnosed with a complex, late-stage chronic neurological disease: *Lyme Borreliosis*, with bartonella and mycoplasma pneumoniae co-infections and Epstein Barr virus—not medically recognized in Canada or covered by healthcare, radical and aggressive protocols (by US specialists) dictated the days and years of my life. Confined to a new city without family or friends, on full medical leave from university, months passed without a visitor or conversation. Hours of every day focused on extensive treatments, often followed by nausea and diarrhea, and always encased in a cold, isolating inhibition. Plunged into "blacker than black" (Hillman, 1997, p. 50), psychologically shattered and physiologically stripped, four long years passed.

This is not a heroine's journey—there is no egoic striving, no return in better shape for the tasks of life. This is a soul movement: The land of black swallowed my "soul into a depth for its own sake so that there is no return" (Hillman, 1979, p. 168). By soul, I mean "a perspective…a viewpoint toward things rather than a thing itself" (Hillman, 1975, p. xiv). Simply put, *suffering through* brings about a "point of view 'beyond' and 'below' life's concerns" (Hillman, 1975, pp. 206–207)—the striving for or the acquisition of things. A warning however must accompany nigredo, for there was a period when I sensed that I might succumb to "the tragic paradox of black" (Hillman, 1997, p. 50). Of all alchemical colours, "black is the most densely inflexible and [thus] the most oppressive and dangerously literal state of the soul" (Hillman, 1997, p. 51). The task even here is to yield. To wait without waiting….

Having seen black, it is now blue that enables me to see *by way of black*; black darkens and sophisticates the eye so that it can see *through*. Alchemists call this the *caput mortuum*, the death head or raven's head. It requires both a *living through* and a *seeing through* suffering. It is a *hermaion*—a "godsend," a gift, a blessing (Hyde, 1998, p. 132), for bearing witness to extremity.

Suffering, like depth psychology and alchemy, offers a way of knowing, a way of seeing, a way with the unsaid of life. Suffering is a way to see by means of black. It seeks to make darkness conscious, however disagreeable and unpopular. Suffering as pedagogical is a move in depth from the analytical mind to soul, a move against the current trajectory in education, the helping professions, and the historical stream of our culture, which embrace figures of light, which fear the "darker shades of existence" (Hillman, 1997, p. 52). Suffering as a vital part of human life is a clear call to hermeneutics as a way to inquire and dwell in the mystery of life.

CHAPTER FIFTEEN

Time

JUDSON INNES

Tender parting and elegant flow,
a silent passing above the forest floor.
Wings raised up to gain favour,
and soften the looming perch.

Triggered now, firm thrust and smooth unfolding,
fell swoop and talon strike.
A mere moment swept away, devoured.
Echoed perhaps in a ripple of air,
or brief shrug of robust bough.

CHAPTER SIXTEEN

Quickening, Patience, Suffering

DAVID W. JARDINE

A FORTUITOUS E-MAIL EXCHANGE

Jodi [Latremouille]: Hi, David, I was reading *The Spell of the Sensuous* (Abram, 1996) and was reminded of that paper you sent us a couple of weeks ago. There is a passage about the Australian Aboriginal tradition of "songlines" or "ways through" the continent, meandering trails, auditory route maps that are composed of a melody with various verses to be sung in different locations. It speaks of the Dreamtime Ancestors, while chanting their ways across the land, depositing a trail of "spirit children" along the trail. They are described as "life cells," children not yet born; they lie in a potential state within the ground. When a woman is pregnant, the actual conception is thought to occur with the quickening, when she steps on a song couplet in the earth. So the spirit child "works its way into her womb, and impregnates the fetus with song."

Wherever the woman find herself when she feels the quickening—the first kick within her womb—she knows that a spirit child has just leapt into her body from the earth. And so she notes the precise place in the land where the quickening occurred, and reports this to the tribal elders. The elders then examine the land at that spot, discerning which Ancestor's songline was involved, and precisely which stanzas of that Ancestor's song will belong to the child. ...In this manner every Aboriginal person, at birth, inherits a particular stretch of song as his private property, a stretch of song that is, as it were, his title to a stretch of land, to his conception site" (Abram, 1996, pp. 166–167).

I woke up this morning way too early and couldn't go back to sleep! Maybe if I send you this I can sleep again :-)

David: Well, I woke up this morning thinking of that paper and how I might either finish it or abandon it again for now. This almost reminds me of what Abram is describing—this fortuitous email just leapt! And that that leap is an ancestral one in its own way—what quickens is not just this life but also the lead lines of song that bear it here. And, as with much of my writing, it reminds me too of Hillman's passage, and Tsong-kha-pa's which are the headers of that paper, about patience.

TO BEGIN, SINGING

There's another word for objectivity, which I feel is much better, and that is 'patience.' Suffering with it. (Hillman & Shamdasani, 2013, p. 156)

It is very crucial that you generate the patience that accepts suffering. (Tsong-kha-pa, 2004, pp. 172–173)

This title term "quickening" is an apt image for something that is phenomenologically recognizable in hermeneutic work—that moment of suddenness, when an idea comes alive and starts to become full of a *life of its own*. It is an apt term because it designates the deep ontology of hermeneutic work: that we live in a living world whose life is, in turns, generated and degenerated, renewed, transformed, handed over, ailing, near death, new-born, occluded, woken up, and fast asleep. And this points to something evident in the work of an alert classroom—that beautiful and difficult and often sudden arrival, when students and teachers alike lean inwards towards a topic, a topography, a place, and feel life rising up in and through its song lines.

Its lives.

Our lives.

It lives and so do we, now, again, caught in its new radiance.

Hermeneutic work is both the "furthering of an event that goes far back" (Gadamer, 1989, p. xxiv) and the embracing of the new such that that furthering and those events henceforth appear differently than we could have heretofore imagined. Both of these insights must be held together—like David G. Smith's (1999) image of "living in the belly of a paradox" (p. 138) wherein the child, the new, the arrival, arrives as both part of us and apart from us. This is why quickening quickens us, because we recognize ourselves in its stirring even though it is not me stirring but rather me being stirred. The purpose of hermeneutic work is not to solve this as if it were an error, but to find ways to abide this ever-just-arriving irresolvable and make it, once again, livable.

Upstartings gone beyond startles to become "possible ways of shaping our lives" (Gadamer, 1986, p. 59). Tough work, this going beyond.

This tough work bespeaks the especial affinity between hermeneutic work and pedagogy.

It summons, too, Jacques Derrida's image of the Seder table's empty chair, awaiting, biding, leaned forward into a future's portend with "hospitality for what is to come [*avenir*]" (Derrida & Ferraris, 2001, p. 31).

This "apart from us" is a locale of great trauma and joy in hermeneutic work as well as the work of pedagogy—an experience of an other, asking us to be otherwise. We could not experience it as apart from us if it were not part of us and us part of it. Paradox. Belly laugh in recognition.

Such giddy composure is both "the path and the goal" (Gadamer, 1989, p. 180) of hermeneutics:

> It's like making a path through the forest. At first it's rough going, with a lot of obstructions, but returning to it again and again, we clear the way. After a while the ground becomes firm and smooth from being walked on repeatedly. Then we have a good path for walking in the forest. (Chah, 2005, p. 83)

Quickening: "*it* draws *you* into *its* path" (Gadamer, 2007b, p. 198, emphases added).

Quickening thus bespeaks the quick of it, that, even though all this work of mine on some particular topography of the world has set out the conditions of possible insight—all the reading, thinking, writing, exploration, repeated mulls and conversations, transcriptions, finding citations and etymologies and dates and names and places, copying things out by hand, falling in love with an image or recoiling into thick nickel-spittle fear and inaction in the face of it, receiving emails and waking up singing unexpectedly, looking and looking through literature, writing things and reading them aloud and scratching them out, revising, rejecting, trying again, reading things to others, trying to memorize phrases and finding these phrases in the voices and faces of those I meet day to day, hoping they will say just the right thing that I need to break the spell, clear the way, or whatever that hesitant block might be called—the breakthroughs and disappointments, and, often, leaving the work behind, for now, in sad abandonment, filed away like a corpse in a cold drawer, darkened and chilled for possible later exhumation, sickened by this thing I'm trying to write, wanting to get away from it, failure, the dark valleys of shadows and death…*all of this* suffered roiling only makes insight *possible* not *necessary*. There is no *necessary* pedagogy to such suffering.

Teachers know this, that the plan does not assuredly *cause* the quick of arrival and engagement. Teachers know this weird gap—like a silence in a songline, suspended—and, if they become experienced, they learn the painful lesson of how to not panic over it. A great trial with its own sufferings.

Patience, here, is necessary, but it never ensures.

"I am willing to endure the shame of falling short as the price of admission" (Berry & Moyers, 2013)—over and over to stand failed in the face of the work I undertake, "outplayed" (Gadamer, 1989, p. 106) all over again.

A hermeneutic secret, then, that my failure to measure up to the work I do is a sign of why *its* success is not *mine*, a sign of how the child must outrun its forbearers if it is to have a quickened life of its own and how, paradoxically, again, my success in such matters is found in precisely this failure. This is part of the careful suffering at the heart of teaching, that students get up and walk away, just like my own child has done, and how this necessarily leaves me haunted by his death even though he is alive and kicking.

Even in walking away, these young things then walk amidst songlines. Thus, caring, in hermeneutics, for the well-being of these lines is my only comfort. It is how the suffering of such matters might just be Noble.

Might be—that "might" is why compassion is always necessary and why sorrow (German, *Sorge*, translated in the work of Martin Heidegger [1962] as "care") always necessarily ensues upon the joy of quickening. This is why the hermeneutic affection for quickening must learn to be about love and not attachment, about compassion, not rescue.

Again, all of this roiling work only makes insight *possible*, not *necessary*. This gap between the possible and the necessary cannot be bridged by an act of will, by methodologism, or by increases in funding, or earnestness, or drive. This bridging, if it happens, "happens to us over and above our wanting and doing" (Gadamer, 1989, p. xxvii):

> The whole leap depends on the slow pace at the beginning, like a long flat run before a broad jump. Anything that you want to move has to start where it is, in its stuckness. That involves erudition—probably too much erudition. One wants to get stuck in the history, the material, the knowledge, even relish it. Deliberately spending time in the old place. Then suddenly seeing through the old place. (Hillman, 1991, p. 154)

And oh the tales that can be told of being simply stuck seemingly endlessly in that old place (that, too, is quite a topic). Just like this chapter that has taken *so* long—it's taking its own sweet time tastes bitter sometimes.

But here is the hermeneutic hope. There can be a moment when the effect outruns such efforts and causes, such erudition and history and material, such relish. It is a moment when *the outcome becomes uncaused by the efforts to cause it,* when it becomes, in the old Latin coinage, *causa sui,* something generated within itself, something with a "life of its own," literally, from the Latin, something that is the cause of itself. Until this happens, I do not have a topic for the work I am doing, only frail and patient suffering and scuttling around in stuckness.

Quickening—with all the startled witlessness that comes with it in the act of composing a text, when it rises up of its own accord and I am asked to act accordingly. I become a follower, a guardian, a cautioner, full of affection for something now both part of me but apart, it turned to face me now, full of "the…intrusive power of a being reposing in itself" (Gadamer, 1977, p. 227). I become an object of *its* quick regard ("it would not deserve the interest we take in it if it did not have something to teach us that we could not know by ourselves" [Gadamer, 1989, p. xxxv]).

I become the outcome, and *it* becomes the cause. It seeks to outcome me, to make me and my words and actions into what it needs. Now I must marshal what I know, what skill I've gained, what experiences I've gleaned, what practices I've practiced, what patience I've tested, and bring them as offerings to this meeting of the quick:

> If one pursues a hermeneutic study it is not enough to write about different things. I must also write differently, in a way that acknowledges, attends and waits upon the agency of the world. Hermeneutics is therefore akin to the opening up of "animating possibilities presented by each event" (Hillman 1982, p. 77). Hermeneutic writing is premised on the eventful ("understanding proves to be an event" [Gadamer 1989, p. 309]) arrival of animating spirit. This is why its name is the name of a god of arrival, of youth, of fecundity and fertility and agency. It is premised on the belief in a resonant, animate world, full of voices and spooks and spirits which require a form of attention that extends beyond one's self, out into the living ways of things. It is premised on the arrival of the young boy Hermes, flitting and flirting. Hermeneutics represents a conversation with the old borne on the breath and in the face of "the new, the different, the true" (Gadamer 1977, p. 9). This is not precisely a leap that I do, even though I must prepare myself through immersing myself in the voices of the ancestors, spend time in the old place [learning of the songlines]. And then, "the leap"—some insight arrives, it seems, from elsewhere, a "provocation" (Gadamer 1989, p. 299) carrying its own agencies and consequences and desires. "To understand…hermeneutically is to trace back what is said to what wishes to be said" (Grondin 1995, p. 32)— just imagine, things *wishing* to be said. (Jardine, 2008, p. 110)

What do you want from me? And what will become of me if I concede to this urging? And, perhaps most telling, what is the right thing to do, now, here, in this turn of a sentence? It is thus that such quickening is linked to the fact that I, as one trying to compose myself in the face of such quickening, must now suffer its arising. Trying then to settle myself and compose in the face of these arising and quickening topics is, in part, trying to figure out what attention I now owe this arrival. I owe these topics something of my life because they are already intimate parts of that very life (part and apart), some of its organs and blood, some of its memory and regret and sudden joy.

This is a deeply ecological occurrence, this recognition that my life is in debt to the surroundings and territories and topographies of its emergence, and that my research is, in this sense, always already underwritten, already "funded" (Latin *fundus* meaning, among other things, "piece of land").

AN ELONGATED POLITICAL AND ECOLOGICAL CHORUS

> The concoctions that are beneficial to the rich and powerful, they'll tend to propagate. The ones that are harmful to the rich and powerful tend to be marginalized and suppressed. But that has nothing to do with the reality of the world. That has to do with how power systems function. (RenegadeEconomist, 2011)

> What becomes of the function of education within the state? Insofar as market logic determines the value of *all* social practices, only forms of education that serve the market have value. Hence the recommendation of Hon. Mike Harris, Premier of Ontario, at the beginning of Hayekian reforms in that province in 1989: "The humanities should be removed from the university, since they serve no economic benefit." More recently, the *Social Sciences and Humanities Research Council of Canada* (2009) has passed policies that give priority funding to proposals that directly serve the interests of the business community. (Smith, 2014)

This matter of a quickening that arrives over and above those things that cause it causes institutions to "waver and tremble" (Caputo, 1987, p. 1) and often respond with disdain and condescension because such institutions are premised, perhaps inevitably, on the market-accountabilities of causation. Unfunded research has become a suspicious waste of time in the faculty I am now leaving. Rarely a minute goes by without the marshaling of workshops to increase the chances of getting grants, getting published, and on and on. Equally rarely does anyone feel that there is any time at all to talk about the territories we are researching—*what is being thought about* rather than the *fact* that it is funded. Flippantly put, if it is funded, *it doesn't matter what it is about*. It is already deemed worthwhile because, in advance, the only object worth whiling over is funding. All of this is premised, of course, on the neo-liberal movements of withdrawing public funds for public work, a fetish for the individualistic privatization of scholarship that equates with linking it to market-economic productivities and outcomes (Smith, 2014). Faculties are now underfunded, so they need external funding. But such externality then feeds the atrophying of the *fundus* of the work itself in favor of the productivity of the outcomes.

Without external funding, scholarship is simply time wasted. Mal-lingering.

Just now, in writing this, overhearing (March 22, 2014, 2 pm, EST) the premier of Ontario, Kathleen Wynne, say at a Liberal Caucus Annual meeting, "in government, impatience is a virtue." "Time is always running out for machines. They shorten our work…by simplifying it and speeding it up, but our work perishes quickly" (Berry, 1983, p. 76). We are instructed to erase any references in our reference lists that are older than five years, because such matters are considered "out of date." Under such auspices, songlines and our blood relation to them are *deliberately being cut*. Their memory traces and language are deliberately being suppressed, marginalized, and ridiculed—too wild and out of view of productivity surveillances and accountabilities—as we rush, instead, into work that is premised on outdated-ness as its deliberate goal. Our work is deliberately designed to not last, to not mature and age well, but simply become disposed of in favor of what's next—the fetish for the new, so odd, as we both recoil from the wild and summon new arrivals at accelerating rates. That is why there is a great analogue, here, to First Nations lamentations and hopes, and to ecological nightmares. Thus, too, the great bullying of market consciousness—when Xi Jinping was announced as the new president of the Peoples' Republic of China, the Canadian Broadcasting Corporation introduced him in its radio broadcast as the new leader of the world's largest *economy*. And, too, distraction becomes the requisite mood (Smith, 2014) whereby a low-level panic is maintained just enough to propel insatiable consumption and production. Satiation, of course, would spell the end of the spell. There must be no "development of the concept of *enough*" (Berry, 1983, p. 79).

A SIDE-NOTE ON AN IATROGENIC LOOP

There is a reason that Buddhists call this world and the delusions that sustain it a Wheel. We find, here, a terrible, heartbreaking loop, where the attempts to ameliorate our troubled situation are suddenly seen to be its causes. Fear of arising leads to panic setting in, and once panic sets in, procedures, rubrics, mandates, and methodologies rush in, in good-hearted attempts to save the day, further foreclosing on future quickenings and further confirming the fear of arising that set this sequence in motion in the first place. Hence "outcomes-based education" and ever-louder calls for "teacher accountability" that are *causing the panics for which they are touted as the cure*, with little or no consciousness of there being ancestral songlines that lie buried under these scurrying surface loops. We then seek relief inside the very loops that cause us to seek relief, unable to decode our circumstances because we've lost track of what might bring relief outside of this loop.

We not only no longer know how to sing. We not only no longer know why singing might help. We've come to believe that singing is the cause of our suffering.

In other words, the loop and its insides are experienced to be all there is, and the promises to "fix" education with this or that or this skitter and skip across consciousness like stones on water. Many teachers I know correctly sense that there is "something else going on" here, but memory has been lost. Meditating on these matters and singing over them is deemed impractical because, of course, we don't have the time, not here, "in the real world." As one teacher noted in a recent class, if you just nebulously sense this iatrogenic loop but have no way of unraveling its spell, if all you have is an ever-new sense of "trouble" with no songline recourses, all you can do is complain. This is why our relationship to the culture of complaint that ravages many schools must be one of love and affection for those suffering from the forestalling of quickening, from the disparaging of patience and the cultivation of "the old place," from the loss of any memory of what has been done to us. The complaint is correct ("something is going on") but incorrect (it feeds on uneasy without recourse to the sort of study, composure, practice, and patience that might ameliorate such suffering, that might lead to some insight and a slowing of the spinning of the wheels of complaint). Complaint then pacifies the complainants by letting them feel an in-reality impotent agency while the powers that be feed and maintain this impotent sense of agency in their "employees" or "clients" (students, classroom teachers, University professors, nurses in hospitals, and so on) by mocking as "unreal" the recourses that might break this spell. Complaint thus becomes a perfect commodity—endlessly bought (into), endlessly promising satisfaction, and endlessly never precisely delivering, thus propelling the perpetual need for "more."

Little wonder that attempts at enlivening any memory or knowledge of this wheeling fix we're in, and suggesting patience in the face of the quickening of the world are often met by anger. We've placed a lot of stake in our attempts to avoid the suffering that comes from learning to embrace the suffering of the world and its arising. It is little wonder that we unwittingly dream of a pedagogy premised on "'a state of perpetual war' (Postel & Drury, 2003), given the perpetuity of the world's [natality and] mortality. After all, a war against our response ('terror') to the very existence of uprising is, of necessity, perpetual" (Jardine, 2012, p. 5).

Little wonder that the scholarship feels so embattled, that many of my colleagues feel under siege and exhausted, that no effort is ever enough. However un- or semi-conscious it may be *perpetuating this state of siege and exhaustion is deliberate*—it is, quite literally, de-liberating. In fact, to enter into such a state of perpetual war is now seen as a cause of great pride in the academy. There is no other way to explain how a university can have "being in the top 5" —i.e., "beating" all but four other universities in some battle, some race to be "first"—as its stated goal. I'm willing to allow that some of those "in charge" are simply living out this wheeling and think it is simply "the real world," or "the way things are these days."

Thus, quickening becomes terror, a perpetual insurgency that must be perpetually fought with ever-new sources of funding. And, as market logic dictates, *it can never be enough*.

This is not a logic of speed. It is a logic of acceleration. The faster we speed over the Earth, the less likely our foot might fall somewhere long enough to experience the leap, the quickening.

Hence, unable to be "interpreted," quickening becomes broken in two. It makes more likely, on the one hand, our increasingly stunned fascination with the skittering surface stimulations of our own latest and shiniest devices (where quickening becomes sheer speediness of access, and promise, and novelty, and flight between one site and another) and, on the other hand, our equally stunned fascination with a world that feels full, as so many recent movies and television series show, of the walking dead, evacuated of the quick but seeming to summon us and our attention nevertheless.

"JUST START DOING IT"

> *Berry*: The country and, I think Vandana [Shiva] can tell you, the world, is full of people who are seeing something that needs to be done and starting to do it, without the government's permission, or official advice, or expert advice, or applying for grants or anything else. They just start doing it. (Berry & Moyers, 2013)

There is no way out of this iatrogenic loop-logic except to simply step out of it. I am on the verge of retiring from my job and realize full well how easy that is for me to say. That ease comes with great sorrow, but rest assured that such ease is hard won and won't come unless it is practiced. Hermeneutics is a practice that must be patiently practiced if you are to become practiced in it.

Just start doing it.

Hermeneutic work (as with worthwhile work in the classroom), in its love of the patient work of attending to quickening ("to know the world, we have to love it" [Berry & Moyers, 2013]), provides a modest way, however embattled it remains in the eyes of the academy.

Along this way, I must suffer the disjuncture between the lingering time called for by such arrivals and what time they need from us, and the terrible market-logic panics that have caught us spellbound and halt with a sense of low-level emergency and a deathly silence:

> *Moyers*: What do you say to those people who ask "Wendell, please tell me what I can do."
>
> *Berry*: Well, you're putting me into the place I always wind up in. And that's the problem, we've tried to impose the answer. The answers will come, not from walking up to your farm and saying "This is what I want and this is what I expect from you." You walk up and you say "What do you need?" and you commit yourself by saying that I'm not going to do any extensive damage here until I know what it is you are asking of me. And this can't be hurried; this is the dreadful situation that young people are in, and I think of them and I say, well, the situation you're in is a situation that is going to call for a lot of patience, and to be patient in an emergency is a terrible trial. (Berry & Moyers, 2013)

This is the trial to which hermeneutics is dedicated. This is why Hans-Georg Gadamer (1989, p. 356) invoked the words of Aeschylus in his invocation of *pathei mathos* as key to understanding the sort of experience and knowledge sought by hermeneutic work: *learning through suffering*.

Sure, we must remain clever in and about the machinations of the world. Go ahead. Just don't fall for it and start believing that the getting of grants is the real work. The getting is the cover story, the lie needing to be told to those who brook no quarter for the truth. So here's the impudence (shush and keep this to yourself). The real *fundus* of this funding must itself be hermeneutic: its "ground" must be the patient and suffered ground of the Earth, the topic, the stretch of song, and the path and goal of composure that such a ground requires of me:

> What we call the modern world is not necessarily, and not often, the real world, and there is no virtue in being up-to-date in it. It is a false world, based upon economies and values and desires that are fantastical, a world in which millions of people have lost any idea of the materials, the disciplines, the restraints, and the work necessary to support human life, and have thus become dangerous to their own lives and to the possibility of life. The job now is to get back to that perennial and substantial world in which we really do live, in which the foundations of our life will become visible

to us, and in which we can accept our responsibilities again within the conditions of necessity and mystery. (Berry, 1983, p. 13)

People whose governing habit is the relinquishment of power, competence and responsibility, and whose characteristic suffering is the anxiety of futility, make excellent spenders. They are the ideal consumers. By inducing in them little panics of boredom, powerlessness, mortality, paranoia, they can be made to buy virtually anything that is "attractively packaged." (Berry, 1986, p. 24)

Any grant will do as long as it is attractively packaged. But hell, get the grant. Shut up. Stay alert. Do what you can. Study. Try not to get in too much trouble with the authorities. Remember that they, too, are suffering under precisely the delusions that they present to you as real. They are not the authors of this delusion, just bit-players in its weaving.

Their suffering is worse. They have to *believe* it or become empty shells, empty shills that feel compelled (for our own good) to pretend to believe it. The purpose of scholarship, its "end," no matter what its topic, is to break this spell. Just give up expecting much thanks in return from those living "in [delusional spell of] the real world."

You will be understood to be causing suffering ("rocking the boat"), not offering a way to ameliorate it.

SECOND LAST MULL

Berry: A lot of my writing has been, when it hasn't been in defense of precious things, has been a giving of thanks for precious things.

Moyers: What are the precious things that you think are in danger right now?

Berry: It is mighty hard right now to think of anything that is precious that *isn't* in danger. But maybe that's an advantage. The poet William Butler Yeats said somewhere "Things reveal themselves passing away." And it may be that the danger that we have inflicted on every precious thing reveals the preciousness of it and shows us our duty. (Berry & Moyers, 2013)

One of my classes this year takes place at a school I've been working with for decades. This fall, for the first time, my hand hit the door and it was locked, and there was a new security camera pointing at me, and a buzzer. That such a circumstance was good-heartedly considered, I do not doubt. That such new arrangements both aim at *increasing a sense of security* while at the same time *increasing the atmosphere of insecurity* in which we now live, I also do not doubt. I just no longer know who to tell about such experiences except you, now, reader.

Sing, if you're able. If you're not yet able, learn. The suffering that comes is assuredly noble.

Such securing takes me back to thoughts of F. W. Taylor, about whom I've written often, but who is making a new appearance that sounds too familiar:

> A little more than a century ago, Frederick Winslow Taylor introduced "scientific man-agement" to American factories. By meticulously tracking and measuring the physical movements of manufacturing workers as they went through their tasks, Taylor coun-seled, companies could determine the "one best way" to do any job and then enforce that protocol on all other workers. Through the systematic collection of data, industry could be optimized, operated as a perfectly calibrated machine. "In the past the man has been first," declared Taylor; "in the future the system must be first." (Carr, 2013)

The links between my faculty's funding fetish and the desire to put scholarship under surveillance cannot be avoided, even though this may be no one's intent. And then this:

> There is, for example, the Hitachi Business Microscope, which office workers wear on a lanyard around their neck. "The device is packed with sensors that monitor things like how workers move and speak, as well as environmental factors like light and temperature. So, it can track where workers travel in an office, and recognize whom they're talking to by communicating with other people's badges. It can also measure how *well* they're talking to them—by recording things like how often they make hand gestures and nod, and the energy level in their voice." Other companies are developing Google Glass-style "smart glasses" to accomplish similar things. (Carr, 2013)

The fear of quickening (like the reactionary ecological fear of "the wild" ["the child," as Alice Miller (1989) noted]) is ripe and rampant.

Kids these days!

A SONG AT THE END OF THINGS WITH TOO MANY THINGS TO SAY ALL AT ONCE

Even though it is difficult, don't panic.

To be patient in an emergency is a terrible trial, but it is the only deeply hu-man prospect.

Hermeneutic insight and all the time and patience and suffering it takes are, I believe, asked of us now more than ever:

> The important thing to do is to learn all you can about where you are, about that place, and to make common cause with that place and then resigning yourself, becoming

patient enough to work with it over a long time. And then, what you do is you increase the possibility that you'll make a good example. (Berry & Moyers, 2013)

The possibility, *not* the necessity. This is the great risk that must be suffered, ventured. This:

> Living in the belly of a paradox wherein a genuine life together is made possible only in the context of an *ongoing conversation* which never ends and which must be sustained for life together to go on at all. The openness that is required is not a vague licentiousness, but a risky, deliberate engagement of the full conflict and ambiguity by which new horizons of mutual understanding are achieved. (Smith, 1999, p. 133)

And then this: "Understanding is an adventure and, like any adventure, it always involves some risk" (Gadamer, 1983, p. 141).

And then "adventure is 'undergone,' like a test or a trial from which one emerges enriched and more mature " (Gadamer, 1989, p. 69). I must add, here, "maybe."

Ah. Do you feel that songline? Fear of the quickening wild child (fear of Hermes) is at once a fear of aging, of "maturing." And a fear of aging, of maturing, is being overly enamored with the child, the new, with "what's next" coupled with a steadfast desire to not learn from such arrivals: Hans-Georg Gadamer (1989, p. xxii) brilliantly named this temptation "the naive self-esteem of the present moment." This is another hermeneutic insight, that we can become simply ravaged by the "onslaught of the new" (Arendt, 1969, p. 185) if we become spellbound by arrival itself and have no time for the patience required to let such adventures ripen us. We fear quickening because we fear mortality.

So the whole of this chapter's venture into quickening now inverts: we are perhaps *too much in love with the new* as a way of forestalling insight into our own mortality, of forestalling our own aging. With patience comes experience, and the impatience of modern scholarship that eradicates old references eradicates my becoming an experienced teacher, an experienced scholar. Just because I've published a lot and got many grants and taught many courses does not necessarily mean that I am "experienced" in such matters.

So, we have here, in the efforts to avoid the great suffering that comes with insight into patience and quickening, a delusional complex that cannot bear the belly of this paradox, actions in praise of the child ("the new," "the latest," "next") while also hating and fearing the child and its quickening arrival, wanting to outrun it. Wanting to no longer suffer.

As a consequence, our well-intended responses, our questions, become Utopian (literally, "nowhere"), Titanic, Gigantic, distorted under ideal eyes raised too high, that no longer know the ground they walk, no longer having the patience to ready themselves for the leap.

What can we do to make schools better?

"We don't have a right to ask that question. We have to ask 'What's the right thing to do?' and go ahead and do it, and take no thought for the morrow" (Berry & Moyers, 2013).

CHAPTER SEVENTEEN

Smart Ass Cripple

W. JOHN WILLIAMSON

What a man [sic] has to learn through suffering is not this or that particular thing, but insight into the limitations of humanity, into the absoluteness of the barrier that separates man from the divine. It is ultimately a religious insight—the kind of insight that gave birth to Greek tragedy. Thus experience is experience of human finitude. The truly experienced person is one who has taken this to heart. (Hans Georg Gadamer, 1989, p. 357)

Words like 'suffering' and 'afflicted with' are demeaning. People who live with Down syndrome lead fulfilling lives; many people with Down syndrome attend college or university, work and get married. (Canadian Down Syndrome Society, 2013, para 1)

Expressing pain and sarcasm since 2010. (Smart Ass Cripple, n.d.)

THE PROBLEM WITH "SUFFERS FROM"

How should we talk about suffering as it relates to disability? Even as it remains in frequent use in media and by the medical community, the phrase "suffers from" in relation to physical or mental impairments (e.g., *suffers from* dyslexia) has been widely criticized as patronizing and demeaning (Snow, 2009; Titchkosky, 2001). Criticism of the use of "suffers from" is often made from the perspective that the only appropriate way to discuss disability is with "people-first" language, which emphasizes the personhood of people with disabilities over their impairments. "*People with*" autism or "*people with*" learning disabilities would be exemplary "people-first" phrases. "People-first" has, with this humble precursor, become the dominant bureaucratic language practice for describing disability (Titchkosky, 2001). While critics have suggested "people-first" conceals its own ideologies of individualism as well as a continued reliance on a medical deficit rubric for understanding disability (Titchkosky, 2001), the argument "people-first" makes against "suffers from" is a powerful one. It is unjust and demeaning to judge the quality of someone's life as less than that of people deemed normal simply because that person has one of the impairments we currently consider disabilities. "Suffers from," in this context, is the epitome of ableism.

SUFFERING FROM FINITUDE

"Suffers from" understandings, that is, understandings that question the quality of life of people with disabilities, have profoundly hindered the inclusion of people with disabilities in public life, and there is some wisdom in pointing to the toxic assumptions (Snow, 2009) that undergird this phrase and encouraging people to avoid its use. Still, despite the incorrectness of "suffers from" when it is used in this way, it seems a painfully obvious statement to note that all people suffer, existentially, from many things. Giving voice to our suffering in its agony and in its mystery, whether through religious texts, artistic representations, or philosophical reflection, is a primary and profound human expression (Caputo, 1987). I do not intend an extensive spiritual discussion in this chapter, but I would point out that the mysteries of suffering and the place suffering occupies in human existence has been a hermeneutic obsession since antiquity. Buddhism reminds us of this in noting that "All is suffering," and maintains that the only transcendence possible from this state is a lived commitment to the conquest of desire and attachment (Boeree, 1997). As Chesterton (1916) has pointed out, in the Judaeo-Christian tradition the book of Job hauntingly asks "What is the purpose of God?" in the context of human suffering before even more hauntingly refusing to give the comfort of a satisfactory answer.

> God comes in at the end, not to answer riddles but to propound them. And the "great surprise" is that the book of Job makes Job so suddenly satisfied with the mere presentation of something impenetrable. …He has been told nothing, but he feels the terrible and tingling atmosphere of something that is too good to be told. (para. 10)

In both of these examples our finitude seems sewn inextricably into the fabric of our suffering; in the former example, the inevitable limits of our having, in the latter, the limits of our knowing. Also—and I would endorse the sentiment of universality, if not the Cartesian mind/body split in Davis's (2002) statement—"what is universal in life, if there are universals, is the experience of the limitations of the body" (p. 32). Important questions remain about why, when it comes to disability, some of the limitations to which Davis referred are marked off as "abnormal," not universal, and about the role ableist ideologies and practices have played in emphasizing the severity, stigma, and visibility of these limitations. It is, nevertheless, on the grounds of the finitudes of having and knowing that "suffering from" might be redeemed to express human suffering, including suffering related to disability.

SUFFERING FROM AND FIGHTING ABLEISM

From a disability studies /disability studies in education perspective, a "suffering from" in need of address is how people with disabilities have suffered from exclusionary practices. The finitudes at work here are not in the minds and bodies of people with disabilities but in the limits of understanding and imagination of the often able-bodied people doing the excluding. Hidden prejudices about disability emblemized in demeaning "suffers from" understandings are the limits that activists interested in authentic possibilities for inclusion seek to transgress.

Responses to "suffering from" understandings of disability have taken the form of activism in the academic community and beyond. Disability studies discourses criticize understandings of disability that fall under the charity model and medical deficit model and propose a social/rights-based model of disability that emphasizes the abilities and strengths of people with disabilities. Suspicious of the gaze of the expert researcher or diagnostician who works from without, disability studies believe that people with disabilities are to be understood as experts, not only regarding their own lives, but regarding disability itself. In fact, many of the disability studies scholars who routinely write of the complexities of the experience of disability identify themselves as disabled and/or have close family members they identify as disabled (Berube, 2003; Gabel, 2005; Shakespeare, 2002; P. Smith, 2006; Titchkosky, 2008).

As the concept of inclusion has itself moved from being a demand and rallying cry of disability rights advocates to a value that most institutions claim to hold and a practice that most professionals who work with people with disabilities claim to be engaging in, critics have sought to help inclusion reclaim some of its radical savour by revealing the inconsistencies and hypocrisies of policies and practices that institutions name as inclusive (Allan, 2008; Couture, 2012; Graham & Slee, 2008, Williamson & Paul, 2012). Titchkosky's (2008) "To pee or not to pee?" analyzed from a sociological perspective reactions to the lack of wheelchair-accessible washrooms in one of the largest buildings on campus at a large Canadian university. More specifically, she studied the anomaly of a wheelchair-accessible sign that had been posted above a narrow and decidedly inaccessible washroom for years. She quoted one able-bodied commentator on this state of affairs as asking "Isn't something better than nothing?" (p. 44) as if the inaccurate sign itself somehow marked a major improvement in social justice. She went on to study the complex assumptions about disability that would make such a statement possible.

As people with disabilities continue to suffer from exclusionary policies, the need for activism continues. When the provincial government of Alberta recently cut 42 million dollars from the P.D.D. budget, funds that support the community living of adults with intellectual disabilities, 1000 people with intellectual disabilities and other concerned citizens protested outside the provincial legislature in Edmonton, with smaller protests outside the premier's constituency office in Calgary, as well as in Red Deer, Lethbridge, and Medicine Hat. While the government has not yet chosen to reverse the cuts, seeking to instead defend their policies in a series of clarifications, the protests did succeed in raising awareness of this issue and challenging the then-premier's commitment to her own 2011 election statement that "a healthy society looks after its most vulnerable" (Climenhaga, 2013, para. 2). Through these actions this community has announced it will not suffer such arbitrary and damaging treatment meekly; present government and future governments would be wise to attend to this announcement.

OUTRAGE, TRAGIC LAUGHTER, AND SUFFERING FROM DISABILITY

Is outrage the only fitting response to suffering from disabling thought and practice? Though he does not pick favorites, indeed suggesting that we are strongly claimed by both, Caputo (1987) did offer an alternative. He has contrasted the genealogy of the religious, which sees suffering as an outrage, with the genealogy of tragic, which regards suffering as naturally situated in life. He does not mean this in the narrow sense that "tragic" is often patronizingly applied to people with disabilities, but as the Dionysian "play of all things" (p. 286). In the former, suffering is not seen as a violation of life but as "a part of life, a movement in its total output of energy" (p. 282). Suffering, therefore, is not to be fought, avoided, or even endured. It is to be affirmed and loved as a part of the "the entire ring dance in which all thing are caught up" (p. 282). Suffering as an inextricable thread woven into our existence, is best loved and affirmed through laughter. Caputo (1987) has explained this as a "Dionysiac exuberance," quoting Nietzsche's claim that "the most suffering animal on earth invented for itself—laughter" (p. 283). Caputo is also quick to caution that when it comes to the suffering that humans inflict on each other, particularly that which the privileged inflict on the less powerful, the accepting, tragic mindset has no value, it encourages the love of oppressions that should be fought. This point is well taken, but in the present case the dialogue between these two mindsets requires additional consideration.

In what ways do these two genealogies of suffering work with disability? When people "suffer from" disability in the sense of disability as arbitrary barriers, a "religious" mindset of outrage that denounces these barriers as unnatural and as having no place seems fitting indeed. Notwithstanding Caputo's argument that it risks an acceptance of oppression as a love of fate, the mindset of the tragic in some ways also offers a voice to "suffering from" disability. In the sense that suffering is a part of every life, is imbued in all our ordinary havings and doings, in our very being, the tragic mindset, in its courage to laugh, seems another potential reclamation of "suffering from" disability. Tragi-comic laughter cannot be directed narrowly at accepting "suffering from disability" in its oppressive aspects. Nor does it suggest that impairment itself is inherently tragic. That would reek of the forms of contemptuous pity I mentioned early. This expression of suffering can only work in the context of disability when its target widens to include all the vagaries of fate a robustly lived life might involve. Insisting on the freedom to suffer, that is, to live, and to give voice to one's suffering, seems as urgent as the freedom from the oppressive and capricious "sufferings from" attitudes and policies inflicted on people with disabilities. It also powerfully affirms the idea that a life with suffering is not an outrage, but an ordinary life.

SUFFERING AND THE AESTHETIC(S) OF DISABILITY

In writing that echoes Caputo's sentiments on these two mindsets towards suffering, the dance between laughter and outrage, Gabel (2005) and Allan (2009) have both written of an "aesthetic" of disability. Drawing on Dewey's theories of the aesthetic, Gabel (2009) has written that "art is intimately and subjectively connected to everyday human experience, perhaps even synonymous with experience" (p. 23) and that its deep authenticity is as if "felt in one's bones" (p. 30). In Dewey's understanding, both pain and pleasure feature prominently in this aesthetic. The aesthetic is formed by the meanings constituted by "the doings and sufferings that form experience…a union of the precarious and the novel, irregular with the set-tled, assured and uniform" (in Gabel, 2005, p. 23).

Gabel suggested that an aesthetic of disability includes

> most importantly body meanings [when] the individual is attuned to what is happen-ing with her body, when she acknowledges the struggles and joys that constitute her life, and when she uses her imagination or her creative forces to make sense of those experiences. (p. 30)

Gabel has given many examples of works that exemplify this aesthetic. Two are particularly illustrative. In the first of these, Sundar, the mother of a severely in-tellectually disabled daughter understands their relationship with the help of her belief in karmic reincarnation: "I think she was my mother in a previous life and now she comes back to give to me the problems I gave to her. …She is teaching me the lessons I did not learn in my previous body" (p. 32).

The second example Gabel (2005) has given is how disability rights scholar and activist Harlan Hahn joked that since every culture "has a food associated with it [the offerings of] fast food drive-throughs are the food of crip culture because they do not require customers to get out of their cars" (p. 33). Both "artists" in this case claim meanings that have political dimensions, Sundar's rejecting an implied ableist claim that her daughter is a burden in the first example and pointing to continued problems with accessibility for people with disabilities in the second, but they also present their experiences in the fullness of lives of joy, suffering, and laughter.

Allan (2009) has discussed a genre of disability arts that not only "celebrate[s] difference" in the manner in which the two former examples might be seen as doing, but that also seeks to subvert the "normality genre" (Darke, in Allan) by forcing able-bodied people to "examine their own normalizing and disablist at-titudes" (p. 42). Disability arts often "unravel the politically correct language of disability [by] using words like cripple and freak" (p. 42). Illustratively, she quoted poet Cheryl Marie Wade. Wade's poem denounced the sterile language of political correctness in claiming "I am not one of the physically challenged." She replaced this empty concept with a series of provocative metaphors that challenge ableist notions of beauty and normalcy while claiming her own sexual/gendered identi-ties. "I'm a French kiss with cleft tongue. …I'm pink lace panties teasing a stub of milk white thigh" (p. 43).

Allan (2009) equated disability art with Kynicism, an ancient Greek form of "pantomimic argument" (p. 45). Unlike cynicism, which cannot help but don an ideological mask when engaged in the rhetoric of critique, Kynicism offered a critique that is, if not strictly speaking, silent in the sense of pantomime, lived and embodied rather than rhetorical.

> Ancient kynicism begins the process of naked arguments from the opposition, carried by the power that comes from below. The kynic farts, shits, pisses, masturbates on the street, before the eyes of the Athenian market. He shows contempt for fame, ridicules the architecture, refuses respect, parodies the stories of gods and heroes. (Sloterdijk, in Allan, 2009, p. 46)

Kynicism refuses to fight oppressive ideologies on their own grounds. As suggested by this admittedly graphic history, it uses the body as a weapon of critique of institutional power, giving it a certain primacy over theoretical argument. It attacks seriousness through the "physiologically irresistible energy of laughter" (Sloterdijk, in Allan, 2009). Kynicism summons life's indignant, embodied sufferings, to fight, with dirty tactics, against the hegemonic forms of suffering ableist discourses inflict.

THE PASSION(S) OF MIKE ERVIN AKA SMART ASS CRIPPLE

I can think of no better chronicler of these complexities than the writer Mike Ervin, who produces serious journalism under his own name and identifies himself on his increasingly popular satirical blog as "Smart Ass Cripple."

Ervin is no stranger to the more earnest forms of protest and activism I described in the prior section. He is one of the "Jerry's Kids" who rebelled and renamed themselves "Jerry's Orphans." "Jerry's Kids" were the children with muscular dystrophy and similar impairments that comedian and philanthropist Jerry Lewis sponsored and "paraded" (Weiner, 2011) across the stage in his many Labour Day telethons to raise money for the Muscular Dystrophy Association (MDA). A group of former Jerry's Kids led by Ervin became incensed with what they saw as the pitying attitudes of Lewis and the telethon organizers. They also objected to the misguided emphasis on curing muscular dystrophy over promoting accessibility and inclusion (Lewis once held up a small child with MD for the audience and said, "God goofed, and it's up to us to correct His mistakes" [Weiner, 2011]), and they began protesting the telethons (Richardson, 2005).

As Ervin described in *The Kids Are All Right* (Richardson, 2005), a documentary about the telethon protests staged by Jerry's Orphans, he became an activist against the telethon when, at the Chicago public library one day he read an article that Lewis had written for *Parade Magazine*. In the article, which the magazine featured as a cover story that week, Lewis speculated what life might be like "If I [he] had muscular dystrophy." Writing from what he saw was the perspective of an adult with MD, Lewis (1990, in Richardson, 2005) made a series of claims that, while addressing some of the real issues of barriers and inaccessibility wheelchair users faced at the time, were written in a tone and style many people with disabilities found patronizing and demeaning. The passage that Ervin said outraged him the most was

> I know the courage it takes to get on the court with other cripples and play wheelchair basketball, but I'm not as fortunate as they are, and I bet I'm in the majority. I'd like to play basketball like normal, healthy, vital, and energetic people. I really don't want the substitute. I just can't half-do anything—either it's all the way, or forget it. That's a rough way to think in my position. When I sit back and think a little more rationally, I realize my life is half, so I must learn to do things halfway. I just have to learn to try to be good at being a half a person…and get on with my life.

Ervin and his sister, another former Jerry's Kids, began to demand Jerry Lewis be fired from hosting the telethon and from working for the MDA in general. They began to hold protests at the Chicago local broadcast of the telethon, showing up uninvited during the filming and disrupting the speeches and musical numbers with chants of "stop the telethon now" and "piss on pity" (Richardson, 2005). They led a campaign to encourage corporate and private sponsors to stop making donations to the MDA during the telethon (though not to lower the amounts of their donations to the MDA overall) (Johnson, 1992). Protests spread to other cities broadcasting the telethon, garnering media attention and eventually prompting Lewis, who was angered at what he perceived to be the ingratitude of the protesters, to make further offensive statements including, "Pity? You don't want to be pitied because you're a cripple in a wheelchair? Stay in your house!" (Richardson, 2005).

And, in a *Time* magazine interview about the protesters

> It just kills me to think about these people getting publicity. These people are leeches. They all glommed on to being Jerry-bashers. What did they have before that?…. There's a million and a half people who depend on what I do! I've raised one billion three hundred million dollars. These 19 people don't want me to do that. They want me to stop now? Fuck them. [He then instructed his interviewer to write his last statement in it in capital letters.] FUCK THEM. (Richardson, 2005)

After initially threatening Ervin and his sister with legal action and publicly denouncing their complaints (Johnson, 1992), the MDA seems to have eventually (though without explicit acknowledgement in any public statement) addressed the concerns they and other protesters and critics had. It announced on August 3, 2011, that Lewis had "completed his run" as both host and national chairman, effective immediately and that Lewis would not appear in the 2011 telethon. Since then, the telethon itself has been radically scaled back in length and has changed its title to "Show of Strength," apparently attempting to move from a tone of pity and emphasis on cure and normalization to emphasizing resiliency of, and accessibility for, people with MD (Muscular Dystrophy Association, 2011; Weiner, 2011). These were among the demands made by Jerry's Orphans during the protests. It seems likely that Ervin and his fellow protesters, by raising negative publicity about the telethons and by provoking Lewis to reveal his ableist attitude more fully, strongly influenced these events. They have recruited their outrage and slowly but effectively reversed the "suffers from," in the sense of pity, discourse of the largest not-for-profit organization for people with muscular dystrophy.

Ervin has participated in other protests, including a gathering in front of the Chicago Mercantile Exchange (CME) over a severe $210 million cut to programs providing home care workers to people with disabilities by the state of Illinois, during the same budgetary year in which the state approved 1 billion dollars of tax breaks to the conglomeration of financial companies that comprise the CME group (Simpson, 2012). In addition to his leadership of Jerry's Orphans, he also works with several disability rights organizations. As a freelance journalist he has written frequently about disability issues including what he sees as the negative consequences of Obama's health care reforms for people with disabilities (2013a), continued reliance on institutionalization of the severely disabled on the part of state governments (2013b), the impact of the Illinois cuts on medically fragile children (2012), and a case of a so-called mercy killing where a mother in her 60s shot her two middle-aged sons who had Huntington's disease because she felt she could no longer care for them (2002). Though Ervin is occasionally sarcastic in this work, for the most part his editorials offer serious critique of the sorts of institutional and discursive barriers that restrict the public life, and limit the value placed on the lives, of people with disabilities. Ervin shows how these barriers, due to their invisibility to many able-bodied people, lead to the misperception that people with disabilities "suffer" mainly from their impairments when institutional barriers are often the larger sources of the suffering. In this he shares in what Caputo has called the religious mindset to suffering, the kinds of suffering he writes about in these examples are an outrage.

SMART ASS CRIPPLE

Ervin's alter ego, "Smart Ass Cripple," the last word of which is a defiant reclamation that he says politically correct language crusaders will have to pry out of his "cold dead fingers" (2012, June 11), is up to something else altogether. Since 2010, he has been using his titular blog to chronicle his adventures of trying to live well as a "cripple" in a world of "verts" (i.e., verticals or non-wheelchair-users). A side panel on his blog quotes Bertrand Russell "those who are solemn and pontifical are not to be successfully fought by being even more solemn and even more pontifical" (n.d.) and his work embodies this theory.

Smart Ass Cripple is very aware of the supercrip stereotype, the narrative impulse to depict the lives of people with disabilities as extraordinarily heroic (Goggin & Newell, 2004). He has noted, for example, that,

> Those people who always expect cripples to be super heroic are easy to please. They think every little thing we do is super heroic, like eating breakfast. Somehow, in spite of the obstacles we face, we still manage to find the strength and courage to eat breakfast. (2011, January 21)

As a result of this, he goes to great lengths to prove how unheroic he is. Trying to debunk stereotypes of people with disabilities, or "cripples" as Smart Ass Cripple says, as chaste and heroic, he writes often of the pleasures of profanity, idleness, scatological humour, sexual desire, revenge, scorn, and mockery. In response to myths among employers that "cripples" are loyal, he says he has gone out of his way to quit many jobs. To reverse myths that "cripples" are teetotallers he has drunk "shitloads of beer" and plans to continue to do so throughout his anticipated retirement in a nursing home. Regarding the myth that "cripples" are meek and grateful as tenants Smart Ass Cripple wrote,

> I also felt great pressure to be a role model when I lived in government-subsidized public housing for cripples. So I threw parties featuring adult piñatas. Adult piñatas are full of adult stuff like condoms and joints and those little airline bottles of booze and cigarettes and furry handcuffs. (2013, September 2)

His only regret, he wrote, is that he has been less-than-successful in fully countering the myth that "cripples" have "no desire to get laid." Though as a twice-married man he noted that he's "gotten around," he sadly never had the stamina to become a "raging omnisexual hedonist" (2013, September 2).

While his editorials as Mike Ervin work through reasoning and argument, Smart Ass Cripple's commentary on the inequities of disabling practice and policies are, like his persona, more akin to kynicism. He uses pre-ideological, embodied attacks that refuse to honour those with disabling attitudes with the rebuttal of serious, lucid argument. When he writes of his demeaning and isolating experiences in the residential/vocational school for children with disabilities where he received his education, the Sam Houston Institute of Technology, Smart Ass Cripple (2012, October 2; 2013, May 31) always refers to its title in acronym form

(SHIT). Remarking on the astonishing fact that the school is still open, "SHIT Still Exists," Smart Ass Cripple (2012, June 20) equates it with the many other exploitive employers of people with disabilities. "These places are like fly paper for cripples. If we land there, we're probably stuck there until we die." He then denounces the argument that many people with disabilities work at such institutions out of free will, given the lack of viable employment and available housing options that many in the community face

> When I hear people make this "choice" defense, I find myself wishing hard that there was a nearby pit full of yak turds. Because I would grab them by the back of their suspenders and hurl them into it. Choice and preference implies a menu of options. …I could conduct a survey where I offer cripples a choice between a) being locked in a meat freezer for three days wearing only a Speedo or b) a kick in the crotch. Four out of five cripples will say they prefer a kick in the crotch. Hell, five out of five cripples will say they prefer a kick in the crotch. (2012, June 20)

Smart Ass Cripple might have plainly and simply argued that, given the lack of viable employment options for many workers with disabilities, the position he is opposing makes a "bad faith" argument about "choice," but, as expressed in this blog entry, a more visceral message lies in the embodied kynicism of his rant. The violence in the blog entry reverberates with the violence he feels was inflicted on him at SHIT, a violence that he feels continues to be a feature of such workhouses.

Sometimes Smart Ass Cripple's reactionary sarcasm captures, aesthetically, the flavor of unease about a controversial issue about disability that ethical or logical arguments cannot fully address. Remarking on the unsettling topic of the ways in which negative perceptions of disability have influenced reproductive decisions since the advent of genetic screening Ervin (Smart Ass Cripple, 2012, July 2) revealed some of the complexities of this issue

> I'm always hesitant to even bring up this abortion shit because I know what will happen. Some right winger will seize it as an opportunity to show that they are really the true friends of cripples. If they were in charge, we wouldn't have to worry about being aborted. They would tenaciously defend our right to be born. They're right about that. No doubt they would guard every crippled fetus like a junkyard dog, right up until the second they are born. After that, you're on your own, Maxwell. That's the American way.

But he nevertheless speculated,

> [S]till, I've always been tempted to form an exclusive cripple fraternity called Coulda Beena Borted. It's a kinship I share with cripples who are born with spina bifida,

Down Syndrome, dwarfism, congenital amputations and all the other stuff obstetricians can spot from a mile away. (Smart Ass Cripple, 2012, July 2)

Invoking the exclusivity of college fraternities, complete with the faux Greek name, plays in satiric brilliance off the complexities of belonging to a community of people with disabilities that are now often routinely screened out through genetic testing. The further characterization of the medical community as border police looking to "catch" fetuses with disabilities (Smart Ass Cripple described himself as a "stealth fetus" who made it through under more rudimentary technologies) heightens the morbid satire. While it is hard to decide, within a disability rights perspective, where the ethical pull of this issue is, Smart Ass Cripple at least engages with the topic in all its discomfort.

Smart Ass Cripple (2010, October 27) sometimes takes a break from disrupting the marketplace of ableist ideologies with his bad behavior to target, with equal scorn, other forms of hegemony that disturb him. Commenting on the continued overt racism of the sports franchise named "The Washington Red Skins" he empathized by noting that, as a person with a disability, he would object if there were teams named "the Detroit Droolers, …Seattle Spastics [, or] Indianapolis Invalids." He then abandoned this vision because team names are supposed to sound ferocious, and although "cripples scare people, [its] not for the right reasons." Realizing that "Red Skins ownership is determined to keep their name for three reasons: money, revenue and cash," he described how he desperately phoned an attorney who worked for the team and proposed that they at least change their logo of a stereotyped Native American to that of a potato instead. "It can be a fierce potato with a menacing snarl and razor teeth. Or it can be a rotten, rancid potato that will give you botulism," he suggested, to no avail, to the team's attorney.

Smart Ass Cripple's writings clearly indicate that he suffers in many ways from living in a society he regards as so bereft of care, understanding, and empathy for people with disabilities, and many of its other citizens as well. Yet he laughs, in the spirit of the tragic, not only at his targets for satire but at his own fate, not in having an impairment, but in having to live amidst such ignorance. Though the writing seems to carry the hope that his rough wit might shake his readership into more inclusive understandings, there is also the tragic realization with every subject he tackles that the examples of exclusion are countless. This is because, in part, such ableist thinking is so pervasive and, on this count, Smart Ass Cripple acknowledges the limits of his own understandings related to disability. He is not only a "cultural vigilante," (Slee & Allan, 2001) he is also, at times, a humble interpreter trying to understand better himself. He makes this clear in a blog entry entitled "Where's the Keeper?" (2002, September 14). His initial complaint is about how, whenever "verts," acting as managers and proprietors in public places such as movie theatres, see "cripples" gathered in the same place they tend to look for the "vert" who brought them there to talk to and deal with. "When a covey of cripples comes in peace, say like to a movie theater or restaurant. The manager has a look of panic. Where's the keeper?" He then moves on to admit that this ableist tendency is dangerously easy to fall into, even for a person with a disability,

> I'm guilty too. I went to see a play. It was some Shakespeare deal starring Down Syndrome people. The play began and the only people on stage in Shakespeare outfits were Down Syndrome people. That wasn't what I expected. I said to myself, "Where's the keeper?" I'm well aware that this means I am an asshole. But acknowledgement is the first step to recovery.

While he is tireless in his efforts to capture examples of ignorance and prejudice in his satiric lens, Smart Ass Cripple isn't always on the attack. In perhaps the most effective protest of all to ableism, he often writes simply of the "the entire ring dance," the "doings and sufferings" of his daily life. Though he doesn't explicitly state this, in naming in his own way and casting as ordinary his "doings and sufferings," he asserts that they are not unnatural, or objects of pity or hero worship, but aspects of a life worth living or, aesthetically, a life well lived. Evoking the language of a professional race car driver, he (2013, June 17) referred to his personal assistants—the "people I hire to drag my ass out of bed every day, make my meals, do my laundry, scrub my toilet, wipe my butt, etc."—as his "pit crew." Several of his blog posts are of the nature of "Pit Crew Members Say the Darndest Cute Things" (2013, July 28). Preferring "quirky" assistants to "mother Theresa types," Smart Ass Cripple (2013, January 3) wrote of one assistant who, in a karate-inspired effort to focus all of his strength on a moment of exertion, always emitted a blood-curdling scream as he lifted him out of his wheelchair. Another assistant helped deepen his understanding of the genius of Leonardo da Vinci in teaching Smart Ass Cripple (2013, July 28) that one of the Renaissance master's lesser known achievements was the reversal of the commonly held but fanciful theory of how mammalian erections happened.

> Brian was giving me a shower and somehow we got to talking about the Mona Lisa and Brian said that da Vinci also debunked the scientific belief of his time that an erection was caused by the penis filling with air, like a balloon. da Vinci came to the conclusion that this was all wrong, Brian said, after he saw a mule fucking a mare. So I looked it up and it's true!

Musing on the legacy of this assistant he noted, "so now, thanks to former pit crew member Brian, in my mind da Vinci is synonymous not with the Mona Lisa but with erection."

On February 17, 2013, Smart Ass Cripple wrote about the upcoming anniversary (February 28) of "The Day I Quit Walking." Forty years before, as a teenager at SHIT, he had wearied of nagging therapists and the uncomfortable equipment and awkward body positioning used to correctly position his body as he attempted to learn to walk. He was also tired of the clinical attitude toward the whole endeavor,

> I also didn't like how therapists referred to walking as "ambulation." Why couldn't they just call it walking? "It's time to ambulate!" I think that word bothered me because I was raised Catholic and ambulation sounded like something a priest would tell me I should never ever do. "Bless me father for I have sinned. This morning I ambulated all over my bedroom."

So he sat down and quit. Far from viewing this as a tragic event, Smart Ass Cripple described it as a liberation of sorts. It was "a big load lifted" to have the "time and energy" previously spent in therapy back for "doing something more fruitful and fun." It "felt good [to] tell walking to fuck off! You can't fire me! I quit!" In writing about this, Smart Ass Cripple claimed an experience a therapist might frame as a failure or disappointment as victory. As an educator who works with students with disabilities I appreciate the challenge offered in this story. Dazzled by an ever-increasing variety of therapeutic strategies and the range of assistive technologies and enamored by the hope that we might promote the "self-advocacy" of children with disabilities by educating them in these possibilities, it is all too easy to forget the perspective that Smart Ass Cripple expressed here. While a dialogic approach with the students helps them understand what's "out there" to meet their needs by way of equipment and therapies, we can't assume the dominant role of the specialist, teaching students with disabilities the "correct" ways of performing their impairments (Allan, 2008). The day Smart Ass Cripple quit walking was also a day in which he, not the specialist, decided which treatments and interventions were best suited to how he wanted to live with his impairment.

As I've mentioned, finitude, the limits of our bodies, our understandings, and, ultimately, our lives is often thought inextricably linked to human suffering. Heidegger (1962) equated the anxiety that pondering the fact of this last finitude provokes with freedom, "impassioned anxious *freedom* toward death which is free of the illusions of the they, factical, and certain of itself (p. 311). He contrasted this with inauthentic being towards death, which is "everyday entangled evasion *of* death" (p. 117). If following a factical existence with the "they" in this case can be seen as something like engaging in an unreflexive traffic of cultural norms as if these norms at least will live on, this does indeed seem a rather inauthentic evasion.

Can activism itself be an illusion of "the they," expression of a desire to replace one certainty with another? Is it for Smart Ass Cripple? This might depend on how Smart Ass Cripple positions himself within his critiques of ableist ideologies. As mentioned, he goes out of his way to distance himself from being considered as a heroic figure. Though he writes in solidarity with the marginalization of people with various disabilities, he has also, in the "Keeper" article, and others, confessed the limits of his own understandings when it comes to other disabilities. Though activism implies ideology, he plays the role of the kynic, profaning instead of engaging in reasoned debate, and often seems coy about articulating a larger political vision. In a blog entry coyly titled "I Was a College Marxist" (2013, October 21) he soon clarified that he was referring to how his emerging world view was influenced not by the revolutionary social critic and ideologue but by the Marx brothers of *Duck Soup* and other slapstick comedies. In the words of one of his kynic heroes, he doesn't seem to want to be a part of "any club who would accept [him] as a member" (Marx, 1959).

It seems fitting to conclude this section of Smart Ass Cripple's writings not with further discussion of his positioning within "the they," but with the thoughts he has expressed about "being towards death" in the most literal sense. In many supercrip narratives, after a life of suffering from and overcoming disability, the supercrip dies heroically. In non-fiction, these deaths are often portrayed as the culminating acts of lives spent inspiring others (Groggin & Newell, 2004). In fictional works such as *Simon Birch* or *The Mighty*, the supercrip is even more directly sacrificial, literally giving away a "disabled" life to save the life of an able-bodied companion (Arndt, White, & Chervenak, 2010). Smart Ass Cripple, on the other hand, described himself as "a fucking baby when it comes to pain" (2013, May 26), and imagined that if he were to come down with a terminal illness there is no way he would suffer his fate heroically or stoically. In "A Perfect People Magazine Death," he noted, "The only way I'll die with grace is if there's a woman dying next to me named Grace" (2013, May 26). Smart Ass Cripple (2010, November 17) has also expressed a couple of thoughts about his send-off and legacy when the day comes. In a conversation with another member of his pit crew, he said he would like simply to be dumped in Lake Michigan before reflecting briefly on the various benefits of having a full funeral in which he was displayed and buried in a gorilla suit. "It would sure make things easier on the kids" and it might "go viral" and "become a catchy euphemism for terminal illness. You go to the doctor for your test results and you say, 'Give it to me straight, doc.' And the doctor says, 'Well, let me put it this way. I think you should get fitted for a gorilla suit.'"

Imagining legacy in longer terms, he has commented on the scientific value his body might have were it to be discovered in a thousand years by an anthropologist.

He is certain they would wonder what to make of his bent skeleton, ravaged by years sitting, "if God intended for humans to sit on our asses all day, she would have made us all Congressmen" (Smart Ass Cripple, February 22, 2013). Perhaps, he muses, they would think he perished because he was unable to keep up with his tribe. In these writings, Smart Ass Cripple playfully rejects any sense of his imagined decline as dignified or of his memorial as solemn and lasting. Though he calls himself a physical coward when it comes to pain, he makes the aesthetic choice of refusing to manage the suffering of finitude by speculating, comfortingly, on how to "have" (Heidegger, 1962) a meaningful death. Instead he "owns up" (Caputo, 1987) to the capriciousness of it all and laughs at his place in the flux.

RETELLING "SUFFERS FROM"

While acknowledging that people-first, "people with…" language does, to some degree, "override" demeaning understandings of disability such as "suffers from," Titchkosky (2001)pointed out that it does so by organiz[ing] a consciousness of disability as a condition of limitation and lack that some people "have" (p. 129). The consequence of this, she pointed out, is that it also overrides

> more political conceptions of disability, such as "I am disabled by my culture"; "I belong to the largest physical minority in Canada"; "I experience my world, my self, and others differently, now that I am disabled"; or "Canada has been built to exclude people like me." (p. 129)

She also pointed out that people with disabilities hardly need to be reminded, by way of linguistic convention, that they are people first. In over simplifying, the complexities and contradictions of disability through the unreflexive use of "people with …," "people-first" language, may, in some ways, overlook the personhood it is trying to assert. While in the strictest sense one would do well to heed the advice of "people-first" and avoid naming a person's impairment with the phrase "suffers from," in the broader sense, to exclude the idea of suffering from conversations about disability robs the experience of personhood as well. People suffer. At the start of the first of three volumes of memoirs, *Angela's Ashes*, Frank McCourt (1996) wrote, "the happy childhood is hardly worth your while" (p. 11), and he went on to chronicle a childhood that, while terrible in many ways, might also have been one of his most interesting experiences. Our best stories all involve various sufferings. It is true that some historical, and, unfortunately, current modes of thinking and writing about people who "suffer from" disabilities engage disastrously in misguided and, at times, contemptuous pity. To ease our suffering from this, many disability studies scholars and disability rights activists, in work that echoes with the mysteries of suffering the philosophical tradition has given us, take on "suffers from" disability in all its nuance. They achieve this in pedagogic expressions of outrage over the ignorance of ableism in its manifold forms. They achieve this as well by chronicling, often with laughter, the various sufferings inherent in their aesthetic acts of living well.

In a rare convergence of opinion with political correctness, Smart Ass Cripple (2012, June 11) admitted to similar consternation with words as the "people-first" movement. While he sees no problem with the word cripple as the label he chooses for his impairment, he objects to its application as an adjective to describe anything that is, in his words, "fucked up"—"the crippled Fukushima nuclear power plant or the crippled Greek economy," for example. His response to this, and the last word in this chapter, however describes a tactic much different than that of "people-first," a tactic we might consider when we next find a phrase such as "suffers from," with problematic associations related to disability.

> I'd rather hammer away relentlessly at the word cripple like a coked-up blacksmith until cripple is forged into something new. Maybe being crippled will become synonymous with being awesomely cool. From that day forward, when people visit the Sistine Chapel, they'll look up at all the Michelangelo stuff and say, "Man, that is sooooooooo crippled."

CHAPTER EIGHTEEN

The Comfort OF Suffering

GILBERT DRAPEAU

"Why doesn't she just hit me?"

A foster child asked me this about his foster mother. The child was unable to deal with or understand the concept of consequences.

"If she just hits me, it will be over, then I can move on."

Hitting, for this child, was a known entity. It was acknowledged and understood as a way of being, no matter its abusive connotations. The concept of consequence, of rational cause and effect, in this case an episodic withdrawal of extracurricular activities, was, to this child, a greater suffering than physical abuse administered incidentally as a timely action understandable within the child's usual familiar context.

In Social Work, whatever the program, an individual is, ideally, moved from a troubled situation to a new, hoped-for, beneficial one. The helper proposes a new avenue where suffering is naught or resolved. One of the great truths of the helping professions that is often ignored is that the suffering will never be ended. It can only be transformed. A scar will always mar the cancer patient's body; the amputee will always be missing a limb; the once-snake-bitten will always err in caution in the desert.

The ultimate current cyclical failure of human services programming fails on three levels:

- The limited understanding of the impact of one's comfort in suffering that which is known;
- The destabilization created by proposing a break in something understood, and;
- The abnegation of the previous suffering to a new paradigm where a different suffering may exist, i.e., the impact of the unknown and/or change upon the person.

To conceive that someone would accept abuse is anathema to most of us. Reactions vary from profound empathy to outright hostility toward the person refusing to withdraw themselves, when allegedly able, from the abusive situation. Understanding is even more challenged when children of abuse seek to return to abusive parents and/or engage in abusive behaviors against those seeking to help. Such responses do not take into account the profound human desire for that which is known: the comfort of the known versus what might be achieved should the familiarity of that which hurts be removed. Set patterns of thinking, of being, in children and adults, can be molded by abuse. That which becomes known and familiar can render change (experienced as an attack on that which is known), challenging at all levels: emotionally, physically, and spiritually. The individual seeks out that which repeats what is familiar suffering, and by extension the social constructs we develop to counter it only serve to bring more suffering sometimes disguised as social constructs to alleviate that which is subjugating the individual. Dr. Bruce Perry's work (e.g., Perry & Rosenfelt, 2013), amongst others, has shown how abuse can physiologically impact brain development, how patterns of intervention on that suffering may create experiential suffering similar to the one that is attempting to be relieved, and that current systems cannot holistically support appropriate healing.

The destabilization created by proposing a break in something familiar and understood brings about an uncomfortable suffering: a further injury. What once was perceived as typical is now identified as injurious and what is proposed is feared. That which is known—a secure albeit negative familiarity—finds itself shaken, pushed toward a new reality where parameters are unknown and potentially seen as a violent countermand to what was a vicious placidity: how dare one propose a new set of behaviours, a new way of being, when a measure of success, sometimes as basic as survival, is achieved on a daily basis? The proposed change now moves the individual from one suffering into another, from the comfort of familiar suffering to the suffering and discomfort of unfamiliar suffering. It is thus perfectly understandable that such movement forward can only be sustained by managed ongoing change processes involving significant unlimited resources, where the further injury can be manifested positively in contrast with the past suffering until it achieves (one hopes) its transformative crescendo.

The abnegation of the previous suffering to a new situation where a different suffering will exist is rarely fully explained to the individual, which can serve to render the past suffering into a known, comfortable entity to which the individual will long to return. Progress, in such social work, is viewed as moving to a new world where what was seen as abusive no longer exists and where suffering will be eliminated if not greatly reduced. That proposition's somewhat inescapable falsehood is rarely discussed with the client. What is often not underscored, perhaps not even able to be admitted by social work professionals themselves, is the suffering inherent in the process of change itself and the comfort that can be found in the familiar, however abusive, situation of clients. This is experienced, in many cases, where multiple appointments are had with a number of individuals where one's life story is repeated *ad nauseum* with false or at least unexamined presumptions as to what such repetition is to accomplish in a scope of accessing help from a system where organizations, management, caseworkers, policies, and practices are forever changing, sometimes for the better, sometimes not. When a lack of adequate ongoing sustained support does not enable the person to appropriately weigh the benefits of the current suffering against that of old, it is only logical that the client, willing to change or not, turns to that which is known, his past suffering as comfort. The helping professions find it hard to admit that the individual was able, in their former circumstances, to sustain a sense of self, even though perverted through extraordinary suffering, yet it was their own, their propriety, their self.

No matter the proposed solution, there seems to be a requirement that we accept the continuity of suffering, that the person will be moved from one type of suffering to another, using the wisdom of past suffering, to, one hopes, support the individual in a productive contemplation of a life worth living. When change is necessary, the comfort of suffering must be acknowledged, allowed to stand as its own entity, allowed to influence the change process. There can be spontaneous recovery in individuals when the suffering itself becomes such that it is no longer inescapable. However, most of the time, easing into a comfortable suffering, or variations of it, may be the most favoured path.

Should this be ignored again, those engaged in a change process will only see their efforts stymied by a return to the relief of what is known.

Acknowledging the comfort of suffering is key to our efforts to relieve it.

CHAPTER NINETEEN

Fragment Four:
"And Yet, AND Yet"

CHRISTOPHER GILHAM, DAVID W. JARDINE
& GRAHAM McCAFFREY

DJ: If I may, attached are two poems written by Judson Innes (see Chapters 4 and 15). I think both of these pieces are absolutely brilliant and breathtaking, and they linger nearby our topic in ways that I find illuminating. Time and the predator's talon strike, and then those suffering calling up to the creators: "we are here; we are here." Two lovely things that will only take up two pages, but that will give a lilt to the voice of suffering.

    CG: Thanks David. I read these poems several times over because of where they took me in my thinking and imagining…almost Koan-like and I think very much related to this work. Timely for me too…just got word two days ago that my Sensei in Japan is dying…been thinking about flying there to say goodbye but it is not the Japanese way though I have been told he would like to see me. He is at home, in his bed most of the time…stomach cancer and it seems the hospital sent him home but he may have wanted to be home as well… At the end of a letter he wrote the following: "Please do not worry. This is how I am now." Those words have been deeply echoing in me these past two days…brewing, like a yet to come eulogy for Sensei on those words which remind me of the poem's line "We are here, we are here."

    "This is how I am now"…. resolve in the face of and comfort for the still thriving… Indeed, sensei's resolve is inherently the way of the warrior. He is comported for what has been coming all along, and is now so near. Quoting Kawabata Ryu (in Niwa & Wilson, W.S 2012, p. xviii):

When the doctor
gives up, the tengu (demon)
is called.

Oh it makes me so sad at once…

DJ: Yes, let yourself go to this spot. Reminds me of this old thing that Gary Snyder (1990, p. 175) cites from Dong-Shan, a 9th-century Chan/Zen Master:

One time when the Master was washing his bowls, he saw two birds contending over a frog. A monk who also saw this asked, "Why does it come to that?" The Master replied, "It's only for your benefit."

GM: And it reminds me of the haiku by Issa that he wrote after the death of his infant daughter from smallpox (Hass, 1994, p. 228):

The world of dew
is the world of dew.
And yet, and yet.

CG: These bring to another level my experiences with *ohanami* while I lived in Japan. Cherry blossom parties under the trees… Some of my fondest memories are of these gatherings with friends and family… Like dewdrops… And brilliant in their radiance… Fleeting as they were… Thanks fellas…

DJ: Ted Aoki would often refer to his daughter who died quite young as a cherry blossom–beautiful, fragrant, yet not lasting long. Fleeting. Like dew. He and I did a presentation at the University of Victoria years and years ago called "The Cherry Blossom and the Rose" to highlight the European pursuit of "the lasting" and the Japanese sense of ephemeralness. It's why I love this Don Domanski passage in an old interview:

> …what the Japanese refer to as "the slender sadness," that runs through every moment of existence, about the fleetingness of lives lived in a world where nothing can be saved[It is] entering that state of being with a joy and wonder that comes from that very impermanency, from the absolute dispossession of everything we love and cherish. The wonder is that anything at all exists. The joy is that it does, even if it is as momentary as a human life. We can live this as a mode of attention, we can live within its movements, its cycles and treasure the phases, the round of it. (2002, p. 246)

> At poetry's centre there's the silence of a world turning. This is also found at the centre of a stone or the axis of a tree. To my way of thinking, that silence is the main importance. Out of it come the manifestations, all the beings we call words. (p. 245)

CHAPTER TWENTY

"Neither They Nor Their Reward"

ALAN A. BLOCK

In his autobiography, *The Confessions*, Jean Jacques Rousseau (1953) narrated how, after a long absence, he returned home to Mme de Warens (Mamma), for whom once he had been, and expected to become again, her singular love, only to find that M de Courtilles had replaced him in Mme de Warens' affection. I personally believe that Rousseau's sense of betrayal rings just a bit false as does the display of his extreme jealousy, since his protestations to Mme Warens affirming his alleged devotion follow soon after his passionate love affair with a Mme Le Lanarge. Indeed, throughout his confessions, Rousseau portrays himself as an avid lover of women, and, despite his protestations and denials, seems rarely at a loss for female companionship. For example, Rousseau told us how Mme de Mably attempted to teach him to do the honours of her house, "but I was such an awkward pupil, so bashful and so stupid, that she lost heart and gave me up. That did not prevent me from following my usual custom, and falling in love with her" (p. 254). Nevertheless, Rousseau bemoaned the loss of the affection of Mme Warens.

At what Rousseau took as Mme Warens' seeming abandonment of him, he suffered. But, Rousseau admitted, though he suffered, yet from that suffering he found reward. Rousseau (1953) commented, "Thus there began to spring up with my misfortunes those virtues whose seed lay at the bottom of my heart. They had been cultivated by study, and were only waiting the ferment of adversity in order to sprout" (p. 250). These virtues of which Rousseau spoke that lay apparently innate within and were encouraged by study, required only adversity in order to develop. Interestingly, he referred here not to a process of fertilization but also to one of fermentation: as if his natural virtues needed not creation—a bringing into being—but required only an action upon being. In Rousseau's context, ferment refers to a leaven, which is the yeast that is added to dough to make it rise. The "ferment" breaks down substances without the use of oxygen to yield energy (and, frequently, gases and alcohol); this process yields a new substance. From a food and nutrition perspective, "fermentation" involves the breakdown of carbohydrates and proteins by bacteria and/or yeast. One product of fermentation is yeast bread: the rise of the dough results from the yeast "digesting" the sugars and producing carbon dioxide. Fermentation is a chemical process that leads to a change in the nature of the product fermenting. When the yeast breaks down the sugars in the juice the end product is ethanol and the yield is wine. Adversity is the ferment that enabled Rousseau's virtues to grow.

Interestingly, in the *Oxford English Dictionary* (1971) the word *ferment* contains within it the idea of suffering: in the OED, ferment is defined as, "Of material substances (in early use primarily of dough or saccharine fluids): to undergo an action of a ferment; to suffer fermentation; to 'work.'" Fermentation turns grape juice into wine (often into fine wines) and transforms mere raw dough into (often elegant) bread. To experience ferment is to suffer it! And "to suffer," I read in the OED (Suffer, 2001), means at least: a) "to have something painful, distressing or injurious, inflicted or imposed upon one; or b) to allow to be affected by, subjected to, undergo an operation or process, *esp.* of change." Since adding leaven enables fermentation, the process that transforms simple substances into prized, edible foods or alcoholic beverages, then Rousseau (1953) advocated here for the efficacy of suffering as a necessary ingredient to the development of his now-virtuous character. As a result of his study (not in itself the cause of suffering), his natural virtues were cultivated *by* his suffering and made Rousseau a better man.

Rousseau's (1953) observation gets to the heart of this present text: the pedagogy of suffering. The question may be asked: to what extent does pedagogy require or inflict suffering in the aim of producing a greater good: the development of the self. This greater good is not inconsistent with the definitions offered by our text's editors for the verb "to suffer": they write that this greater good may be defined as "a process of *becoming someone* that is undergone, endured or suffered" in the act of coming to know about oneself and the world. John Dewey asserted that education proceeds by the participation of the individual in the social consciousness of the race, a process not dissimilar to the editor's definition of this greater good that is education, though I suspect that Dewey would not equate education with suffering. For our editors here, education would require the ferment of suffering to transform simple substances into products more highly valued. Rousseau announced that his confessions are a record of his growth and development—his education—and that he required adversity to bring his virtues to maturity. By writing *The Confessions*, Rousseau informed the reader, he intended to record his self-development, and would in the text "display to my kind a portrait in every way true to nature, and the man I shall portray will be myself" (p. 17). *The Confessions* is, he said, "the history of my soul that I have promised to recount" (p. 262). This autobiography narrates the soul's fermentation and the development of the individual from its embryonic state through the efficacy of suffering.

As the editors of our text comment, this site of becoming someone because of the experiences one has undergone is the site of learning through suffering: this development requires a type of "undergoing" or "suffering" in which one risks becoming changed and having to learn to live with consequences.

Rousseau's (1953) confessions suggest that his sufferings have led him to know himself and the world about him. "I warn those who intend to begin this book, therefore, that nothing will save them from progressive boredom except the desire to complete the knowledge of a man, and a genuine love of truth and justice" (p. 263). To read *The Confessions* is to read the record of the development of the soul of a man. Rousseau's suffering, though uncomfortable, was beneficial in his process of developing.

For Rousseau, suffering was necessary to produce growth and change. But here I want to question whether the confluence of suffering and development is productive to pedagogical thought. I want to consider if it is true whether, indeed, suffering is necessary for growth, or if suffering occurs in the absence of growth and does not facilitate it. Does suffering really have benefit? Need suffering always be accompanied by pain? Without pain, can the state be referred to as one of suffering? And if education means change, must suffering necessarily accompany it? If education might be thought of as a metamorphosis, I think of the butterfly whose remarkable transformation reveals little evidence of suffering.

I want to offer an opposite perspective on suffering, and one that suggests that suffering has neither meaning nor value. It has nothing to add. That is, I want to suggest that though suffering exists it has neither instrumental nor existential purpose; suffering is a means to no end. Indeed, suffering is not even a means. A story is told: Rabbi Johanan went to visit Rabbi Hiyya who had fallen ill. Rabbi Johanan sat by Hiyya's bedside and said to him, "Are your sufferings precious to you?" You see, Johanan's question was based in the belief that sufferings in this world might lead to comfort in the next; that suffering has its rewards either here or there. But Hiyya responds unequivocally, "Neither they nor their reward." Then, Rabbi Johanan fell ill, and Rabbi Hanina paid him a visit. Sitting by the bed-side Hanina asked, "Are your sufferings precious to you?" and Johanan responded, "Neither they nor their reward." Finally, Rabbi Eleazar fell ill and Rabbi Johanan came to visit him. In the midst of a conversation about mortality, Rabbi Johanan asked Eleazar, "Are your sufferings precious to you?" and Eleazar answered, "Neither they nor their reward" (Babylonian Talmud, *Berakoth*, 5b [Note: all editions of Talmud are similar: citations are to folio location and not to page numbers.]).

Clearly, these Rabbis understood no benefit to be derived from suffering. For them, suffering does not serve as a ferment to anything.

I might offer another perspective on suffering that also does not consider it a necessary accompaniment to change and growth, and suggest that suffering has no pedagogical value. In this view, neither suffering nor adversity are leavening agents that act on natural human seeds, but are merely elements intrinsic to the very nature of human life. We might rationalize suffering, but it is mere rationalization that affords it any value. Suffering is. A founding Western myth argues that Adam and Eve can only actually experience the world when they are banished from the garden, and out there the humans must make effort to achieve anything and everything. Outside of the garden is not paradise: that is the point of the story! In the Stone edition of the *Tanakh*, God says to the two humans,

> accursed is the ground because of you; through suffering shall you eat of it all the days of your life. Thorns and thistles shall it sprout for you, and you shall eat the herb of the field. be the soil on your account, with painstaking labor shall you eat from it, all the days of your life. Thorn and sting shrub let it spring for you, when you [seek to] eat the plants of the field! By the sweat of your brow shall you eat bread, until you return to the soil from which you were taken. For you are dust, and to dust shall you return. (*Bereshit*, 3:17–19)

To Chava, the human's wife, whose name means life-giver, God says "I will greatly increase your suffering and your childbearing; in pain shall you bear children" (3:16), and condemns her to painful childbirth. From the beginning, suffering and death was part of the human lot, but there is hardly a hint here that suffering leads *to* anything or encourages learning. Perhaps we might say that suffering partakes of everything but adds nothing to it. Suffering just is! To dust you shall return!

What does Job learn from his suffering? If it is that there are more things in heaven and earth than are dreamt of in his philosophy, then I might suggest that this was something he already knew. After all, Job has become a wealthy and satisfied man and there must have been others about him who did not enjoy his comforts. And the *Book of Job* offered no hint of the effort Job had once made to become so comfortable. That the suffering now occurs to him must have come as some surprise: after all, his life had been one of privilege and good fortune prior to his suffering. I think, instead, that Job realizes that his suffering leads to no learning. To Job's question, "Why me?" God appears to answer, "Who are you to demand some answer? Yours is not a legitimate question." God provides no answer to Job's question, nor I think would any answer suffice. If Job had been changed by his experience, then what he has learned is that he does not, indeed, he cannot, know why he suffers, and that his ability to know very much in life remains extremely limited. Job acknowledges, "Therefore I declared, yet I understand nothing. It is beyond me. I shall not know" (Scherman, 1996, 42:3). For the acknowledgement of his ignorance, Job is rewarded. But can we say that from the learning that derives from his suffering Job has changed?

As a teacher, I am interested if learning requires the ferment of adversity to develop. I wonder if suffering must accompany learning. In the classroom, my students say they suffer; I suffer in the classroom! But I think, as my grandmother might say, "What else is new?" If the Rabbis recognize that suffering is endemic to life, then suffering must simply be borne and adds nothing to existence. Neither it, nor its rewards! But if the Rabbis acknowledge that suffering may have no purpose, I think that they also recognize that it can be relieved, as it were. And perhaps it is in the idea of relief that the relationship between learning and suffering may be explored. I have spent my life in the classroom, and I am now considering whether I have really suffered there, or has my suffering been relieved there? And I wonder: is it to relieve my suffering that I have learned? Is this what I teach? How?! Or was it in study that I caused my suffering to depart?

A story is told in *Bava Metzia* (83b): one day Rabbi Elazar met an officer of the government who had been charged with arresting thieves. Rabbi Elazar asked the soldier, who was not at all familiar with the community, how he might be certain that those he arrested were, indeed, guilty. After all, said the Rabbi, like the beasts of the forest, don't the wicked hide during the day and come out only at night and under cover of darkness? "Perhaps," Elazar commented, "you arrest the righteous as well as the wicked!" The soldier moaned and said that alas, he had no choice: he was simply fulfilling the orders of the king. Elazar leaned close to the soldier and confided to him that he had a method that might legitimately distinguish the wicked from the righteous. "Come," said Elazar, "and I will teach you what you should do. Go at the fourth hour to a tavern. If you see a man drinking wine and holding a glass in his hand and dozing, ask about him. If he is a rabbinic scholar and is dozing, he rose early from his studies. If he is a worker, he rose early [and] did his work. And if his work is [done] at night, he was stretching [metal wires.] And if [he is] not one of these], he is a thief, so arrest him." And so the soldier set to try Elazar's method and found it to be remarkably effective, and when the soldier's superiors inquired of the source of his system, the soldier mentioned that he had learned the technique from Rabbi Elazar. And Elazar was hired by the government to catch thieves!

One day a certain laundryman met Elazar and reviled him, referring to him as Vinegar, son of wine. Elazar took offense, and declared, "Since this man is so impudent, he must be a wicked man. Arrest him!" The man was brought to trial, convicted and hung. And Elazar experienced a heavy sense of guilt. Indeed, he had not practiced his own approach to detective work, and he had accused a man of thievery and the man had been executed. Elazar lamented: perhaps he had been wrong and he had condemned an innocent man. His students assured Elazar that not only the man, but the man's son's, were grievous sinners and they were obviously guilty, but Elazar was not comforted. The Rabbis tell us he suffered. "Every night he accepted upon himself afflictions. …In the evening they would spread for him sixty felt mattresses, [and] in the morning they would draw from under him sixty basins of blood and pus." Elazar's wife urged him not return to his study; she insisted that he remain in bed. But every morning Elazar would awaken and say to his sufferings, "Go, because of neglect of Torah." To his sufferings he would demand, Be gone! It is time to return to study. And at once his sufferings would disappear and Elazar would engage assiduously and pain-free for the day in study. And when in the evening he had completed his study he would invite back his sufferings: "Come, my brethren, my friends." And he would spend the night in misery. Here Elazar's study dismisses his sufferings. And his sufferings, his friends, as he calls them, occur at the end of study! His "friends" torment him but they do not provide ferment. I wonder what his sufferings could teach him, in fact, when his study occurs during the day and his sufferings are dismissed?

Suffering is very much on the minds of the Rabbis: after all, they had been living with the reality of exile and oppression throughout most of their lives. Both Temples had been destroyed—the first by the Babylonians in 586 B.C.E. and the second razed and sacked by the Romans in 70 C.E. The Roman occupation had been particularly oppressive; it is from this era that the crucifixion of political prisoners derives. The suppression of the Bar Kochba revolt in 132–136 C.E. had resulted in a genocidal campaign by Hadrian to rid Judea of the Jews. To suffer seemed the fate of the Jews. The Rabbis are much concerned with the existence of suffering. And so they wonder: when will come the Messiah and usher in a new world and bring an end to the sorrow? Rab says that the Messiah will not come until all of the Jews in all of the world have been held in captivity for nine months. Only then will the Messiah arrive. It is an auspicious period of time, I think, this nine months, and the travails that precede the birth are severe and (especially in this time) dangerous. There is much suffering. The students of Rabbi Eleazar wondered if there was anything one could do to avoid hearing the birth pangs, and he responded, "Let him engage in study and benevolence" (BT, *Sanhedrin*, 98b). Once again, as with Rabbi Elazar, study obviates suffering. And in this case, study leads to acts of benevolence!

Suffering rests central to the thought of the Rabbis. The destruction of the first Temple by the Babylonians in 586 BCE and the subsequent (and seeming permanent) exile and homelessness to which this defeat led; the loss in 70 CE of the Second Temple and the sack of Jerusalem, and of Jerusalem and the genocidal massacre and enslavement of the Jews by the Roman occupiers, led not merely to immense suffering but also produced an existential crisis for Judaism. The loss of the Temple threatened the central symbol of Judaism. In the aftermath of the destruction of the Temple, the Rabbis had to reconstruct the religion to maintain its viability in the absence of its center; Judaism had to learn to exist without a center. Of course, the Rabbis would wonder what might have caused such a tragedy to occur, what had led to all this suffering, assuming, as the Rabbis always do, that human action must have been responsible for the event.

And to our purposes here, often the Rabbis link the suffering not *to study* but to the *failure to study*. More, suffering occurs as a result of the people's de-sacralization of study. A story (*Bava Metzia, 85a*) is told: in their study the Rabbis wonder why Jerusalem was destroyed. Quoting *Jeremiah* 9:11 the Rabbis seem perplexed by this puzzling line: "Who is the wise man that may understand this, and who is he to whom the mouth of the Lord has spoken, that he may declare it, for what the land perishes." Jeremiah wonders why the land suffers, and the Rabbis search for an answer to Jeremiah's plaint. Interestingly, in the next verse an answer seems to be proffered by none other than God, who says, "Because of their forsaking My Torah that I put before them." It would seem obvious why the suffering occurs: the people have abandoned study and the practice that derives from that study.

But the Rabbis have quoted only part of *Jeremiah* 9:12. In the remainder of the verse God adds to God's indictment "they did not heed my voice nor follow it." Since for the Rabbis every word in the Bible is sacred, then there must not be needless repetition in it. Thus, the Rabbis must distinguish between the accusations "forsaking My Torah" and "did not heed my voice nor follow it." And Rav Yehuda offers a fascinating distinction: Rav Yehuda says, quoting Rav from whom he has first learned this explanation, that God's accusation here refers not to the fact that the people did not study, nor even that they had engaged in immorality, but that before they began their study period they did not recite the blessing for the Torah first. Study had become secular and not sacred. Study had lost its base in wonder and awe and had become mundane. Ordinary. Lifeless. Prosaic. Suffering has been caused by the abandonment of the wonder of study!

Some history: Following the Babylonian exile and the destruction of the Temple in 586 BCE, the study and obedience to Torah had, indeed, been neglected. But Cyrus had soon invited the Jews back to Palestine, and they began the construction of the second Temple that was finally completed in 519 BCE. The celebration of its completion was held before the building with a first public reading of the Torah in many years. The entire people gathered before the Water Gate as Ezra the Priest brought the Torah scroll out before the people.

> Ezra opened the scroll before the eyes of the people; and when he opened it, all the people stood silent. Ezra blessed God…and all the people answered, "Amen, Amen. …" They read the scroll in God's Torah, clearly with application of wisdom.

Over seven days the entire text was read to the people, and Ezra and his colleagues helped the people to understand what had been written down. And what is significant here to the Rabbis and to me in this description is that at this auspicious occasion, the first words that Ezra speaks are not *from* the text itself, but were a blessing *over* the text: "Ezra blessed God!"

Prayer raises the mundane to the level of the sanctified. Prayer reflects the awareness that we live amidst daily miracles and that there is more to the world than we will ever know. Abraham Joshua Heschel (1959) wrote "The beginning of awe is wonder, and the beginning of wisdom is awe" (p. 52). Prayer is an expression of awe; prayer sacralizes the mundane. Prayer transforms this public event from mere study to an engagement with that which is holy, with that which inspires awe and wonder. A blessing is a moment of insight, a change of direction. This blessing raises study to the level of the sacred. To engage in study is to be brought near to the holy. The blessing before Torah "Blessed are you, Adonai, our God, Ruler of the Universe, Who has sanctified us with your Commandments and has commanded us to engross ourselves in the words of Torah" makes of the public reading a sacred event.

Indeed, for the Rabbis, the practice of study rests at the center of social order. Its absence answers why Jerusalem was destroyed. Other possibilities are proffered: Rabbi Judah suggests that Jerusalem was destroyed because scholars were despised in the City, and he quotes, *II Chronicles* (36:16): "But they mocked the messengers of God, and despised his words and scoffed at these prophets until the wrath of the Lord rose against his people till there was no remedy." Suffering was caused by the disdain *of* study and not *by* study. Misquoting *Jeremiah* 6:11 the Rabbis say that Jerusalem was destroyed because people "neglected the education of school children" (BT, *Shabbat*, 119b): for it is said pour it out (God's wrath) because of the children in the street." The children should have been in school! The Rabbis search for a motive for suffering, and it often seems to be linked to the failure to study! It is said that every town without school children will be made desolate and suffering will exist in it (BT, *Shabbat* 119b). For the Rabbis, learning seems to be central to the well-being of the place. Study prevents suffering.

And what does all of this have to do with my classroom? I think now that it is in there that I guard against suffering and destruction. Rabbi Hannuma has said that Jerusalem was destroyed only because the people neglected the education of school children. Suffering occurs not because of the classroom, but from my failures in it.

The scholar, of whom I may be one, suffers; we recognize our lives for what they are and the world for what it is. Like Abraham, we search for 10 righteous people—fully aware that we may not be one of them. We acknowledge our share in Sodom and suffer for it. And our suffering derives from love and not from detachment. It must be borne silently and banished in the morning so that we may continue our work in the world. And that work ought to be the world's repair. But our suffering derives. The question for the pedagogue is how to make the study sacred.

A vibrant pedagogy always involves risk, and hence, it is argued, suffering accompanies study. But the Rabbis suggest that the opposite is true: a vibrant pedagogy dispels suffering. The hypochondriacally depressed Jean-Jacques Rousseau (1953) said, "So little are we formed for happiness here below that of necessity either the soul or the body must suffer if they do not both do—and the prosperity of either is nearly always harmful to the other" (p. 235). Rousseau lived to be 66 years of age. Like Elazar, Rousseau invited his sufferings upon himself, but declared that,

> The *vapours*, being the malady of happy people, was therefore mine. The tears that I shed for no reason, my alarm at the fall of a leaf or the fluttering of a bird, my changes of mood amidst the calm of a most pleasing life; all these were signs of a surfeit of happiness which leads to boredom, and, so to speak, to an exaggerated sensibility. (p. 235)

Rousseau suffered, but his suffering has no meaning outside itself.

What is suffering? Elazar suffered and the filled bowls of blood and pus are indicative of a reality of his anguish. And Rousseau (1953) suffered, though it would seem that much of his discomfort arose more from his psyche than from actual physical ailment. Rousseau's sufferings were not pedagogical; they were psychological. "Far from being astonished at finding myself to be dying, I was amazed still to be alive, and there was not an illness of which I read the description that I did not imagine to be mine" (p. 235). At 60 years of age, Rousseau, "racked by pains of every description," claimed to have acquired "more strength and life in me with which to suffer" than he felt when he was in his youth. There seems little connection between Rousseau's suffering and his learning; indeed, he seemed to have studied despite his sufferings. So, too, for the Rabbis: they suffer but this suffering is not of a pedagogical nature. A story is told (BT, *Bava Metzia, 85a)*: Rabbi Yehudah HaNasi's sufferings were brought on by an unkind act: a calf bound for slaughter laid its head in Rabbi's lap and shed a tear, but Rabbi dismissed the calf: "Go, for this you were created." For his lack of compassion Rabbi, as did Rabbi Elazar, invited sufferings. "Rabbi said, 'Sufferings are precious.'" But the preciosity of Rabbi's sufferings derive not from the learning they inspire but from the punishment they inflict. This suffering partook of no pedagogical nature but was entirely punitive. The preciosity of the suffering consisted of the pain it inflicted and not the learning it inspired. It did not inspire learning but reflected an awareness of learning that had not been practiced.

Rabbi's sufferings were relieved by an act: once, when his maid was sweeping out the house, she swept up some rats who were scurrying about on the floor. And Rabbi said to her "Let them go," and he quoted from Psalms (145:9), "His mercies are over all His works." And the Heavenly host said to each other, "Since he shows compassion, we will have compassion on him." But in the text there is no indication that Rabbi's compassion here reflects learning derived from his suffering; rather, his compassion stems *from* his enactment of prior learning. I think that it is the ubiquity of suffering that this story suggests and not its efficacy. Like a diamond, suffering has no intrinsic value except what it is given: in and of itself, suffering is meaningless.

How to avoid the birth pangs of the messiah? Engage in study and benevolence.

CHAPTER TWENTY-ONE

"Nobody Understood Why I Should Be Grieving"

DAVID W. JARDINE

Near the end of the film, near the end of his life, Benjamin Kasparian, once a respected professor whose identity depended on his research and finds, sneaks into the university lab after hours. He steals a brain, bones, some blood. At a place outside the city Benjamin digs a pit in the ground. He lays out the image of a running figure, a brain on legs. After covering this strange grave with earth, he lays down upon it and falls asleep. When Benjamin awakens, his memory is gone. He has gifted himself, his life, his work, back to the layers of the earth already taking him into its own meaning. (Seidel, 2014, p. 150)

Nobody understood why I should be grieving. (*Disenfranchised Grief,* Dr. Ken Doka, Springer Publishing Company, 2013)

I

I'm nearing the end of teaching a course on Hans-Georg Gadamer's *Truth and Method* for about the 25th time. I've often been asked, and often mulled myself, about how I can go back to the same text over and over again.

One colleague half-joked, years ago, "It's not the only book, you know?"

Another, years ago, spoke of a course in seminary where the year's readings consisted of re-reading the same biblical text every day, over and over and over again and nothing else besides.

And then Ivan Illich (1993), in his brilliant meditations on the work of Hugh of St. Victor (1096–1141) entitled *In the Vineyard of the Text* (1993), spoke of how lovingly and repeatedly reading a text brings it to a glow, and this glow of the text casts its light on me "so that [I] may recognize myself" (p. 17): "studious striving …teaches a commitment to engage in an activity by which the reader's own 'self' will be kindled and brought to sparkle" (p. 17).

"Approaching wisdom makes the reader radiant" (Illich, 1993, p. 17). I have sung, already, in praise of radiant beings and how sitting with something, persistently, making "common cause" with it, resigning myself to it (to re-coin the words of Wendell Berry [& Moyers, 2013]), is a necessary but not in itself sufficient cause of such radiance. It's that odd marriage, in scholarship, in study, of patience and exuberance.

I've also had this other odd experience with this book that comes, perhaps, from age, perhaps from running out of reasons to run. Gadamer's hermeneutics does not answer every question, does not address every woe. But, in the face of the onslaught of texts that surrounds the work of scholarship—I think of Hannah Arendt's (1969) "onslaught of the new" (p. 186)—and in the face of education's fetish for "the latest," I've found that it'll do, as imperfect, clumsy, elegant, and blind as it is. It befits, and, of course, has shaped, my own imperfections, clumsiness, elegance, and blindness. These are not simply the words of a scholar who has given up the panicky race and who faces the imminent end of a career (although it is partly that). I've simply decided to stay put, and I've found that something happens if you do. Staying put, itself, is far more difficult these days than it might seem, keeping away distraction and the fretful suffering that ensues from believing that panic and acceleration will help. "Only by staying in place can the imagination conceive or understand action in terms of consequence, of cause and effect. The meaning of action in time is inseparable from its meaning in place" (Berry, 1983, p. 88). Staying put lets something else come to glow. It is its own way of approaching wisdom. "It is not the only way. It is one way" (Berry & Moyers, 2013):

> The good worker knows…that after it is done work requires yet more time to prove its worth. One must stay to experience and study and understand the consequences— must understand by living with them, and then correct them, if necessary, by longer living and more work. It won't do to correct mistakes made in one place by moving to another place … or by adding on another place, as is the fashion in any sort of "growth economy." (Berry, 1983, pp. 70–71)

This, of course, is harder than ever before to imagine in the contemporary academy. But don't worry. I get it. I used grants as a cover story so that I would be left in peace to do the work I would have done anyway.

II

So all this links up to an undeniable fact, here, at the tail end of what might turn out to be my last offering of this class. Every time I teach this class, something almost always *happens*. Part of doing hermeneutic work itself is awaiting such happenstances, settling, composing and readying oneself, studying intensely so that breakfast conversations, radio programs on the way to work, off-hand colleagues' comments, a gesture, a fragment of text, a glance … we await, in the smallest of circumstances "where it seems like one life hardly matters" (Wallace, 1987, p. 4), the glow and work on behalf of its arrival.

So, anyway, here's what happened. Several students in the Gadamer class this term responded positively when I suggested that we continue into the spring term. We had done this last year, and it was approved as a teaching overload. This year, we were met differently. New rules. No more teaching overload. The proposed course was not offered. It is something like this: no one is allowed to teach overload because some employees have been taken advantage of and forced to do so, others have taken advantage of this circumstance unfairly, and, also, overload teaching cuts back on the work available for sessional instructors, and so on.

Let me continue by saying that this, of course, is a most trivial event. What this incident cued off is, I believe, not quite so trivial.

This incident made understandable in a new way all that stuff at the beginning of *Truth and Method* about the humanist tradition, about cultivating character and becoming someone because of what you know and do (*Bildung*), about judgment and tact, about *sensus communis*—the "common sense" that is build up through living in a community, and the moral tone that then comes, about the ability to make a good decision about what the right thing to do might be given the case that asks for good judgment from us. Such knowledge is eminently practical and substantive, but in a particular sense. Such knowledge is gained only through the practice of applying it to the cases and circumstances in which one is called to act, to think, to carefully consider, and, by such means, becoming practiced in good judgment and in the judicious and careful application of a rule. As Immanuel Kant (2009) said, there is no rule for the careful and proper application of a rule and only a fool would ask for one. To be gained, such knowledge must be exercised, over and over again. Even something like "careful and proper application" (from the sentence above) is, therefore, not an abstract universal idea or ideal, nor is it a method that can be simply handed over without any expectation of the recipient that he or she will have to practice this idea for it to become available, comprehensible, and understandable. "It cannot be taught in the abstract but only practiced from case to case" (Gadamer, 1989, p. 31). It is a knowledge only "won by a certain labor" (Ross & Jardine, 2009).

What emerges, here, is what Gadamer (1989) queerly named a "concrete universality"—a "sense that founds community" (p. 21). It is a deliberate, continued cultivation of good judgment regarding what it is that binds us to our common work. In such a community—such as, for example, a Faculty—we are not simply identical "individuals." Some of us are more experienced than others, experienced in different matters, more patient, more angry, more tolerant, more well-read, more forgiving, more suspicious, more trustworthy, and each of these differentiations is itself experienced differently by all concerned. This complex, ongoingly negotiated, contested, worn-out, and re-woven fabric describes what a community is like. It is not a fixed given but "always must be renewed in the effort of our living" (Gadamer 2007, p. 244). As Hannah Arendt (1969) so clearly put it, all we can do is strive to act "in such way that a setting-right remains actually possible, even though it can, of course, never be assured" (pp. 192–193). A living community thus lives within the shuddering of such lack of assurance and the endurances, labor, and patience that it requires.

Individual cases that arise in such a milieu arise in a particular way: "the case which functions as an example is in fact something different from just a case of a rule" (Gadamer, 1989, p. 39). A case of a rule simply falls under a universal and is governed by it. A case that functions as an example, on the contrary, calls that rule to account, illuminating it, supplementing, co-determining, and correcting it (p. 39). Of course, simply falling under the rule makes things easier: the case either falls or it doesn't. Experiencing a case to be exemplary requires opening the rule up to the conditions of its authority and governance and asking whether, in this case, the rule must give way to the practical knowledge of the community's well-being, and, if so, in what ways, for what good reasons and to what extent—in *this* case, and given the rules that govern us, what is the right thing to do? Who shall have a say in what this might be? Simply strictly and unwaveringly following the rule *might* be the right thing to do, but it might not (consider in this light the zero-tolerance policies in some schools). This openness of the rules to the vagaries of common sense is not a "vague licentiousness" (Smith, 1999, p. 139), but is, rather, a practical and practiced knowledge that Gadamer (1983) identified with an old Aristotelian understanding of *phronesis*: "the knowledge in terms of which one thing is preferred to another" (p. 131). Note that this is deemed to be a type of hard-won *knowledge*. One does not gain such knowledge simply through affirming one's right to have an opinion, or one's membership in a community. It is not just a matter of letting some people get away with breaking the rule and not letting others (although it does necessarily and unavoidably run this risk of being vulnerable to the vagaries of power, favor, and the like). It is a learned recognition that those in the community are not just abstract "individuals" who all fall identically "under the rules" but that each person in the community is someone—practiced, experienced, marginalized, foolish, trustworthy, unreliable, oppressed, authoritative, inexperienced, knowledgeable, a bully, a victim—not just an anonymous "anyone" and, moreover, not just the same "someone" one was yesterday or a year ago or in other circumstances or conditions or in light of different demands and occasions. Thus, such knowledge is not only tough both to win and to practice, it must also be constantly in the process of renewing itself and giving a good account of itself to the community so that good judgment doesn't atrophy into old prejudices and presumptions.

But then again, in giving an account of itself, something is also expected of those *to whom* such an account is given—that I will not just "react" or "give my opinion," but that I will attempt to have a good, well-informed, measured, and tempered opinion. Being part of a community, then, involves pedagogy: learning to understand what is going on, what is being said, what conditions are in play in our living together and not letting the simply willful assertion of individuality hold final sway (although this, too, is sometimes the right thing to do). Such practical knowledge, then, is retrievable and accessible only from its repeated practice, and the questions posed by this case will have to be reposed with the arrival of the next case. This vulnerability to interpretation is at the core of the practical knowledge that defines the humanist tradition as it finds its way up into contemporary hermeneutics in Gadamer's *Truth and Method*. A concrete universal proves its universality through its susceptibility to the next case, to being taken up again, re-thought in the face of the arrival of the new. And this proves itself through the well-being of the community that is thus woven over time. Its substance links to Gadamer's invocation (1989, p. 21) of Vico's idea of *topica*—a, so to speak, "topographical" knowledge of a place or locale that is gained only by venturing (German *Fahren*, "to journey") in that place and "learning one's way around" (p. 233). It is only thus, by venturing in one's "topic," that one becomes "experienced" (German *Erfahrung*) in its ways and learns, of course, that others have been there before, ancestors (German *Vorfahrung*). We learn, too, that this territory is often full of contestation, and inherited troubles, prejudices, occlusions, marginalizations, and the like). Becoming practiced and experienced, in such a venture, "does not consist in the fact that someone already knows everything and knows better than anyone else. Rather, the experienced person proves to be…someone who is particularly well-equipped to have new experiences and to learn from them" (Gadamer, 1989, p. 355), i.e., someone prepared to do the work necessary in order to have the next case be able to demand good judgment regarding its character and merits. And, here, again, "being experienced" is not an abstract but a concrete universal, the cultivation of which differentiates us rather than making us more and more identical. I, for example, should sensibly *never* be in a position of administration, given my impatience and inability to muster certain required forms of tolerance, judgment, and leeway. These admirable abilities are not my fate or my practice.

This is why I have so much enjoyed Thora Ilin Bayer's wonderful "Vico's Principle of *Sensus Communis* and Forensic Eloquence" (2008), in which not only eloquence is articulated as part of the humanist tradition inherited and transformed by Gadamer, but also, tellingly, *prudentia, temperantia,* and *decorum* as a key to knowledge thus understood as the practical and ongoing work of working for the well-being of a community and the effected and renewed sense that "we belong to it" (Gadamer, 1989, p. 358). It is near hilarious to imagine eloquence, prudence, temperance, and decorum as anything but objects of mockery and suspicion in our contemporary circumstances. Bayer (2008) spoke, too, of *sensus communis,* including, in the work of Juvenal, the idea of "thoughtful kindness" (p. 1138), which casts me over to another recent love, Wendell Berry's new book, *It All Turns on Affection* (2012), and from there back to an old adage of the Angelic Doctor, where Thomas Aquinas paraphrases the *Ad Herennium*: "It is necessary that a man should dwell with solicitude on, and cleave with affection to, the things which he wishes to remember" (cited in Yates, 1974, p. 75).

There is a root visible here, that this knowledge of the well-being of the community is linked to memory and its cultivation and well-being. The indiscriminate application of rules or following of rubrics bypasses the cultivation of memory. We're linked back, then, to Benjamin Kasparian and the drift of his memory into the Earth. Here lies the shock:

> We know full well that th[e] Great Council [of memory and practice] that shows up surrounding…any one of us… is not Absolute, that [I am] surrounded (I would suggest, *necessarily* surrounded) by a dark and irremediable penumbra of absences. We don't learn everything. None of us is everyone. None of us is cut out for living just any life, and none of us will live forever. We are not perspectiveless and timeless beings whose knowledge floats [identically under the rule of law] and whose life is a matter of indifference. I am defined by what I can thus remember, what necessarily exclusive and incomplete host of voices haunts my inner life and work and therefore haunts the world(s) that open in front of me. This composed and cultivated memory constitutes my openness to what comes to meet me from the world. No amount of effort allows any of us to avoid this process of suffering through the remembering and forgetting

of the world and becoming someone in the process. As memory increases, so does this suffering. I become more susceptible to the world's affect as I become more experienced. This is basic. (Jardine, 2008, pp. 56–57)

III

If one's sight is clear and if one stays on and works well, one's love gradually responds to the place as it really is, and one's visions gradually image possibilities that are really in it. Vision, possibility work, and life—all have changed by mutual correction. Correct discipline, given enough time, gradually removes one's self from the one's line of sight. One works to better purpose then and makes fewer mistakes, because at last one sees where one is. Two human possibilities of the highest order thus come within reach: what one wants can become the same as what one has, and one's knowledge can cause respect for what one knows. (Berry, 1983, p. 70)

It used to be that our administrators were allowed, in fact required, to at least attempt to make considered, sound, defensible judgments about the matters facing them. Discretion. Of course, such discretion still exists, but we all have to keep it secret, because if it becomes visible in a "community" governed by rules, it can only appear as rule-breaking or "favoritism." I, for example, am near retirement, I'm not being forced to do anything, I'm not taking work from something a sessional could do, I am, dare I say, a bit of an expert in the content of this course, 15 graduate students wanted this course to continue, and so on. Again, this is a profoundly trivial example except for this: the rule indiscriminately applied now precludes the relevance of any of this. In other words—here is another layer—under the rules and rubrics, I become simply one employee among others, an F[ull] T[ime] E[quivalent] cluster who, to be treated "fairly," gets treated like "anyone." Otherwise, under the rule, those applying it would be discriminating. These, then, become the alternatives. Either the community is prejudicially discriminating (understood only negatively, of course, as bias, favoritism, collusion, and the like) or it operates indiscriminately under the law. This perhaps accounts for the fact that I come, then, like I have over the past years, to feel faceless, anonymous, replaceable at a moment's notice. But something gets hidden here.

There is an iatrogenic "loop" that frightens me and sends me grieving, and in all this, a transformative shift that gets occluded. A passage from Sheila Ross' brilliant essay "The temporality of tarrying in Gadamer" (2006):

The possibility presents itself that such deference [to rules simply anonymously followed] prevents or obviates the occurrence of a kind of experience…the human hermeneutic experience that Gadamer calls tarrying [a form, we might say, of "staying put"]. The Gadamerian dystopia is not unfamiliar. In his version, to be glib, little requires human application so little cultivates it. Long alienated form abiding in inquiry as a form of life and way of being, a restless humanity defers to models, systems, operations, procedures, the ready-made strategic plan. (p. 111)

But here is the great tragedy. Our deference, here, *creates* restlessness in its attempt to overcome restlessness. It attempts to replace the alienation from the community that it has caused with obedience in the zero-tolerance application of rules.

Once there is a fixed "rule" that no fecund case can correct, supplement, or vary, cultivating good, careful, thoughtful judgment is no longer "asked for."

The fixity of the rule thus replaces the difficult cultivation of the wisdom of practice.

Therefore, the practiced ability to make such good judgments is not exercised.

Therefore, that ability atrophies.

Therefore, since no one is practicing good judgment, it cannot be relied upon.

Therefore, a fixed rule becomes necessary.

The imposition of the fixed rule creates the conditions for its being needed by transforming the community in which it is applied into a locale with no wise, practiced, trusted, or considered alternative to such fixity. Rules thus create the conditions for which they are then touted as the cure. Because it falls outside of the surveillance purviews of fixed rules, the suggestion of "good work" becomes nothing more than an object of suspicion, and those touting it seem simply out-of-date, old-fashioned, self-serving, and out-of-touch.

And hence, one last turn in this iatrogenic looping—the great ontological disguise, where such anonymous ruled-governedness, and its consort, the abstract and anonymous "individuality" of those thus governed, become trumpeted as "the real world." Thus aligned, assessments of our labors are, of necessity, reduced to market-economy logics and zero-sum calculations—the number of articles published and number of pages and the sheer amounts of external funding that have been secured, whatever the topic, whatever the real or perceived worth (this latter matter is now either rendered "subjective" ["who is to say what is worthwhile?" "What is worthwhile to you might not be worthwhile to me" and so on] or is simply equated with the brute fact of funds being received). Enduring the labor of cultivating good judgment about good work (a suffering that just might lead to composure, compassion, thoughtfulness, patience, and the like, even though, recall, "it can never be assured") is replaced with the insufferability of living in a world where the very idea of good work seems like a dream and thoughtful practice is not only no longer needed, it is also no longer *possible* within the confines of the academy.

So, if I may, and as a parting gesture, hermeneutics is important, not just because it helps us get a glimpse of this loop in which we are caught. It also points to the terrible fact that the living worlds of our work are being reassembled, right before our eyes, in order to eliminate the need for application and its cultivation, and therefore atrophying and marginalizing hermeneutic acuity. Once we all become unpracticed, we will all be glad of the rules, since any other recourse has died off. We will find that obedience is our only comfort.

And a sort of unnamed, collective grieving, perhaps. Would that I could believe that this whole matter is not deliberate, even though those perpetrating it are caught in and spellbound by this circumstance as much as any of us.

Hermeneutics asks us to think, just for a moment, about who profits from such a circumstance and to what ends. Hermeneutics does not promise to make our suffering less, but only to make it, however briefly, utterable—to turn what is now a silent, suppressed, and panicky malaise into the refuge of scholarly commiseration.

Nobody understood why I should be grieving. Thus, I steal a brain, some bones, some blood, and place them carefully upon the Earth, readying myself to lie down.

CHAPTER TWENTY-TWO

"God's Sufferings Teach God Nothing": Some Emails

ALAN A. BLOCK & DAVID W. JARDINE

David: Date: Sunday, April 13, 2014 at 8:16 AM Attached [a draft of Chapter 21,"Nobody understood why I should be grieving"]

Alan: We should talk a great deal about this paper. So let me start: You say, "I am defined by what I can thus remember …" but I wonder, can we be defined also by what we choose to forget—that forgetting is an active process and not a passive one? And why do you want to call the effort of remembering and forgetting—of becoming—a suffering?

David: Yes re: forgetting—formative process, not just indiscriminate storage for later access. And as to suffering—I keep blurring my way between enduring, undergoing, traversing, feeling, passing through, all the way to the nurses I work with in pediatric oncology, where suffering is still all of these, but magnified. The reason I keep blurring this is because of the tendency in education to try to get away from the old regimes of punishment and "a lesson he'll never forget" by cleaving to the equally bizarre belief that everything should be easy, that nothing is gained through patience, endurance, perseverance, discipline, and so on…

Alan: But as the Rabbis ask: are your sufferings precious to you, and the answer is neither they nor their reward (inelegant and ungrammatical but that is what they say!). Suffering exists, but does it have meaning in and of itself, or must we impose meaning on it to endure. And is suffering just life and life only—Dylan's line. Life is sad, life is a bust, all you can do is do what you must/You do what you must do/ And you do it well. …It interests me how Jewish Dylan sometimes seems.

Is patience, endurance perseverance discipline equivalent to suffering—is suffering comprised of these elements (there is a better word but I don't have it right now.) For me the effort of studying—as you do say in your paper—study relieves suffering.

David: Studying relieves unnecessary suffering. But why do I persist in it when it is sometimes so difficult? Why don't I just drop it? Because enduring its difficulty relieves, but only if I let myself go through with it…so yes, it is not as if there is an intrinsic value to suffering. It is simply life and life only. All life is suffering. But if we let ourselves not baulk at this and step towards it, studiously, we can ameliorate some of the suffering caused by our fearful retreats from the basic suffering of life and life only. This is why the nurses I work with talk about stepping towards suffering instead of away.

Alan: Agreed—but then what is the relationship between suffering and pedagogy? Is suffering pedagogical?

David: Attending to the life-world—life and life only—and coming to understand its ways (study)—so not just suffering the life-world but taking on the task of study, coming to know…transforms the suffering/undergoing of life into something to be known, to be praised, in fact, and therefore, suffering itself isn't pedagogical necessarily, but if suffering/life is taken to be that which we study, yes. There is a relationship. Suffering *can* teach, but not necessarily, not unless we break the spell of the life-world (as Uncle Buddha says, break the spell of Samsara) and our attachment to it. Meditating upon our life/world, and becoming wise in its ways—this, too, must be endured, repeatedly, but it offers a way of relief. It is not as if my anxiousness over my child disappears, now. But it "lightens" and becomes what it "is"—a worldly endurance that teaches me about love and why love is not attachment, perhaps.

David: BTW, I think, perhaps, that my suffering *is* precious to me, because without it, study would not be induced and I would lead a lesser life. I seek it out with an eye to studying it and, in the process, becoming more able to endure what is to come. With the always pretentious hope of becoming wiser, not just older. Like that paper I sent [Chapter 21], if we are cut off from the world in which care, good judgment, thoughtfulness etc., are called for, our patience, perseverance, etc. atrophy. Like the paper I've never written, "compassion loves suffering" [see Chapter 23]—I was going to add that we study because we, unlike God, must make our way through this, but I recall you mentioning to me ages and ages ago an image of heaven where even God studies Torah? Hah!

Alan: Yes, suggesting that the Torah existed before the world—that God had an instructional manual—interestingly, God suffers too—God makes all kinds of mistakes—and miscalculations. Destroys the world once and almost destroys the Jews but gets talked out of it by Moses.

God's sufferings teach God nothing.

CHAPTER TWENTY-THREE

Compassion Loves Suffering: Notes ON A Paper Never Written

CHRISTOPHER GILHAM, DAVID JARDINE,
& GRAHAM McCAFFREY

Chris: I've been wanting to get to our shared work and well, it's been just so busy here. Today is the last day of classes…and I've become something of the open office door guy for students so I get a lot of traffic here…very hard to get into anything…now I realize why lots of faculty are not here much…but I like being present and helping and believe me, some of these students need help…little bits and pieces of suffering…much like being in a high school…privileged work to be trusted…I often think of you sitting, listening, nodding and being attentive… being careful with your words…dropping insightful comments to shift a direction or mindset…I try to do the same…this life needs our attention, for sure, in order to be well with and for one another. Love this work!

David: I love it too, but. It becomes a matter, too, of how to not simply exhaust ourselves at this un-healable breach. That is the real trick, that sense of balance where I can maintain my ability to be attentive and be attentive as well. Again, of course, this is always judged event by event, as Graham's paper [see Chapter 2] notes. This is why the compassion/mindfulness stuff only makes sense once the exigencies of practice are entered into. Both are a great "idea" but both are not livable or sustainable as ideas, only as ongoing practices to be suffered. Interesting, then, how compassion *as practice* requires suffering. Mindfulness *as practiced* requires suffering. Both are not simply "cures" for it, but embodiments of it. *That* is why people come to your door—not just for the cure, but for an embodiment of what is, in fact, a Noble Truth! This is N.B. Compassion is, in the end, a love of suffering itself, because it asks us to "undergo."

Graham: I find a resistance to this sense of practice at times among nurses—one of the most helpful borrowings from Buddhist traditions to me is the sense of practice as a kind of Sisyphean labour ("We must imagine Sisyphus happy." Albert Camus). The bodhisattva vows from Zen and I think other traditions embody the idea of endless practice ("Dharma gates are endless, I vow to enter them," etc.). I know resistance from the inside, which is the point—practice exposes just those perfectly modulated points of pressure *against* staying compassionate and mindful—"individualized care" indeed. But at another level, I have found a non-listening to trying to say something about practice in this sense—maybe our self-identity as "practice disciplines" is so ingrained it is hard to shift, and maybe there is for some people a reflex unwillingness to take these aspects of Buddhist thought seriously.

David: This unwillingness is important. I recall a thing I never properly wrote about, how facilitation need not mean "making things easy/facile" but rather "being at ease with."

I remember, too, being in a Grade One class where the children where struggling with writing and, in those old days, getting that hot burning spot on your middle finger from the pressure and the sweat.

I said to them, "Do you know why you are having so much trouble learning to write? Because it's difficult." As they turned back to the task having shed a certain burdensomeness about it, writing wasn't now "easier," but they were more at ease with their suffering its demands. The suffering was recognized as *real*, not just some error or personal failing. This is the strange relief of practice.

CHAPTER TWENTY-FOUR

"Isn't All Oncology Hermeneutic?"

NANCY J. MOULES, DAVID W. JARDINE, GRAHAM McCAFFREY,
& CHRISTOPHER BROWN

The impetus for this paper arose during an Alberta Children's Hospital pediatric oncology research day in November 2012 in Calgary, Alberta, where dedicated researchers presented the work they were currently conducting in efforts to cure, treat, and make sense of childhood cancer. Most of the research presented was that of bench and natural science, understanding the progression of tumours, the impact of radiation on mice, randomized control trials, or evidence of the potential of a new chemotherapeutic agent. Dr. Nancy Moules, Alberta Children's Hospital Foundation and Research Institute Nursing Professorship in Child and Family Centred Cancer Care, presented her research on understanding the impact of childhood cancer on lives and relationships, and her research approach of hermeneutics. In this context with this audience, it is a shared understanding that there is a very human experience of cancer and an appreciation that bench science offers one way of knowing that must be translated into another kind of knowing that is handled in the day-to-day practical decisions, judgments about, and interactions with those undergoing such experiences. Cancer is readily understood as an affliction that can affect all aspects of a person's life, a phenomenon replete with complex and often contradictory cultural, historical, and personal/familial understandings, assumptions, hopes, fears, and expectations. There exists a whole world of lived experience that precedes bench science and provides it with the contexts of its application and the conditions of its value.

Moules, in her description of hermeneutics as a legitimate research method in understanding cancer, moved past the very public cry for finding "cures" for cancer and into the lives of people who have cancer, who may or may not be treated successfully, who may die, who may suffer losses to their sense of self, their body image, or their peace of mind. There is something inherently difficult when we add this mention of suffering. Over and above the sought-for clarities of bench science, doctors, nurses, and other health professionals must learn to live with what they know and to handle this knowledge well, with a sense of dignity and proportion that is acutely aware that this knowledge inevitably invokes a whole life-world of experience and faces medical practitioners and patients and families alike with the experience of suffering. In the valuation of research that seeks for cure, there is hope and fear, and an awed waiting upon the presumed inevitable triumph of science. Hermeneutics is a form of research into the effects of cancer on individuals and families, as well as the effects of cancer on those treating such individuals and families, a method that opens a way to inquiry into all of these considerations, in all their awkwardness and difficulty. Yet, in this context, as in many others, hermeneutics is again and again required to account for itself, while all along addressing the suffering that is attendant upon childhood cancer. Hermeneutics is frequently asked to live up to the ways, means, and methods of the natural sciences.

In addressing the issue of numbers and power in this kind of research, Moules briefly outlined some of the ideas in Dr. David Jardine's (1992) "The Fecundity of the Individual Case" which demonstrated the strengths that surround hermeneutic work and the vital importance of hermeneutics as a way to understand the living character of our living professions. It is in the power of the particular—in the recognition of one voice, one experience, one diminishment of suffering, one experience of healing—that our professions have always found their real power and their real, living knowledge. It is in the moment of being present at the death of one child; or watching one patient walk for the first time on artificial limbs; or the privilege of being present while *this* family hears bad news or good news. It is in the richness of the power of these individual, particular moments of grace, kinship, and human relationship where the professions have always found their own graceful and powerful place—in the context of one human life, here and now, in *this*, and *this,* and *this* (Wallace, 1987).

In this forum and in reaction to this sketching out of the nature of hermeneutic knowledge and its place in our profession, Dr. Peter Craighead, Professor and Head of the Department of Oncology at Tom Baker Cancer Centre, rose and said, in response. "Yes, this makes sense to me. Isn't all oncology hermeneutic?"

A part of this response was rooted in Dr. Craighead's respect for a recently deceased colleague. Dr. Robert Buckman died at 63 years of age on October 9, 2011.

A renowned medical oncologist, author, and comedian, Dr. Buckman was known for his unorthodox approach to illness and death. He was reported to have once commented that it was the individual person who changed his practice every time. In this regard, Dr. Buckman was arguing for something subtly hermeneutic about his practice and about the knowledge that arises only in practice. It was not simply that the individual patient was more important than his aggregate knowledge of oncology, but that the confrontation with the individual, the particular, always enlivened, challenged, and informed that very knowledge, keeping it awake, alert, and in proper perspective. He held his amassed professional knowledge with a certain readiness and "lightness," as could always be seen from the often sheer delight with which he greeted "the next case." The next case always seemed to arrive as an opportunity to open up his vast knowledge and to let it be susceptible to what enlivening difference this new arrival might make. He embodied this openness with his patients, with the general public, and in relation to his own suffering. Dr. Buckman provided us with a strong confirmation of the vitality and importance of hermeneutics to professional life and practice, as demonstrated in the title of one of his books, *Cancer Is a Word, Not a Sentence* (2006).

For the experienced practitioner, the arrival of "the next case" involves its arrival into a territory of knowledge and experience for which that case provides a live and rich occasioning of our attention. The experienced practitioner is one who must remain open to such arrivals and the differences that can be made to them, to us and to the life and well-being of the living discipline(s) we are inhabiting with our patients and their families. The word "case," long since incorporated into medical, legal, and other professional speech, has this sense of arrival in its origin. Case derives from the Latin *casus,* meaning a chance, occasion, opportunity; accident, mishap. Literally, it means "a falling." In the 13th century, it had the meaning of "what befalls one" and in the 18th century began to be adopted by medicine (Online Etymology Dictionary, 2012). A case is something that has befallen one. Despite the professional control implied in the "case history" or the "case study," when a doctor or nurse meets a person with cancer, something "befalls" the professional too. The next case of a patient is not simply an "existential" matter of it being this person and no one else, and therefore a matter of the irreplaceable life of this individual who is not replaceable in their suffering with anyone else. All this is certainly true. The issue is what *difference it makes* to those of us who already know much about such suffering, who have already witnessed a long line of symptoms and presentations and varieties of heartache or fear or bold readiness to do "battle" with the invader.

The issue is how our knowledge is not simply "amassed verified knowledge" (Gadamer, 1989, p. xxi) anonymously held in some figurative storehouse, so that this new arrival simply gets slotted into the right locale of that store. Our knowledge is also a form of readiness for new experience it opens towards this new arrival in anticipation of being called to account, of being summoned and needing to respond professionally, "properly," in ways that Gadamer (1989) described as "relations of responding and summoning" (p. 458). This describes the profound *vulnerability* of our professional carriage that we deliberately make ourselves and what we know susceptible to the subtleties of what is arriving. More than this, it is *because we are experienced* that we are able to find this carrying of ourselves practicable, day-to-day. This susceptibility is a matter of how we experience our experience; whether we can see ourselves not only out of the authority of our expertise, but also as being experienced by the other. Experience in this sense includes humility; it is permeable and reciprocal, and inevitably attendant upon that which it does not produce from itself and its own storehouse of knowledge.

As Gadamer (1996) noted in his essay *Hermeneutics and Psychiatry*, "…the doctor needs more than just scientific and technical knowledge and professional experience" (p. 172). The doctor or the nurse also needs a well-honed sense of practical knowledge and practical judgment, wherein individual cases are treated with a sense of proper proportion borne of practice itself (what Aristotle called *phronesis* rather than *techne*). These two forms of knowledge are not in a battle with one another for the same territory or voice, but neither is one simply replaceable for the other or able to do the work of the other. "Although the expertise of a technical knowledge…has a proximity to *phronesis*, technical knowledge does not ask the question of the good or the just comprehensively, or it does not allow us to act comprehensively in each situation" (Gadamer, 2007b, p. 232). An experienced hematologist/oncologist colleague offered this view:

> I deal with very nasty malignant diseases. Fatal if our therapies don't work. Each of these diseases can be categorized under broad headings and, as our knowledge advances, increasingly narrow sub-headings. Such a degree of organization implies that a process of inquiry about this disease has revealed enough to form the basis of a broadly accepted approach to the disease, a therapeutic plan, a management strategy. For many disease entities we have such an approach. "You have disease X and the book says do this." It doesn't always work as well as is hoped but at least we have a plan. This makes medicine sound quite formulaic and from a biomedical perspective this is what we strive for – the magic formula. A moment of reflection will reveal that these formulae provide strategies for managing diseases. But diseases exist in people and our magic formulae rarely take that into account.

Hermeneutics provides a form of research geared to precisely such difficult accounting. It does so by reformulating what it means to "apply" what one knows in a specific case. It is not that those who practice within the natural sciences and help to develop such knowledge that provide formulae do not care about individual cases; they do this work because they care deeply. Hermeneutics, however, maintains that the difficulty of these cases and the complexity of the human experience of them can be understood and known. Science might question the study of such things as perhaps only subjective, private, and even indemonstrable, or that if they are to be studied, they must be subjected to the particular rigor of the scientific method. Hermeneutics provides a way to study human experience that does not subject it to the demands of the natural sciences, but still provides dynamic, rich, compelling, and detailed understanding and description that leaves all of their difficulty and ambiguity in place and makes it available to thinking, communication, sharing, and a deeper understanding of, and sensitivity to, the subtleties of lived experience.

Hermeneutics also provides ways to improve practice through studies of lived experience by pointing to the layers of ambiguous entailment in which we live with our patients—the coming of the death of a child *is* troublesome, terrible, surrounded by myriad tales, images, and fears. Understanding this in detail improves the practice of oncology, not by "nailing down" something more securely but by honing and shaping our ability to be aware of and articulate our lived surroundings.

In *Truth and Method*, Gadamer (1989) demonstrated how understanding, in this hermeneutic sense, is "more a passion than an action" (p. 366). It is not the application of a rule to a case but more like the application of a case to a rule. Our already established "magic formulae" must befall and respond to the demands that the new case brings and expects of such knowledge. This knowledge is something we must therefore "undergo," something we must "suffer." In choosing to work in an area such as oncology, one agrees to this hermeneutic wager, to a willingness to not only suffer but to "suffer together" in the way that Moules (1999) wrote of compassion as a hermeneutic endeavor that is willful and deliberate.

This is why Gadamer suggested that at the heart of this living knowledge is an old Greek adage: *pathei mathos*: "learning through suffering" (Gadamer, 1989, p. 356), an idea itself inherited from the Greek tragedies of Aeschylus (c. 525 BCE). The hermeneutic tradition recognizes that there is something inherently difficult and transformative in the act of becoming experienced in the ways of the world, and from such a process "no one can be exempt" (Gadamer, 1989, p. 355). This claim about experience extends across the whole gamut of human life, from small, exhilarating interruptions of one's expectations (moments of inquiry, learning, engagement, investigation, questioning) to traumatic experiences of mortality, impermanence, and illness (moments considered "life changing"). In all these cases, the learning and teaching that ensues is understood as "an adventure and, like any adventure, it always involves some risk" (Gadamer, 1983, p. 141), including, of necessity, "moments of loss of self" (Gadamer, 1977, p. 51) wherein who I understand myself to be and what I understand of the world might have to endure suffering change. This is why, as professionals, we are drawn towards the suffering of others because it is *there* that we experience a deep insight into our shared human lot. This, again, recalls the example of Dr. Buckman and his willingness to step into the suffering of others and to use his own suffering as way to help others:

> Application is neither a subsequent nor merely an occasional part of the phenomenon of [hermeneutic] understanding, but codetermines it as a whole from the beginning. This does not mean that…he first understands [some pregiven universal] per se, and then afterward uses it for particular applications. Rather, the interpreter seeks no more than to understand this universal – i.e., to understand what it says, what constitutes [its] meaning and significance. In order to understand that, he must not try to disregard himself and his particular hermeneutical situation. He must relate [it] to this situation if he wants to understand at all. (Gadamer, 1989, p. 324)

This next patient, this next presentation of symptoms, these next uttered words of concern, do not simply "fall under" general principles or established knowledge, but ask something of this knowledge. They ask of the general principle that it proves itself "in this case" to be adequate to such a case. This ability to deftly judge the relationship between established knowledge and the arrival of a new case is itself a type of practical knowledge that does *not* operate in the same way as the establishment of that natural scientific knowledge itself. It is, rather, a cluster of contingent practical judgments. One can become practiced in such judgments, but one cannot give a set of rules for how to make such judgments because those rules, in turn, would require cultivating, in practice, an understanding of their application:

> *Each patient is embarking on a difficult journey on a road that is unknown to them. A part of our responsibility as physicians is to prepare our patients for the journey and then walk with them. That comes partly by providing them with insight about what may lie ahead and the likelihood of having to change plans according to what happens on the journey. The conversation needs to be ongoing and open-ended. Things change. I start such a conversation by asking the patient and family to explain to me what they know about their disease and what is being offered. For me, it defines the starting point and strategy of our ongoing conversation and it is often a unique starting point and **always** a unique strategy.*

The hermeneutic object of interest is the ability, in practice, to recognize a case *as* a case *of* some general principle, as a case that exemplifies it, modifies it, defies it, or "nearly fits" or demands that our established knowledge gain more subtlety, differentiation, and acuity. This judgment is not a matter of simply applying the general principle to the case, but allowing the case to "speak back" to that already-established knowledge in such a way that the case puts the principle into question and demands that the knowledge already established gives an account of its applicability in the face of the demands made by the case:

> The ordering of life by rules of law…is incomplete and needs productive supplementation. At issue is always something more than the correct application of general principles. Our knowledge…is always supplemented by the individual case, even productively determined by it. The judge not only applies the law *in concreto*, but contributes through his very judgment to developing the law. [Our knowledge] is constantly developed through the fecundity of the individual case. (Gadamer, 1989, p. 38)

> The individual case on which judgment works is never simply a case; it is not exhausted by being a particular example of a universal law or concept. Rather, it is always an "individual case," and it is significant that we call it a special case, because the rule does not [and cannot] comprehend [this individuality]. Every judgment about something intended in its concrete individuality (e.g., the judgment required in a situation that calls for action) is—strictly speaking—a judgment about a special case. That means nothing less than that judging the case involves not merely applying the universal principle according to which it is judged, by co-determining, supplement, and correcting that principle. (Gadamer, 1989, p. 39)

Negotiating this susceptibility of established knowledge to the arrival of the next case is the work of hermeneutics and it is the work of oncology. "*The true locus of hermeneutics is this in-between*" (Gadamer, 1989, p. 295). This is how professions, of necessity, are not simply the impervious and imperial wielding of "amassed verified knowledge." Professionals seek out instances of suffering or undergoing, instances of susceptibility where the locale of meeting a challenge to our knowledge is at once a locale of meeting our patient "in" this suffering, "in" the locale of taking seriously their arrival as requiring us, with all our aggregate knowledge of, and familiarity with, such matters, to engage *this* arrival. We, like them, must allow what we know to come into play with the person that has arrived with questions, knowledge, fears, concerns, evidence, foibles, resolve, and all the particularities of presentation. This is the negotiation that is at the heart of diagnosis, that our aggregate knowledge is not simply a slot into which the new patient fits, but is, rather, something that must, with great subtlety, respond *well* to that arrival and let that arrival do the work proper to its particularity. We know, as professionals, that we can, with those new to our profession, lay out the criteria of a particular pathology, but we cannot outrun the difficulty of recognizing *this case* as an example of *that* pathology:

> *I met with the patient and family to discuss what we had to offer to treat the leukemia and our chances of success. They asked insightful questions. I was told, "if my number is up there*

is nothing I can do about it but let's try our best." There was a peace in the room. The treat-
ment went well at the beginning but then went off the rails. Each challenge was faced with
determination and a calmness as "the number" came up. Our conversations had remained
easy despite the increasing gravity of what we were discussing and often we had shared a
laugh. After many weeks of struggle, the patient passed away with the family at their side.

This is a practical form of knowledge that cannot be amassed theoretically, nor can it be simply handed over to another professional without that person having to now cultivate this knowledge for him or herself.

A common adage in the work of oncology is the "experienced" practitioner. Hermeneutics identifies how "becoming experienced" is not a matter of simply an increased expertise in "amassed verified [bench science] knowledge" (Gadamer 1989, p. xxi) but an increased deftness in how one "handles" such knowledge in practice. Being experienced does not culminate in knowing more and better than anyone else (the sort of required expertise in the "amassed verified knowledge" of one's field requisite of being "knowledgeable in the field"). Hermeneutics points to another vital and essential form of knowledge and experience that are not of the same kind of knowledge as this expertise. "Experience has its proper fulfillment not in definitive [amassed] knowledge but in the openness to [new] experience[s] that is made possible by experience itself" (Gadamer, 1989, p. 355). An experienced doctor or nurse, therefore, is not simply someone who has been in such a profession for many years. Being experienced, in hermeneutics, is connected with an old concept from the Humanist tradition: *Bildung* (Bruford, 2010; Gadamer, 1989; Pinar, 2011; von Humbolt, 2000), a German term meaning self-formation, that is, the endured process of *becoming someone* in the act of coming to know about oneself and the world. This site of becoming someone is the site of *pathei mathos* because it requires a type of "undergoing" or "suffering" in which one risks becoming changed and having to live with the consequences.

I met with the patient and family to discuss what we had to offer to treat the leukemia and
our chances of success. They asked insightful questions. I was told, "if my number is up there is
nothing I can do about it but let's try our best." There was palpable fear in the room and the
patient looked truly terrified. The next questions were, "what will happen to me?" and "what
are my chances?" I started over again and tried a different approach. The treatment went
badly from an early stage. Each challenge was faced with determination but the terror never
left the patient's eyes. I was never sure if my conversations were answering their questions
or addressing their needs. After many weeks of struggle, the patient passed away with the
family at their side.

This situation started and ended the same as the one described before it, but in the middle of it something changed, something that called the oncologist to realize that no amount of amassed and aggregate knowledge or mastery of such knowledge, no "magic formulae," could save him from the "deliberation and decision" to move and act differently in this case (Gadamer, 1983, p. 113).

CONCLUDING REFLECTIONS

When a diagnosis is confirmed for a patient, or particular symptoms are described as such, the oncologist is able to "hear" a wide range of possibilities and probabilities. There is an ability to know, from long experience, something of a patient's possible future(s) and possible future suffering in ways that someone without this expertise simply could not. This is not exactly the same as simply "having the facts" but rather knowing that the facts alone will not save you or address the situation. There is that wonderful/terrible weight of then having to decide what might be best to say or not say, to indicate, or clothe, or to be straightforward about. This sort of judgment and its soundness and trustworthiness is an amazing thing. As professionals knowledgeable in our fields, we sometimes hold back in having a patient bear all the weight of what could be said, not to be dishonest, but to be measured and to try to act properly, in proper proportion to the best reading that can be given of the full breadth of the circumstances.

This is something of why and how we are professionals and not only technicians in possession of amassed scientific knowledge:

> The way of life of human beings is not fixed by nature like other living beings. Knowingly preferring one thing to another and consciously choosing among possible alternatives is the unique and specific characteristic of human being. The knowledge that gives direction to action is essentially called for by concrete situations in which we are required to choose the thing to be done and no learned and mastered technique can spare us the task of deliberation and decision. (Gadamer, 2007b, pp. 230–231)

Even though we, slowly, through practice and experience, become more receptive to the arrival of the next case and the difference it will bring, it always also feels like the first time as well; it feels brand new – this family, that child, those odd descriptions of symptoms, real, imagined, dreamt, feared, or seen with terrible clarity. As Buckman reminded us, walking into the room of the next patient will forever change our practices, but this requires an awareness that something has changed as well as an opening not to just find what fits with what we already know but what informs us anew. Gadamer (2007a) suggested that "[the world] compels over and over, and the better one knows it, the *more* compelling it is. This is not a matter of mastering an area of study" (p. 115).

This is the practical knowledge or "being experienced" that is the object of research in hermeneutic work and it:

> does have a certain proximity to the expert knowledge that is proper to technique, but what separates it fundamentally from technical expertise is that it expressly asks the question of the good–for example, about the best way of life [or about what course of action would be better than others]. It does not merely master an ability, like technical expertise, whose task is set by an outside authority [e.g., the methods of natural science in producing experimental results, or the simple rote following of procedures in a hospital unit] or by the purpose to be served by what is being produced [e.g., given we have to reduce wait times, do this instead of that]. (Gadamer, 2007b, p. 232)

Robert Buckman knew something of suffering, but perhaps his greatest wisdom was that he did not claim to know it with certainty and finality, because he understood that that is not our lot, as humans, to know once and for all. Even knowledge that has been pinned down with great precision by natural scientific methodology does not help us avoid having to decide, contingently and carefully, as to whether *this* is a case of *that*, and if it is, what we might now best do with those whose suffering is in our hands. Buckman saw suffering as the thing that could only be approached through a hermeneutic wager that the next "case" would indeed change the face of understanding the minute the door was opened.

Oncology is world of discovery, of devout care and intense search for cure. The natural and biological sciences are responsible for significant decreases in cancer morbidity, long-term cure, and longevity of life. This world of science and discovery is vital, but there is another world inherent in oncology—a world of the individual case, the n=1. This is a particular world of suffering that is not disembodied or detached from the rest of the world of scientific discovery, for it is fecund with its own kind of discovery, where fear shows or it does not, and even if the outcomes are the same the process of getting there never is. It is the argument for the innate fit of hermeneutic inquiry and research into the worlds of particulars, worlds that do not stand alone but have always something to say to the next door as it opens.

CHAPTER TWENTY-FIVE

"They Are All WITH Me": Troubled Youth IN Troubled Schools

ALLAN DONSKY

Words strain, Crack and sometimes break, under the burden.

(ELIOT, 1943, P. 19)

THE SPACE IN-BETWEEN

As a physician with over 30 years of "practice" (at once a noun and a verb), half of them as a Child and Adolescent Psychiatrist, I was, and continue to be, in the midst of pain and suffering. Students and parents invited me into their space to be with and witness their lives, both in the relative comfort of my office and at school. I was lured, both metaphorically and literally, into schools in an attempt to more fully "be with" their suffering.

As I spent more time in classrooms, the layers and complexity of suffering continued to show themselves, a kaleidoscope of relating and related fragments. It was only with careful and gently attuned attention I was able to see how I could explore the interwoven richness and interpretability of suffering. An understanding of the causes and conditions (to use Buddhist language) of this suffering is never really fully grasped, it seems. Each moment, word, perception, sense, idea, and wondering is so fleeting. Life cannot be stopped long enough to dissect each frame, as if somehow I could treat lived experience and suffering as I would a surgical incision. Perhaps some experiences enable this decisiveness, and yet, in this work, the work of being with the lived suffering of children, youth, and their families, there are complexly woven threads of interpretation demanding attention. Dissection is then, in any case, not entirely possible. Clarity is not often arrived at. There has been an ongoing flow of interaction between what I perceive as my internal world and what is "out there." Without doubt, this work has helped me to see just how much of our lives are co-generated by the interaction of the two. The profoundness with which my life has changed and continues to transform from being with suffering "others" is difficult to capture in words. There is, however, a space or "in-between" this co-generative action that, in noticing and holding well, may shine some light on the beginnings of a healing and a deeply thoughtful pedagogy.

HIDDEN TREASURE IN THE TROUBLE ITSELF

Arriving for the first time with excitement at the opportunity to offer my services in a high school Mental Health class, I introduced myself to two students sitting on a well-worn and welcoming sofa. I enquired as to the name of the boy sitting beside them. I had, on purpose, wanted to let him know that I saw him and he was important to me, even though we had not met. His head was downcast, perched powerfully atop a strong body, covered by a brown hooded sweater. In a very long and intensely growing moment of embarrassment, the head rose to reveal the face, now glaring, of what appeared to be a female.

All eyes were on me: the stranger who had invaded their space. My embarrassment peaked immediately. Our eyes locked. In that moment I was aware of an awkward, unclear connection between us. I had caused her pain. I was unable to know the full nature of her discomfort and, even if I asked her and she agreed to answer, her words might have strained and cracked under the burden of her lived experiences. In that moment of intuitive recognition I knew it was important to be present for her. I had the sense she felt witnessed and acknowledged by me through our mutual gaze, borne out of a moment of my doing that called us both forth. This sense I had about the moment was at once also comforting. I relaxed into it, trusting that what would happen next was already happening. I continued to be present for her without responding to my own strong urges to say something flippant or to justify my mistake or to turn away. The moment declared a need to slow down, to contain and be contained by the odd paradox of comfort within discomfort. What was called for could only be found by staying right where I was, in the suffering of my embarrassment and her need to declare whom she felt I had not seen.

My initial presumptions about gender had been thwarted. The brief gaze that had connected us had overturned my expectations for what was to come next. We had been identified by this experience; moved along life's journey in ways we could not have predicted up front. The intensity of her stare was matched only by the expectant silence of the entire room. With deliberation and that gaze she stated, "I am a girl!"

I lowered my head, slowed my voice and bowed deeply in supplication, stating, "I am not worthy!" She smiled. She told me I should not do that again. I agreed and stated I would do my best in the future. That was enough. The tension dissolved. Our shared experience of being mutually called forth in that uncomfortable moment was also a sufficient condition for healing. A bridge had been co-generated between us. In that in-between, ever-so-brief space of embarrassment and perhaps acknowledgement of years of her own suffering over gender and identity issues, we connected. Something of the unworthiness of my own presumption made me also worthy of being forgiven. During subsequent encounters, we were always at ease with each other, having shared an unscripted painful moment that, in hindsight, had been collaboratively forged in the heat of a tough moment.

She shared her suffering with me. Such suffering might be a gift we want to open more often. It is unpleasant, messy, unbidden, and burdensome. Yet this present offers us chances to be more fully alive, awakened in the intensity of a moment to a deeper expanse of understanding for being with one another. The key to navigating troubles might just already be here, hidden treasure in the trouble itself.

SUFFERING'S COMPLEXITY

The story is told of a kindergarten student who on being woken by his eager parents on the second day of school wondered aloud why he had to go again. After all, he had been the previous day. This amusing yet telling anecdote hints at the suffering that arises from having to do anything we do not want to do. It reminds us of the idea that suffering occurs when we want the world to be other than it is right now.

For some children, school is a place of sanctuary, wonder, and joy. For others, school is less so. The broadest definition of violence is the imposition of one's will on the other. As such, some children experience school as a form of violence. For them, it may be felt as a violation of the sanctity of freedom and choice, possibly the most cherished value in our culture. This in no way suggests that we are to let children do whatever they want all the time. Yet could a measure of youthful democracy add something of value to the educational system?

We thus encounter an incredible web of seemingly intolerable tensions. Education and schools are important, adults are "in charge," children are seen as vulnerable, immature, and incompetent, and yet violence, as here defined, is done unto them. Sometimes, the ways we understand childhood itself can create a razor's edge upon which school and family life must balance. Children and youth can lose their balance when living within highly structured and inflexible pedagogical experiences.

At the same time parents and teachers are, in some sense, the cause of and witness to this suffering. I believe that even though schools are necessary and maintained by justifiable and admirably good intentions, in no way can the suffering be avoided. Yet why should or would we want to avoid all suffering? If the messy work of human life involves understanding through misunderstanding, as was the case with the student and me in the mental health class, maybe what is called for is practice at being more comfortable with discomfort, or making suffering sufferable.

I hold some measure of accountability in perpetuating this suffering because of my profession, too. As a therapist and by the powers vested in me, I am brought to bear, as witness and potential healer, to situations in which I may not be welcome. For some I am seen as a savior. I do not always save. I sometimes fail to deliver on those expectations. I have then failed in the quest and added to the pain. My role can become counter-productive in such situations. When seen, on the other hand, as unwelcome, my presence is a painful reminder that something in someone loved is wrong or broken.

As I grew in my work, the increasing awareness of not being welcome was painful. It raised doubts about my abilities, my worthiness to do my work, my sense of self. It was strange to recognize that I was suffering even while I was doing what I wanted to be doing in my work and, at the same time, the people I was hoping to help were suffering too because of what I represented to them. The idea of healing required an acknowledgement of suffering, which in turn, for many, perpetuated their suffering, and increased my own. Before I could even begin my work there were deeply counter-productive forces at play. Yet, were these truly counter-productive all the time and in every case? My awareness of this served as a gentle and then firmer hand in guiding me toward a deeper understanding of suffering.

"THE MEASURE OF ALL THINGS"

How much are we burdened by being evaluated, measured, marked, labeled, scored, and graded? What does it mean to be "good at"? The work of a physician is called medical "practice." Every performance is a practice and every practice is a performance. We are each unique and diverse, uneven and changing. This keeps well with the Buddhist notion that all is impermanent. Children face ever-changing academic, behavioral, cognitive, developmental, emotional, familial, linguistic, physical, psychological, social, and spiritual demands. The second decade of life is arguably the most difficult. Additional demands are manifested and magnified. These include identity, peer pressure, exponentially complex academics, puberty, sexuality, and pressure to identify life goals and financial worries.

Often neglected is the realization that school can be seen as an additional burden to the already Sisyphean tasks of childhood, as we have constructed it. At a time in their lives when youth may be ripe with unfulfilled potential, they are the recipients of a defined set of adult expectations that tests many domains of functioning at once. All things seem to be measured and only in their measurability are they of value. As much as adults appear to provide seemingly understandable, rational, and excusable reasons for this state of affairs, it can be of little solace to youth.

For many students, especially those I have worked with, school can be an overwhelming, confusing, frightening, unpleasant, unrewarding, unwelcome, and lonely place. Too many students experience school as not much more than an extension of parental authority where fear of failure, constant judgment, and often-unpleasant consequences are a daily occurrence. Schools are filled with all manner of complex sufferings. School failure can be seen as the result of laziness, poor motivation, and oppositional, defiant, attention-seeking, or manipulative intent. How often is the response of others one of disappointment, frustration, irritation, or anger? How quickly can that lead to the "blame game" and fear of and for the child who is not doing what they should be? The ways we see children and youth can determine how we are with them, in classrooms and school offices, in homes at dining-room tables, and in psychiatrist's offices. How we interpret their lives in the greater context of school's purposes and measured demands can also deeply co-generate suffering and understanding at once!

What if, in moments of judgment, we asked ourselves a different question? What sort of space could we create and what could it hold, if we explored a richer understanding of what might be going on for a student in a moment of tension or challenge? What could we learn if we stopped and examined our language in describing those children? What could be the implications and outcome of such an encounter with ourselves and the space we inhabit with the other? What would we see if we shined light on ourselves, our institutions, our daily practices? What would we see anew that perpetuates or even precipitates suffering? After all, it is much easier to focus on the pathology in the child.

MINDFULNESS IN EDUCATION

A sufferingly shy high school student whom I tried to engage over a period of two years in a Mindfulness-based group was mired in the rigidity of seemingly logical but unhelpful thinking. In regards to school he stated, "Prove to me it's going to be helpful and then I'll do it!" Perhaps, after years of being told what to do and how to do it, he was saying something true about school experiences. On the other hand, maybe his family life had played a role in his demand to see the direct connectivity between learning and life. His mind was made up; so much so that his rigidity impaired his ability to thrive in other classrooms. He at once evoked images of a pedagogy of poverty and an inability to respond in ways that helped him work well with what was before him. Maybe though, just maybe, he too was rigid. That co-generative power resulted in mental health diagnosis and placement in a highly specialized classroom setting.

He was also, like some other teens, dis-engaged from the painful richness that life has to offer. School hours were spent reading a book in the safer confines of a mental health class, a specialized setting for students with internalizing disorders such as depression or anxiety. He had never taken public transport, had little contact with his alcoholic father and was following the path of an older brother, whose life in his early 20s consisted primarily of playing video games. School attendance was good, maybe to escape an unfulfilling solitude at home. Should I assume he was unfulfilled? Did he know he had some choice? Had the sufferings of school and family life paralyzed him so much that he could not see possibility? How many youth are done unto and reach adulthood with no sense of choice or the free space to create and inhabit? The mindfulness work I have been doing in schools for many years now is an attempt to recover that space, for students like this.

In 1979, Mindfulness was arguably birthed into mainstream North American culture when Jon Kabat-Zinn founded the Stress Reduction Clinic and the Center for Mindfulness in Medicine, Health Care, and Society at the University of Massachusetts Medical School. While articulated in great breadth and depth by the Buddha and considered by many to be a Buddhist practice and at the heart of Buddhist meditation, mindfulness is not owned by anyone and is available to everyone. It can be nourished, practiced, fine-tuned, and applied by young and old.

In his seminal work *Full Catastrophe Living* Kabat-Zinn (1990) offered "simply put, mindfulness is moment-to-moment awareness" (p. 2). The challenge of being fully aware in any moment is the reality we face when we realize our minds are constantly on autopilot, filled with chatter and noise, despair and hopelessness. On autopilot, we may be unaware of this, seemingly under the command of a merciless mind as it darts all over with thoughts, ideas, feelings, perceptions, memories, plans, fantasies, and ruminations. The content of this endless production line is, for the most part, focused somewhere in the past or the future.

When living in the past, our mind is often filled with unpleasant memories, regrets, perceived or real failures, self-critical self-consciousness, pain, disappointment, hurt, or frustration. When we are preoccupied with the future there can be, and often is, fear of the unknown, perceived or real threats, and a sense of foreboding. It can be challenging to be more fully present for what is unfolding in the moment, to be here now. Even when we are able to be present in the present moment, we are often more concerned about "doing," typically spending less time attending to "how we are" doing what we are doing. Mindfulness is thus more about how we do what it is we are doing. It is both an end in itself and a means to an end.

The practice of mindfulness, that is, the capacity to be present moment-to-moment on purpose and with a witnessing equanimity enables new space to open. With the moment held there is a pause, an opening, a chance for deeper listening to what is being asked of us, what is being told to us. This potential inner space is always there, waiting, unexplored by the blindness of normative and well-practiced mental habits. This space is brought forth when we let go of wanting things to be other than what they are in the present moment.

There is no room for anything fresh or enlightening if we do not question our biases, judgment, and knowledge of what we believe is good for children and youth. We learn something vital when we are vulnerable, when we do not shrink from the unpleasant suffering of cognitive dissonance, when we relinquish our usual ways of knowing. Mindfulness involves practice at getting used to "not knowing." It is the door we need to enter, the dark forest to explore. We need to let go of the old and invite the unknown. This is hard for many, given engrained patterns of reactivity. The good news is that mindfulness can be found in every moment. Mindfulness provides groundedness in the now, replacing the sometimes unhelpful ways we cling to the past or long to control the future.

It exposes us, in the words of the late Charlie Seashore, to our "core of rot" (Murphy, 2013). This rot goes by many names. Freud called it the unconscious, Jung spoke of the shadow, and Buddha captured it in part when he spoke of delusion. It is the autopilot, untamed and wild Ich (Id) that wants to be in control and make the world other than it is. It rages long into the night against our perceived reality. It is continually fed by that powerful drive to seek pleasure and avoid pain. It is a universal and seemingly automatic human response. It is biologically wired in our hindbrain, from where adrenaline rushes to flood reason as soon as any discomfort or confusion arises. It is why many thoughts of that uncertain place called the future are often accompanied by fear. It is at the heart of the fight-or-flight or freeze response. It is the mortal in all of us wanting to make it all right, all good, and all nice. Of course, this is truly delusional, for it is unachievable. Yet we continue to want pleasure, control, and a painless life, just as many students do not want to be at school.

The struggle inherent in this tension is both the cause and the result of the suffering that arises when the ego does not attend to the present moments we find ourselves in. It is the defensive wall we vainly try to build in an attempt to ignore the first noble truth, that life has suffering. It is the alienation resulting from being disconnected from our heart, as well as not seeing the multiplicity of life as it presents itself now. The capacity to connect to painful moments—to the hearts of our suffering matters—is at once painful and the key to unlocking the riches of hearts of compassion and understanding. There can be no growth in our comfort zone and sometimes no comfort in our growing zone, I suggest.

"I Just Knew I Had to Do It"

The Mindfulness group, of which the shy student was a regular attendee, included sitting practice and learning to pay attention to the passing phenomena of life, both internally and externally. We practiced noticing our senses, our thoughts, bodies, ideas, emotions, and the fleeting nature of the parade of experience. Training the capacity of attention to what is going on enables us to see that in the moment we have a choice to be in the driver's seat of our internal lives or to let whatever "pop ups" (to use a computer metaphor) carry us off to unwelcome and unhealthy "websites" or thoughts. These websites are masterful at enticing us with the three horsemen of the emotional apocalypse, those being anger, depression, or anxiety. The latter two frequently trampled the student.

In conversations with students, we explored confusion and "not knowing" as a wonderful thing. When asked a question to which they did not currently have an answer, students often responded with almost shameful hesitation that they did not know. I responded with joy and celebrated the moment. This was usually met with quizzical staring because the conditioned response is to feel stupid when we don't know, to feel inadequate, and that we should have somehow figured it all out by now. Students are often instantly relieved to see that ignorance is universal, that the moment of uncertainty and confusion has much to offer. Such moments can be the first steps to further learning. In this way, ignorance is full of possibility. What a relief to be able to look forward to the unknown future. Instead of fear, we were able to replace ignorance with new ways of seeing the world, our relationships, and ourselves. Students in the group have told me, without hesitation and with wisdom they were surprised at, that life would be boring if we already knew everything. With moments of mindfulness, ignorance becomes a welcome guest whose presence is cherished rather than suffered.

This was the case with this shy and rigidly thinking student. After many group sessions without ever offering a spoken word, and my best attempts to engage him with open-ended invitations, I noticed a shift in his presence. He lifted his head more often, made fleeting and then sustained eye contact that was followed by a few tentative quiet words. It appears he was aware that no matter what had happened in his past, he had the power to choose how he responded in this moment. One morning, following another argument with his mother, he declared, "I just knew I had to do it."

Only after being with his experience for long enough, dwelling in the suffering and letting the suffering tell him what was wanted and needed, was he able to cross this threshold. He had reached his limit. That day and for the first time, he took public transport, enrolled in online courses and engaged in schoolwork. He discovered his own power, being active in his own life rather than observing. Changing himself was his key to ending some of that suffering. He witnessed the potential of a mindful moment as a means to opening possibility. The suffering spoke loudly enough to do its own wanting and doing. In letting go of the delusion that he was in control by saying no to the world, he found the freedom inherent in listening to the pain. That attentive listening pointed towards a new path. He had reached the end and in it was a beginning. Only by embracing his suffering did it perform its pedagogical work. In being more fully with himself his healing arose, unbidden. Mindfulness was a state of being that created the space for new doing.

"I Cannot Do So"

> "I believe that no man ever threw away his life while it was worth keeping."
> David Hume (original 1755/2005, p. 10)

It may not be coincidence that given the demands of childhood most adult mental health problems have their origins and onset in the teen years.

By the time they reach age 25, approximately 20 per cent of Canadian children and youth will have developed a mental illness. To help prevent serious mental health problems later in life, early intervention is essential. Child and youth mental health is a collective responsibility: it requires the engagement of parents, educators, health professionals and community organizations. (Mental Health Commission of Canada, 2014)

The importance of mental and psychological wellness has direct impacts on academic achievement. Research suggests that 46% of the failure to complete secondary school is attributable to mental disorders (Hoover, 2007).

The recognition of and the wrestling with this suffering is the only way we are going to find a way through what is a troubling state of affairs for young people. That youth suicide occurs too frequently can only be a measure of what should be an imperative for us. That is, a deep, tough plunge into suffering. Nothing a child psychiatrist ever faces is more challenging and painfully suffered than to feel you have failed when hearing the news of patients who complete suicide.

I have permission from the parents of two such youths to allow their children's voices to speak. I have strong memories of conversations with them, their voices in my head, emotions in my heart, all of it past and yet also very present. These courageous youth are among the bravest I have ever met, being completely honest with their lived experience of what it means to be human. I stand humbled by their directness in telling of their beliefs with strong conviction while my adult ground was shifting under the realization I had so little control. After all, healers are meant to heal, I think I can heal, have all the training that society says I need to do so, but no one could ever prepare me for their deaths. Maybe no one did because they could not.

I had no choice but to be open to the intelligence, insight, and clarity-of-purpose these youth displayed. Both sets of parents, years later, still ask unanswerable questions, enduring their hurt and confusion. I too felt what these parents reported about their children embodying calmness and anticipatory relief before they died. The parents and I, having openly discussed our own responses to our helplessness, had no choice but to watch in horror the unfolding of what turned out to be inevitable. This was not a path we the adults would ever choose, and it was unfathomable for us that this is what we would witness. Mindfully, painfully, they saw the outcome and were powerless to change the course.

Yet these parents navigated and found a centre or a point at which they knew there was nothing more they could have done. These courageous parents weathered a storm of unimaginable ferocity, of being nowhere other than where they were, in the midst of impending doom. From this there was no escape. There was only endurance. "Now" was the only time and place. At times when I felt completely helpless to do anything more, I felt incredibly buoyed and strengthened by these youth and their parents. There was wisdom in this suffering, too, despite how tragic these circumstances were.

The boys did not seem to flee life in the way we sometimes assume. While there was much about humanity they did not like, it was not a push to get away from it all. They were not forced to anything. I recall, with clarity, my own frailty during conversations with them, their strength and grace in contrast with my own trembling being. My terror was all sorts of horrible. I was looking at people who I knew would soon be dead. They were mirroring my own inevitable demise. I was confused. I could not help them because they did not want it, nor did they think they needed it.

I am unclear to this day as to why they continued to see me. I did my best to witness them as whole, not fragmented or diagnosed. Maybe they just came to chat, to be with someone who listened and did not judge, did not expect. I found myself having to resist the urge to do something. And then I realized the something I needed to do was to be with them, one on one, witnessing each other, allowing the moment to create itself from itself, with no expectations of things that we knew were not going to happen. I offered them a view of their potentiality, both having much to offer themselves and the world.

Yet they were simply not interested in what the adult human experience had to offer. They reported feeling in control, valuing their autonomy to make what to them was a rational choice. They were fully aware of what their paths would be and acted accordingly with what they felt and knew. From a psychiatric and legal point of view, they were "competent." Neither was psychotic in the sense of being out of touch with reality. Not being able to live life on their terms, they felt inauthentic in their being, untrue to themselves, and thus made fully conscious choices. They lived and died in the only authentic reality they valued. Invoking Buddhist language and understanding one wrote:

> Karma! God! Well, obviously people wish the same thing as me, but have come up with explanations and reasoning to convince themselves it's true, life is fair in its own complex and massively majestic way. They must be happier for it. I cannot do so, though. What majesty to stand one's ground, to be who you are and live it. What majesty indeed to live as authentically as that! (Personal communication, 2006)

He continued:

> What for though? Life will end either way, and it makes naught of a difference if I die the savior of mankind or some kid in a ditch, as the universe as we know it (in other words containing life) will end in time as well. Shut up other part! I'm trying to be optimistic here! Yes, yes it is hard to say what is me and what is a foreign entity of thought attacking me. I am all of it, but it is not all one. (Personal communication, 2006)

And again: "What we perceive and how we interpret it creates our individual universes, not of course physically" (Personal communication, 2006).

Here are moments of profound self-awareness, an understanding of attachment to our own stories, the meeting of a threshold of possibility and the realization of impermanence. Here is a letting go, a falling into the well. These youth needed no one to teach them mindfulness. In reality, they gave me plenty of mindfulness practice without even knowing it at the time.

Without doubt, the greatest tragedy, and by implication, the greatest suffering for survivors, is suicide by and of a young person. Such pain there is to acknowledge that a child might see life as unworthy. What has society created and how can it be viewed as other than filled with suffering, when a young person wants nothing to do with it? As we drop into this dark well of suffering and ponder its depths, important matters present themselves. It seems to be necessary to live at the threshold of not knowing our entire life, to stand at the edge knowing we need to enter its darkness. We need to cross this uncomfortable threshold.

All of us have this capacity when we "drop in" to the present and see it for its wonderful(ly terrifying) finiteness. Perhaps one of the challenges for us is to see all mental phenomena as, quoting one of the youth again, "based on a bunch of neurons pulsing electrical signals to each other in incredibly complex patterns." We are not, and yet are, more than our thoughts. Of course we are more than pulsing signals. But what more is there? How deep does the well go and what do we find? Quoting again from one youth:

> You know, I wonder how it felt to worry before human beings started teaching their offspring words. Strong images and feeling? Like instinct? How deep could your thought even go? Do words give you a different perspective of the world? Thoughts do and without learning some words, many thoughts would never be thought. Maybe it's time for some pointless over analysis on perspective. (Personal communication, 2006)

And so, recursively, back to suffering and the complex ways it manifests itself. What shall we say, with Herbert Draper (1900), in his *The Lament for Icarus*, about the boy who knowingly flew high and fell?

LETTING GO, LISTENING FOR THE IN-BETWEEN

As long as we are alive, it is not possible to be without suffering. The potential for suffering is built into the eternity of time in the moment that "human emotions can never be just right" (Cleary, 1989, p. 48). While the reptilian response to fight or flight or freeze is hard-wired and understandable, it is often neither helpful nor healing when considering the potentiality of the human condition and our potential for growth and change in the tough times.

Not only is a "flight" response inappropriate because it is often exaggerated by the delusional belief that pain and suffering must be avoided at all costs, it also deprives us of what the moment may be able to teach us, if only we stayed around long enough to learn. In flight, we move from engagement to disconnection from the moment and close the pedagogical door to a richer understanding of what can be learned. Of course we need to run from the sabre-toothed tiger, but sometimes as one truth we see pain as a dis-ease, a discomfort that must be banished further into the darkness, rather than allowing it to be the source of light that chases away the dark.

The first requirement for being with suffering is to be with it. The only way out of it is through it. Suffering usually elicits avoidance, a tightening and tension, as if a stiff upper lip will suffice. What is more vital is connecting to the soft underbelly and warmth of the heart. We need to embrace the darkness, the pain, the unknown, the despair, the longing, and the fear.

We need to accept that we are powerless when we think that thinking is all we need in the moment of suffering. Having a vague idea of what is going on is not sufficient when the heart and spirit are speaking. The language of the heart is beyond words. The yearning for resolution and healing are in the silence under and between words. Only a degree of release from our wanting and doing opens the space to connect with the healing well of compassion, kindness, forgiveness, understanding, and love.

When we fall freely and with surrender into the well of our unknown, we might discover what has been looking for us. The need for and the embracing of mindful practices in the West has been a response to the loss of heart and spirit over the past quarter century, I believe. Many have forgotten the language of joy, love, and beauty that can help make the journey of being alive more sufferable. The sense I had with those suicidal youth was that they did not have joy or pleasure while alive, and actually had made effort to find it. It was not for lack of trying. After all, their writings speak to the richness of their expeditionary efforts into their internal worlds. I am no longer puzzled by the fact they did not find peace in their mindfulness. Mindfulness is not about finding anything in particular: it is about clarity of vision.

So what are we to make of youthful death when seen through the eyes of the living and those who are about to die, already dead in their own mind? For those watching and who are to be left behind consolation might sometimes be found when the clarity of darkness is realized. From that blind place, the first tentative steps of healing have the space to proceed with the eternal wondering if anything else could have been said or done. Could it be said that those boys found consolation or healing from their pain and suffering? Did their calm and peaceful dispositions just prior to ending their own lives bespeak a timeless and final resolution to their quandary? Could we live with seeing their lives and deaths as a source of comfort, paradoxically challenging the prevailing belief that suicide is bad?

An elementary school teacher may have had it right when she said: "Own it, fix it, show some learning" (Personal communication, 2010). The order of these instructions is important. What do we own when we see suicide as the ultimate mental health enemy when the participants seem, at least on the surface, to be able and willing? What suffering is evoked and provoked when freedom to die in our own time is not valued as an individual truth? Whose suffering is being relieved or perpetuated in vain attempts to keep all alive at all costs? Am I not already sentenced to death by virtue of my living? In holding this ultimate truth, perhaps I can find the greatest liberation from suffering in living my life as it unfolds in the moment.

The female-I-thought-was-male, the shy student, and the dying are all with me.

"The opening of the heart without fear takes place in the crossing of this threshold" (Simms, 2000, p. 62). We must enter a portal surrounded on all sides by fear and the unknown. We are blind as we walk here, without map or guide, empty of the delusional self-reliance that usually serves us. As the title of a Russian fairy tale suggests, we are bound to "Go I know not where, fetch I know not what" (Zheleznova, 1966, p. 79).

There is much to find in the heart that is alive within us. Growth and transformation arise when we are in a state of tension between the permanent and the changeable. The process must be allowed to do its work on and to us. Only with a wholesome mindful presence, accompanied by equanimity, trust, and letting go, can we be with and understand things anew.

Again, there is also fear in staying as we are: the fear of stagnation and withering, losing hope and drowning in despair. There is fear in embracing youth's suffering and being with it, knowing we are all in some way responsible for it. We retract in and from fear, aware of our own frailty and inadequacy in fixing the unfixable. "Every limit is a beginning as well as an ending" (Eliot, 2014). So we find ourselves constantly walking a narrow bridge, not falling off to either the side of despondency and ineffectiveness or the delusional belief that everything is controllable. Perhaps this is how we might describe what is now so popularly labeled as "mental health." This is that razor's edge: life.

For myself, mindfulness has offered hope. As leader of the Velvet Revolution in Czechoslovakia, Vaclav Havel spoke of hope as follows: "Hope…is not the conviction that something will turn out well, but the certainty that something makes sense regardless of how it turns out" (Wheatley, 2009, p. 81). There is a need for effortless effort, a non-doing, non-striving, non-forcing, and letting-be of that which cannot be changed. I strive to be constantly in the question, always alert to the possibility of my own limits, what is and is not possible, and trying to know when and what kind of effort and action will embrace suffering's pedagogy. The hermeneutically informed moment transforms suffering into equanimity only when we mindfully let go of that we cannot control. In every moment suffering tells us we have both hope and despair, and there is a choice for how to live in and amongst those two choices. Are we listening for the in-between?

To end, I offer more writing from one of those wise youth:

We can fall in love with another because of their differences from all others, because of a single human's uniqueness (that mixed with pheromones and hormones of course), and that can create the illusion of meaning for us as powerful emotions tend to do. Hell, a war someone really believes in creates one just as readily. The illusion of such is all we can truly hope for, as a universal definition of meaning can never exist and we can only create our own. (Personal communication, 2006)

CHAPTER TWENTY-SIX

Happiness IN Bricks

ALEXANDER C. COOK

Maslow (1962/2011) could not have been more right when he developed his Hierarchy of Needs. Humans are a multi-faceted and complex problem, and breaking them down was his analytical response to ease that complexity. That is a kind of response that can only be found in a moment of true Self-Actualization.

For the rest of us, we can be found scattered between Physiology, Safety, Belonging, and Esteem. Moments of victory bring us closer and closer to the seemingly mythical Self-Actualization, while pain is the great destroyer—tearing us back down to our most basic elements, and back to the foundations of Maslow's Pyramid.

I am no stranger to the victories of spirit, stepping up the great stones of Maslow's Pyramid with the aims of reaching the light, and I am no stranger to the failures of the mind and body, stumbling and tumbling back to the pits. I would argue that none of us are strangers to that ebb and flow as we work our ways through life, but I can only speak for myself, and what has been my evident progression and regression, through Maslow's eyes.

THE MIND

The mind is an amazing thing. It enables us to achieve great feats of intellect and emotion, and it works independently of Maslow's supposed Pyramid. If we consider a "normal" person with "normal" ups and downs, Maslow's Pyramid may provide an apt example. I, however, am not one of those "normal" people (is anyone?).

At any given moment a person could be standing on any of the steps of the pyramid. If they are "normal" people we would expect them to follow Maslow's Pyramid rather closely. For example, if they have already achieved physiological well-being and a sense of safety we would expect them to gain that sense of belonging (moving them up the pyramid) or losing that sense of safety (moving them back down). This is reasonable, and no doubt when Maslow finessed his theory these were the people he had in mind. Even if there is a catastrophic event in a "normal" person's life he or she would still be expected to follow the Pyramid in a linear fashion. Look at a person who has just found her belonging in society. If she were to be injured in a motor vehicle accident she would be ripped from belonging, through safety, and be carelessly discarded at the base of Maslow's Pyramid, where she had not even satisfied her physiological needs. On that same line of thought, a lottery winner would be expected to boost herself a few steps up the Pyramid. Perhaps money can't buy happiness, or self-actualization in this case, but it can certainly help satisfy physiological needs, find that sense of safety, and even a sense of belonging (albeit possibly insincere).

I would put forward that Maslow's Pyramid is an exceptional tool to use in the evaluation of "normal" people, but that the mind can break the example and endlessly disprove the tool. This is where my experience comes in. I have been diagnosed with bi-polar disorder, and as is commonly known, that means that my mood goes through cycles of mania, and cycles of depression. If one day I have a "normal" mood, and then my mood naturally shifts upwards to mania, I can very quickly find myself climbing Maslow's Pyramid. Maybe I don't have all my physiological needs met, but maybe I don't care. Maybe I am feeling confident in such a way that my inhibitions vanish and what was unsafe becomes safe. Maybe I feel that everyone loves me and that I fit into and belong in any group. Maybe I believe, no, maybe I know, that I am better than average at everything I do. Maybe, I am the best I can be, in all ways, and I have reached that pinnacle of self-actualization. With bi-polar disorder I could find myself sitting atop Maslow's Pyramid in a number of weeks, and if anyone thinks that I don't belong there, or that I haven't achieved all of Maslow's stepping stones, well, they're wrong.

See, self-actualization isn't so hard. Maybe I can't achieve it in reality, but does that matter? Is there any reality more real than what I see? What I know?

We can take this idea in the other direction as well. Maybe I have legitimately reached self-actualization. Maybe I am at my best on all tiers and am being a flawless, functioning, and enormously contributing member of society. Maybe, but bi-polar disorder is a coin with two sides, and in a few weeks I could find myself falling from that pinnacle of self-actualization (legitimate or imagined). How can I have reached self-actualization if I'm not good at anything? I'm not the best I can be. I don't deserve self-actualization. I can't do anything right, and what confidence or esteem I have was grossly misplaced. There is no belonging. No one understands, and if they do, they don't want to help me. They don't want me. There can be no safety from others while there is no safety from oneself. I don't care if I get mugged, or beaten; on the contrary, I might turn on myself to try and grasp some level of physiological control; but what control can there be when you've dragged a blade across your own skin and found yourself off Maslow's Pyramid entirely? The answer is: who cares? It's not a question, it's not a plea; it's an exclamation of desperation.

See, self-actualization isn't so hard.

It's impossible.

What you've just read, well, it's the story of my life; but there is one more complication. I have also been diagnosed with borderline personality disorder. Long story short, it means that instead of going from that manic state to depression in weeks or months, it means that I can go from one to the other again and again and again in the span of a single day.

Where is Maslow's Pyramid now? I have so little grasp of the "truth" of my life, as everything I see is through the all-encompassing lens of emotion—good or bad. Maslow's Pyramid is just a myth to me. I find myself bouncing so quickly between Elysium and Tartarus that I have no awareness of my feet even touching Maslow's earth.

This is the lens I look through, but the mind is capable of bending anyone's vision.

Reading this again, that jump from mania to depression would be exhausting, and doing it again and again. ...There is no time for self actualization, more accurately, there is no such thing. While my life is perceived through the lens of my emotion there is nothing beyond that lens.

Bipolar disorder is treated through medication. Medication can smooth out the ups and downs and can clear the lens so reality can become visible once again. It's not easy to find the right treatment plan, but through adequate treatment people looking through that lens can hopefully become "normal."

Borderline personality disorder is a bit different. It is not a chemical imbalance that can be addressed through the addition of a few medications; instead, it is an emotional intensity and instability that can only be addressed by careful control of actions through the intricate scrutiny of the lens of one's life. A specific type of therapy has been developed to assist people with borderline personality disorder

(Dialectical Behavioural Therapy), and at its centre is a specific concept that can bring everything back into focus.

MINDFULNESS

Mindfulness is how I am able to put my feet back on Maslow's Pyramid to use it as a tool once more. If it is the great lens of emotion that pushes us off the "normal" track, it is mindfulness that can push us back on. There are many definitions for mindfulness, but I can only show you the working definition that I have acquired through years of effective, and ineffective, use.

To me mindfulness is the ability to reconnect with the body. It is a form of moving meditation that enables the body to take over, and to calm the mind. It is an awareness at the smallest physical level that can become so all-encompassing that it can drown out the mind.

For several years I have been speaking with educators about my condition, and about mindfulness. I have an example that I have used many times that is an apt description of borderline personality disorder, and of the effective uses of mindfulness. I know no better way to demonstrate these two concepts than to share the example with you.

Borderline personality disorder is emotional sensitivity, regardless of context. That means that something devastating could happen in your life (such as the death of a loved one, the end of a relationship, etc.) or something menial could happen in your life (such as getting the wrong order at a restaurant, losing a piece of stationary, etc.) and they could trigger the same response.

For example, imagine I'm a student. I'm sitting in class, doing my work, and the girl next to me says: "Can I borrow your eraser?"

The comment seems innocuous enough, but suddenly I feel like I'm King of the World; hell, I'm pretty sure I am King of the World! Here's this girl, maybe she likes me! True love?! So, I look into my bag and…

And….I can't find my eraser…suddenly I can feel the world collapsing around me. I can feel that world that I'm King of starting to fall apart. I don't have an eraser. That girl, she's going to be mad at me. She's going to hate me! The world…my life…it's…it's…it's over.

This is the kind of emotional intensity and instability that you see with borderline personality disorder. It's as if every emotion is magnified *regardless of context*. This is where Mindfulness comes in, and where Mindfulness can push us back towards that "normal" track.

Where were we? Ah yes. My world is falling apart. Maybe it was the loss of a relationship, or maybe just the loss of that eraser. It doesn't matter. Big or small, they feel the same. I can feel myself tripping down the steps of Maslow's pyramid, but where I should stop at physiological needs I keep falling further and further into depths that only I know.

But wait. If I can return to my body, and release my mind, I can get my bearings once more. I can feel my toes in my shoes, and air in my lungs. I'm not in any danger. I'm not in any pain. Come to think of it, if I use the faculties of all my senses, I'm fine.

If you can get to this place, to be Mindful of the situation and to watch the emotions pass before you without partaking in them, you can ground yourself, and you can place yourself back onto that "normal" path. You can use Mindfulness to bypass the barriers of mental health, to create Safety, and to enable Belonging and Esteem—thus using Mindfulness to climb Maslow's Pyramid.

Still, it's not so easy to climb that pyramid. To control a mental illness it takes an enormous amount of work and an enormous amount of support. There are many tiers of support and having several is crucial. One of the many issues with mental illnesses are that it needs to be identified to be treated. I'm not just talking about doctors and medication, but to fix any problem the problem needs to be identified. This is one of many challenges in seeking that crucial support. Some people's illnesses are so severe that identification is easy, they stick out, and as the old adage goes, the squeaky wheel gets the grease. For others their issues are less visible, and those issues gnaw at them piece by piece as they fight their way through what they think should be a "normal" life. Some of those people get help, and some don't. I was one of those people who didn't get help, and my issues gnawed on me like some fatal parasite. I wasn't supposed to have issues—I was supposed to be "normal."

I had the support of my friends, and my family, but they didn't know what they were supporting—no one did. There were tears, and painful arguments, and blood. They stood by me, but we all stood in the dark. That kind of support should be available to everyone, and with it, with love, people can survive most anything. Survive. That wasn't enough for me, and it still isn't.

My issues would not remain hidden. Like some beast they tore through me until they reached the surface and were staring out my eyes. I hope my friends knew it wasn't me, not the *real* me, but I wasn't in control. Maybe I was, but if I was, it was the darkest corner of my being. I fought myself, I cut myself, and I found myself in and out of the emergency room again and again. When you are suicidal they tell you to go to the emergency room. They tell you not to risk it. So I went, again, and again. The psychiatrists in ER could see my issues, they could see the demons I was battling but they couldn't identify them—until they could. I had been diagnosed with bi-polar disorder and the psychiatrists worked with that, but, it didn't explain my behaviour, and typical treatment clearly wasn't working. After one visit to the ER I was visiting a psychiatrist as an outpatient. I had my appointment in the morning, but that evening I had returned to the ER, and I was suicidal. It was that event that illuminated a critical piece of information for my psychiatrist, and that darkness they had been fighting, visit after visit, was finally brought into light.

Bi-polar disorder, even rapid cycling bi-polar disorder, means going through a single cycle in a few months and not a few hours. It was this, this little piece of illuminating information that set me on a course to right my life. My psychiatrist came to me with a list of symptoms, asking me if I thought I had any of them. I told him that I thought I had a few. He looked at me, wryly, saying "I think you have most of them." I was diagnosed with bi-polar disorder type II, borderline personality disorder, and with his support, and a new line of treatment, I set about righting my life.

That was the climax of this little misadventure. I had my family's support, my friends' support, and now I had professional support. The work part would come, but at once I had the support I needed, not to fix my mind, but to live with it.

I was failing four of my six classes in university that semester. Maybe it was luck, maybe it was hope, but I like to think that it was my new treatment and the support of those around me that turned things around. I managed to salvage three of the four courses. The people around me were apologetic that I had failed a course, but at every bit of sympathy I smiled inwardly; that single failure was the greatest victory of my entire life.

I didn't do it alone; I did it with the support of those around me. This story might not fit in with what is deemed "normal," but I'm not so different. I laugh, I smile, I cry, I love. I do what all "normal" people do; I just do it a little more. There is still significant stigma about mental illness within our society, and still much discrimination against those who face it. It is as if those people on Maslow's Pyramid think that because the climb is a little harder for people with mental illness they ought to be shunned. It's uncalled for, but it's something we humans have done for all our time. But what is different? Am I different because to reach my greatest potential I need medication to help quiet my mind? Is someone different because instead of having perfect vision they need to wear glasses? What's the difference here? They need something to help them survive, and so do I. We don't think anything of someone needing glasses, so why do we think differently of someone needing medication, or mobility assistance, or anything? This example often helps open people's eyes. There are people all around us, no one is the same, and we are all *different*. Maybe that's not so bad. I remember this example opening my eyes. At the time I was refusing medication due to having a bad experience with my previous medication. I didn't want to touch the stuff. I wanted to live as me, and be "normal." My counsellor, Donna Hughes, of InnerSolutions, helped me to understand that there is nothing wrong with needing a little extra support. People with glasses need a little extra support, they were made slightly differently, just like everyone else, and there was nothing wrong with that. So I too was made differently—what was wrong with that? I've borrowed her glasses metaphor and share it with everyone I can. To further the example, my mental illness is the lens through which I see the world. As someone with poor vision needs glasses, I too need to have my vision corrected. Psychiatrists and counsellors are the optometrists of mental health.

I won't be fixed, I won't be cured, how can I be? I can't cure me. I am me. Sure, I've got my quirks, as we all do, but with the support of those around me, I'll make it.

I already have.

THE BODY

As the brain is an amazing control booth, what it controls is no less amazing. The body is comprised of a bazillion components, all of which can be controlled by the mind to do great things. That being said, Maslow gave priority to the body over the mind on his Pyramid for a reason. If you cannot fulfil your Physiological needs you cannot pass go, and you cannot reach Self-Actualization.

In many ways, Maslow was right. Your body can have a profound impact on your mind, and your mood. One interesting example is how when you are sad, if you can manage to smile it will make you feel better (a bit at least). We smile all the time, and there is a certain muscle memory and certain association that goes along with it. If you can manage that smile, your body tells your brain "hey, we're having a good time here, feel better!"

Unfortunately, your body can also send your brain negative or painful messages. Again, I will draw from my own experiences to try and augment this discussion. In a work accident I herniated two disks in my back. In this case the hernias (bulges in the disk) pressed into the soft tissue in my back. This resulted in the nerves sending a message up to my brain saying "hey, we're not having a good time here, stop doing whatever you're doing!"

Relevance? As long as I was in pain I was grounded on Maslow's Pyramid. I couldn't fulfil my Physiological needs, and I could never ascend to Self-Actualization. The pain would act as a constant reminder of my state in life, and let me tell you, living on the ground floor of Maslow's Pyramid is not all it's cracked up to be.

In Maslow's eyes you would simply need to address the Physiological needs first and then you would be free to ascend once more. To me that meant that I needed to recover from the injury and then all would be well. That sounds easy enough, but in practice that can be very difficult. The doctor told me that in one to three months my disks would recover. They didn't. Ok, ok, give it a few more months. Any better? No. Add in some physiotherapy. Any better now? Still no. More physio, more better? No. So then you're stuck (according to Maslow).

In that position you have a few options, but let's look at one of the easiest. The doctors couldn't help the injury so the next step is to drown it out. If your body is sending un-fun messages to your brain and that's the issue, how can we stop the messages? We lie. We throw some extra chemicals into your system, pain killers, anti-inflammatories, muscle relaxants, and we make it so your brain can't even feel whether you are fulfilling your Physiological needs or not. Can't feel it? Must not be an issue!

Alright, so that lets you take a good run at Self-Actualization…that is, if you can attain it in four-hour increments. As the effect of your medications waxes and wanes, varying levels of the Pyramid are open to you. Even if you could completely suppress your pain I'm not sure that's what Maslow had in mind when he suggested you fulfil your Physiological needs. Still, for some of us, it's all we've got.

In my case, bad went to worse. No amount of physiotherapy could repair my disks, and even more drastic pain management techniques (x-ray-guided cortisone injections), could not suppress the fires generated by the hernia pressing on my sciatic nerve. I couldn't even see Maslow's Pyramid. If I missed taking painkillers by even an hour I would find myself completely immobilized by pain. Fuck Maslow. And his Pyramid too.

The doctors had a surgical option, and they took it. They opened me up and cut out a portion of one of the damaged disks (microdiscectomy of L4–L5, leaving L5–S1 untouched). Aside from the anesthetist not providing sufficient pain medications in recovery (woke up screaming, likely gave a few other people in recovery heart attacks…a story for another day), the surgery was supposed to provide lasting pain relief (if causing a structural weakness). What I would call decompression of the nerve was some of the most painful months of my life (two months immediately following surgery), but eventually the pain waned and after months of physio I was back off the pain killers and back on Maslow's Pyramid.

The pain was "solved," and I was back on the "normal" path. Unfortunately, long-lasting injuries tend to wreak havoc on the body. In my case it was nerve damage, atrophy of the multifidus, osteoarthritis in the lower back, scar tissue surrounding one rib head, bruscitis and condromalacia patellae (tendonitis and cartilage damage to the knee—likely due to compensation), and an irritable attitude (which I have to this day). There goes Maslow's Pyramid out the window again. My life has gone back to painkillers and nasty pain-relieving procedures (x-ray-guided cortisone injections to be followed with some nerve zapping for good measure).

So now what? Now I sit here, writing this discussion, letting the painkillers silence my body to type out some cohesive and comprehensive (hopefully comprehensive) thoughts. But it's not enough. Here I am again, surviving.

To add one layer of complexity, if we think of the smile that tells your mind you're having a good time, and the pain that tells your mind that you aren't, well, I'm getting that message all the time. Again, where's Maslow's Pyramid now?

At least Maslow was right about one thing; if you can't satisfy your Physiological needs you can't climb the Pyramid. If you can't stop the pain, you can't find happiness—or can you? He is right about pain communicating negativity to the mind, but can he really be right about not achieving Self-Actualization? If he is right that means that my life isn't life at all. It means that my life will just be fighting day after day to survive; just surviving.

I said it before. That's not enough.

The benefit of learning how to deal with my mental health is that I picked up a number of tools along the way that can help me deal with not only my mental health, but also with everything. The treatment for borderline personality disorder is called Dialectical Behavioural Therapy, and its roots are in a practice called Mindfulness.

I've already mentioned Mindfulness, and this certainly won't be the last time. Mindfulness is one of those things that has endless uses. For my mental health I have been able to use it to ground me in situations with extreme emotion, enabling me to manage those situations that may once have sent me to the Emergency Room. With my body there too is a use.

The issue with chronic conditions is that they are chronic. They can last for exceedingly long durations, including forever. If you are faced with mental illness, say depression, or chronic pain, say disk herniations, your mind is constantly under a barrage of negative signals. If that's all that your brain sees, bad can quickly turn to worse. The truth is that a little happiness, or a little freedom from pain, goes a long way. This is where Mindfulness comes in. Part of it is creating openings for those moments of freedom. For emotion you can ground yourself in your body, but what if your body too is in pain? Then you ground your pain in the environment. You focus yourself away from the pain, on the air, the breath, the action. You focus on something, nothing, so intently that the focus consumes your emotion. The focus consumes your pain. Somewhere your mind is screaming for you to draw that blade across your skin, and somewhere your body is just screaming, but they are so far away. A moment can last forever, and in a few seconds you can find that freedom. I was trained by my counsellor, and she taught me that breaks from depression, or pain, are important. They are crucial. They do not need to be long breaks, but at every instant of happiness, and every instant free of pain, they need to be enjoyed. It's the absence of depression or pain, it's the enjoyment of that moment. It's taking a few seconds of freedom and unlocking a lifetime of enjoyment. If you are depressed for long enough it will wear you down, but if you can break it up with moments of enjoyment, moments of true pleasure, you will never be worn down, you will survive forever, and I daresay, live. Pain is the same. If you can find those moments, you can find freedom, and in those moments you can live.

MINDFULNESS IN EXTREME PAIN

Those glimpses of freedom, of happiness, are crucial. My pain has grown, and it gets harder and harder to manage. I'm in poor practice of my Mindfulness skills, but as I write this my mind is opened to the possibilities. I can't let the pain wear me down. I must find those moments of happiness, and I must enjoy the shit out of them. Then I can bear the pain again, for another moment. Life is full of moments, and I need only to live from moment to moment. If I find myself in a moment of extreme pain then I need only live through that moment.

Above I mentioned a story for another time, the story of my waking up after surgery. When I went in for surgery it was a perfect experience. They admitted me; everyone was effective, efficient, and courteous. My surgeon explained the procedure and confidently said he'd see me on the other side. They put me on a gurney, and they rolled me into the operating room. As the team of people around me began moving about the room and going about their business a woman placed a mask over my nose and mouth. It was one of those count-to-30 things knowing that you would never get there. I looked at her, at that confident smile, and the last thing I heard was "you're in good hands."

It was perfect.

I closed my eyes and opened them. Then I was there, in recovery, lying on my side and facing the bars of the gurney, and I was aware of only one thing: the pain. I screamed. I screamed aloud and without any control. The pain raged through my spine like an inferno and I felt it not only in the incision, but in my very soul. I screamed. I had cried out in pain before, or yelped, but never screamed. I exhausted my breath, filled my lungs once more, and screamed. Agony roared through me and there was nothing else. Somewhere at the edges of my awareness I could hear a nurse. She told me I needed to let go, I was cutting off my IV. My awareness grew to my hands, which were locked on the railing of the gurney. My muscles were seized as my brain sent out signals to lock down everything in a hope of protecting itself from the pain. I could see my rigid fists and I could see the intravenous line protruding from the top of one hand. I had to let go. I could hear my voice, and I could feel fire in my lungs. It took all of my focus to release my fingers from those bars to let the IV flow. It felt like forever, and as I screamed and cried and saw that glimpse of the truth of my soul, I heard the nurse speak once more: "We've given you all the morphine we can, we need to wait for a doctor."

She stayed with me, her hand on me, as I survived the worst pain of my life. Forget depression, forget loss, there was just pain. There was no Pyramid, no Maslow, just the pain. I don't remember much, but I remember her caring. I remember her as a focus point so that I could find something, anything, other than the pain. I remember that moment. I remember infinity.

I didn't see the doctor, but I remember the nurse telling me that they were giving me something else. It felt like years, but it must have been just another moment as the medication set in. I heard my desperate screams wane. Like a child tired from crying, the calls grew shorter, more desperate, and then they turned to moans. Then they turned to nothing.

I was on the edge of consciousness, but all I could think of to do, seeing the other end of that moment, was to thank the nurse who carried me through. I never got to it. The darkness came, and compared to the blaring lights of the recovery room, and the embers burning through my body, it was welcome.

When I woke I had a new nurse, being unconscious for the shift change. I was still limited in my faculties, but I asked, almost pleaded, for her to thank the other nurse for me. With a smile she said she would.

When I made it out of recovery they said that as long as I could go pee (to make sure none of the hoses were kinked) I was free to go. Free to go? They just let people leave after being in recovery for what, 15 minutes? No, that instant, that moment that I had survived through had been six hours—a well-supported, well-loved, six hours.

Where's the lesson here? Sometimes you can't beat it. Sometimes it beats you. Sometimes your body screams so loudly that you can't do anything but listen. And sometimes, people will be there to give you that light in the dark. Sometimes those people will give you something to focus on outside of yourself, and though it might not free you from the pain, it's enough to get you through. It's enough to survive through that moment.

That nurse gave me something to focus on, something other than the pain. It seems such a simple thing, but it made that moment bearable. It gave me a focal point for Mindfulness, a way to transfer my pain to my environment, letting it go so that I could survive. No, I couldn't turn off the pain, but Mindfulness isn't about on and off. It's a spectrum, it's about focus, and it's about acceptance. I knew when we were waiting for the doctor that I had to wait through the pain. I knew. I knew it was the worst pain in my life, and you know what? That's ok. Like the worst I've faced with depression, the pain is seemingly unbearable, but pain won't kill you. Sure, you've got to survive through those moments, but you will, you just have to wait it out.

So I waited, I saw the surgeon on the other side, and I survived; now it's back to living.

LIVING WITH PAIN

It gets hard to see where the pain ends and you begin. There are times when you don't want to manage the pain, or the depression, or the whatever, because to you it seems more you than anything else. I still have that side of me, and it is as real as any other side. I still want to self-harm, I still want to fall into despair, and I still want to collapse under chronic pain. That's ok. I will die one day, but not by my hand. I might not like it all the time, but I'll survive. I'll use medication or glasses if I have to, and I'll let Mindfulness be my way of life. Do I deserve this depression, or this pain? Do I deserve saving? I've hurt so many around me, and done so much harm, and do you know what? That's ok too. The truth is we are all worth saving. We all have our ups and our downs and we all have our good days and bad. The trick is to live lives that we can each live with. Do more good than bad. Love more than hate. Smile. Always smile.

What I've learned in all this, in my troubles, and talking to people about theirs, is that we all face our own issues. There is no "normal," there is just the facade that we all show to the world. It's the largest conspiracy of all time, and we're all part of it. Underneath it all we are all fragile, and flawed, and there is nothing wrong with that. Our individuality defines our humanity, and whether you wear glasses, or ride in a wheelchair, or take medications to combat your own demons, you are human, and you are perfect. It's not about changing us, it's about embracing us. It's about managing your challenges and getting past them. Sure, I am in pain most of the time, but I'll take those painkillers, be mindful, crack a joke about it, and move on.

So, we are all flawed—there is no "normal." Where does this leave our friend Maslow? He's right you know, he looked at the facade of humanity and said, let's make generalizations, let's look to see how people work. He identified his Pyramid with some simple steps to reach true happiness. Maybe some people can climb Maslow's Pyramid, but I think he forgot something. Pyramids are made of bricks, hundreds, thousands, of bricks. The ones from the top could have been the ones on the bottom if the workers placing them there had just chosen differently. Those bricks are our stories; every brick is an event as we each build our own Pyramids. The layers of my Pyramid aren't as identified by Maslow, no, my Pyramid has no layers. Instead, each brick I place on it could be categorized as Physiology, Safety, Belonging, Esteem, and Self-Actualization, as I build my own way to happiness. My Pyramid will not be the same as yours; mine will be unique, just like everybody else's. I'll find my happiness, but not like Maslow said. I won't find one big layer of happiness when I get to the top, instead I will find moments of it, instants of it, as I place my bricks one by one. So there is a brick of pain, followed by a brick of compassion, followed by a brick of freedom, followed by a brick of Self-Actualization, followed by this…

A brick of words.

Pain, mental, physical…it's just pain. Just another moment. Just another brick. Put it on your Pyramid, and then brick it in with happiness, pleasure, love, or anything else that you enjoy. Forget about it. Sure it will always be there in your history, and the bricks of pain may keep coming, but put them down, cover them in a brick of smiles, and build your way to happiness.

Like I said, fuck Maslow.

This is my pyramid.

CHAPTER TWENTY-SEVEN

Suffering "Like This": Interpretation AND THE Pedagogical Disruption OF THE Dual System OF Education

CHRISTOPHER GILHAM

SUFFERING AND SCHOOL FAILURE

What do we do next year? This can't go on *like this*.

GARY, SCHOOL ADMINISTRATOR

Every word breaks forth as if from a centre…

HANS-GEORG GADAMER (1989, P. 454)

James, a young boy, had climbed high up a tree, again. Gary, the principal of the school, had called me and the police. I went to the school to support Gary and his school team, to see how I might be able to help. I was a regular visitor that school year because James and most of the other students in his class were often in distress.

At the time of the event, I worked for a large urban public school board as a specialist. My main work was to support schools in their work with students with severe emotional and behavioural disabilities (EBD). The severe EBD status came from diagnoses that are found within the American Psychiatric Association's Diagnostic and Statistical Manual (DSM). The DSM diagnosis allowed the school board to apply a codification system to the students which identified them as having severe EBD status and in turn, permitted the allocation of special funding to the students. That funding was used to create the specialized classroom and others like it (Gilham & Williamson, 2013).

I also supported several specialized classes for students with severe EBD. These classes were spread across the city, and in recent years had grown in number, considerably. James was a student in one of those classes. Ambulances and police had been called several times that year to attend to one or more of the nine students. James often climbed dangerously high trees near the school. Another student ran around the open concept school screaming in distress. Yet another student seemed to be perpetually fighting or crying, or both at the same time. Worse perhaps, the students in the class often fought amongst themselves. Their fights spilled out into the hallways and classrooms around them. Some of the students had to be physically restrained and escorted to a smaller room where they could calm down.

This class was one of the most resourced and supported classrooms I had been in; there was a full-time teacher and support worker, as well as weekly visits from a therapist, and a family counsellor employed by a non-profit organization. A pediatric psychiatrist visited monthly. Even with this support, the specialized class and school team were often in crises, as Gary, the school administrator attested:

> As the year went on and the kids were supposed to be integrated (into regular classrooms) we saw a lot of breakdowns in the kids, in their congregated setting they were kind of poking at each other…there was strain, and anxiety, and then there would be blow-outs that would impact all the children and so on a day to day basis we had numerous things going on in there…it was a constant battle and it really wasn't working. (Personal communication, August 28, 2012)

Specialized classes such as this were intended to create conditions in which students could begin to thrive in learning. It has been my experience that, students who are placed in specialized settings have complex histories of suffering in multiple classrooms across multiple schools. Student cumulative files are often thickly filed with teachers' anecdotal records which reveal the intensely difficult situations both students and their school teams are trying to understand and work through. Specialized settings are often seen as the best places to ease or ameliorate the complexity of these situations through the application of special education practices. In turn, students are expected to eventually re-integrate into regular classrooms, a practice known as integration (Winzer, 2009). Gary's perspective on this particular specialized class exposed an increase in suffering amongst the children. I too had been witness to this suffering.

For example, some students would hide under desks at the mention of learning particular subjects, like Math. Other students felt extreme discomfort around people they did not know, or large groups of people. Yet others did not speak in school at all. Some kicked and cried as they fled the classroom. As I moved among this class and many other specialized classes in the city, I re-affirmed my understanding of how complex the students and these situations were, and the tremendous resources and efforts that were being put into their education with the belief that they would begin to thrive in schools. I also began to see this differently.

My understanding of the work I was involved in had changed considerably over the previous few years because of my graduate work in interpretive studies. My previous belief systems, filled with what Hans-Georg Gadamer (1900–2002) called pre-judgements—which are a part of who we all are—offered a limited horizon of understanding (2004). I had been swept up in the special education discourse for a time, without any ability to see children and youth differently: Children had deficits or disabilities that we needed to support and sometimes change. Interpretive studies, particularly Gadamer's Hermeneutics as taught by Dr. David Jardine at the Werklund School of Education in Calgary, Alberta, created the space in which I was able to see teaching and learning and the lives of educators and students more ecologically and historically. What had once been a horizon of understanding limited to seeing what was wrong within children and youth, and even educators, had expanded into a horizon much more multi-vocal, complex, and inter-woven.

Put differently, I started to see my work and those I met as interpretable. Something about the comfort of speaking about essential truths for children with "disabilities" was dislodged for me. Now the work could be seen as a multitude of complex threads, woven together, taking on something of the sense of Wittgenstein's family resemblances (1958). Although there may have been strong agreements between me and educators on the struggles that they and their students' faced, the resemblances among cases could not be distilled to final all-encompassing truths often reduced into neat and tidy disability categories. As a result of this expansion of my understanding—which included my past beliefs, also described by Gadamer as the coming together or fusion of one's fore-structures or pre-judgements with those of another into a larger horizon (2004, pp. 269–272, 304–305)—I felt as though my work should primarily focus on teaching and learning.

I did not have to always believe and rely on the discourse of special education. I could talk about what I saw and heard in classrooms from multiple perspectives, and I could also place myself within this seeing and hearing, too. At this point in my work I began to spend much more time in classrooms observing and writing down everything I could see and hear and notice. In team meetings I shared these observations, which served as the starting place for dialogue. This was different than telling teams what I thought was wrong with students or educators, for that matter. My work was liberated in a sense, from the confines of one way of seeing and being.

This is how I arrived at my work at Gary's school. I lived in an in-between place where, talking about understanding as I have above would have been met with glazed-over looks. Returning to discussions about teaching and learning likewise, were difficult adventures. When I arrived on the scene, most educators wanted me to talk about special education and strategies to ameliorate or change student behaviour. With my new sense of possibility or interpretability at hand, I could see teaching and learning as part of the conversation. Students were no longer deficit-ridden in and of themselves. They were part of a complex ecology and history that demanded we stop and ask how the structure of schooling itself played a part in their suffering. I believed that one of those structures was often special education: the very discourse intended to help students thrive in schools was playing a part in exacerbating their suffering. Gary's class was an exemplary case of this and as I have mentioned, not irregular in my experiences, by any means.

Thus, despite the well-intentioned efforts of educators, including Gary and his team, there was the sweeping "*like this*" within Gary's question and claim which spoke of student suffering and school failure. He and his team and many other school teams I had met were suffering, too. Students endured or bore the weight of being put under conditions that did not permit them to thrive in schools and often educators found themselves in conditions that seemed impossible for teaching and learning. A desperate cycle of counterproductive clinging to essential problems that needed fixing or changing accelerated the sense of urgency and fragmentation in complex situations. Specialized classrooms tended to be places where this clinging to the need to find the way to fix or change the child intensified or completely shut down. I grew weary of walking into specialized classrooms to see students in tidy little rows with their binders of photocopied work. Some were surrounded in high cardboard tri-fold walls, and would peek out from the sides when I entered. In the very places we hoped to slow down and be well with our students so that we could all thrive in teaching and learning, these pernicious extremes often resulted. Gary's experience with this class, and my own within special education work across the city was often "*like this.*" He and his team suffered as a result of the suffering of the students. Likewise, the students suffered further from the desperate attempts to isolate and change targeted behaviours or, the absence of any presence for teaching and learning.

Despite my almost weekly visits with Gary and his school team, including the families of the children in the class and the professional supports of partner institutions, it seemed we could not help the students. Was all of this about being located in a specialized classroom? Could the situation be reduced to place? I knew there were several students who often found ways to provoke one another. Was this also part of the story of ongoing crises? Several students suffered from extreme anxieties. If the specialized classroom tended to be a place of conflict, then it was no surprise that some students would run from the classroom, and school. Gary often wondered if some of the students needed to be placed in our specialized schools. Could it have also been, as special education scholars have argued, that we were not engaging in evidence-based special education practices (Kauffman et al., 2007)? The ecological interpretability of this case posed challenges for us all, as it has provincewide.

In a telephone interview with an Alberta Education representative I learned that for every ten students categorized as having EBD seven of them would not complete high school (Personal communication, Antaya-Moore, 2012). Data from the United States also points to a larger phenomenon of suffering known as the school-to-prison pipeline (Valle & Connor, 2011, p. 34). I knew this phenomenon too, as I tracked several of my previous students (I was a special education teacher prior to becoming a consultant) as they entered the local Young Offenders Center. Given all this, what did Gary's "*like this*" reveal about our attempts to help students thrive through both traditional special and regular education? What broke forth as a result of our collective suffering?

COUNTER-PRODUCTIVITY

Despite the caring and sincere efforts educators put towards supporting "special" or "exceptional" students, there were deeply troubling consequences arising from stigmatizing structures inherent to that very support, I suggest. For example, Lydia, a grade 4/5 classroom teacher in Gary's school, who would sometimes take particular students from the specialized classroom into her "regular" classroom for certain subjects shared:

> They were very separated. On the playground they would be in one part of the yard where they were all away from the other kids, umm, in the school the other kids didn't know them at all. They didn't know their names. They didn't understand who they were. We had a lot of conversations because there would be kids crying in the hallway or yelling and things like that that year. So we had a lot of conversations about, because kids had no clue who they were, they just saw these kids in the hallways and upset and…having meltdowns and so they did not understand what was going on so we just had conversations about them and about who they were and things like that but they were very separate. My kids did not socialize with them at all. (Personal communication, March 7, 2013)

At the time I wondered, along with Gary, if the "poking one another" and "strain" and "anxiety" in the classroom was a result of placing the students together. The students knew they were placed together because of their diagnosed pathologies, in a classroom for "whatever." Isolation from the school community ensued, despite the belief that the students would be successfully integrated into "regular" classrooms. This case was particularly acute because the students were not placed into a classroom environment rather they were housed in what was once the school's infirmary. At the start of that school year I attempted to address this placement with Gary. Gary took me on a tour of the school to show me that there were no classroom spaces available for these students. Gary also shared that the very recent placement of this specialized class in his school was not a decision he was involved in. Gary shared that he was very open to receiving our advice and support throughout the school year because, as an educator, he had not worked before in a school with a specialized classroom within it. It was also his first year as an administrator. The situation was complex, indeed.

Interpreted through my own nascent understanding of some of Michel Foucault's (1995, 2003) and Ivan Illich's (1976) work, I offer the following: A segregated classroom within a community school with the aim of integrating students into the normal population can be a highly counterproductive institutional structure. In this case—based on my conversations with Gary and his school team, and my participation throughout the school year in classroom activities, crisis response, student and family meetings, and ad-hoc informal conversations with students—a binding, co-dependent and counterproductive *dual* gaze emerged. Contained together in the classroom, as well as when they ate lunch or were on the playground, the students in the specialized classroom were the stigmatized who gazed *at* the "normal" school population, wanting to have a sense of belonging in the greater community. At the same time they were gazed *upon* by that normal majority.

Despite being in the same place, the structures of special education fragmented the school community into the normal and abnormal. I imagine that the children's gazes at and upon one another produced immeasurably difficult and confusing emotions: From longing and loathing to curiosity and retreat. Because of this counter-productive, community fragmenting structure inherent to the school system, the students in the specialized class retracted from both the segregated classroom and the regular classrooms by expanding outward into the school's spaces, including the school yard, as James would often do. If they were asked about this I wonder if they might have said something like, "We just want to be like them, but they stare at us as if we're weird or something. I want to be with them and I don't at the same time. I think I don't want to be here at all, actually."

The student's expanding retreat from their mixed world of special and regular education could be read as a result of the amplification of the stigma attached to the Western world's sense of fixed, individual and importantly, *ill* or *abnormal* selves. Again, the amplification is inherent to special education and is lived out in codification regimes and the physical displacement of students from community classrooms. Such structures create further distance between the majority normal student population and the strange and foreign abnormal population. The dual gazing served to solidify the students' perception of an "us and them" on both sides of the unhealthy binary. This revealed the co-dependent and viciously counter-productive nature of the relationship between regular and special education. The abnormal students were both in and out of the school, on many levels of understanding and interpretation.

The students' turn inward towards seeing themselves as objects of sickness and, knowing that others saw them this way too, created a frustration that could not be contained. That counter-productive energy expanded outward into the school as confusion, frustration and anger, I offer. In other words, the retraction into a false sense of self, in this case, a very negative ego entrapment (Jardine, 2012), created an internal pressure that exploded outward into the community. It was as if the students' anger shouted that the very idea of a self-existent and deeply troubled or *mental* ego in isolation—and in need of visible, physical isolation under the banner of "congregation" because they were "exceptional" and thus it was all *"for their own good"*—was deeply flawed.

The students had been *othered* by special education's codification and placement logic which in turn created self-identities that worked to further alienate *themselves,* including their sense of self in relation to the community. The situation was counterproductive to special education's aim of congregation for the amelioration of suffering or the changing of negative patterns of behaviour. Another interpretation suggests that this "technology of the abnormal" (Foucault, 2003, p. 316) was doing precisely what it was intended to do that is, regulate and reinforce the normalization of inherently diverse populations through sustaining the classification of those considered mentally sick or ill.

A Pedagogy of Suffering

The suffering of the students and its manifestation throughout the school as anger and dangerous retreat was also pedagogical. This is where Hans-Georg Gadamer's (1900–2002) hermeneutics serve to help read Gary's *"like this"* as a kind of reprieve from that counter-productive, co-dependent production of suffering inherent to the dual system of education. Here, suffering can be read as pathei mathos: "learning from suffering" (Gadamer, 2004, p. 351) understood by the ancient Greeks, particularly the tragedies of Aeschylus (c. 525 BCE). The children in Gary's specialized class thwarted the embrace of special education's expectations and specialized structures in such a way that Gary and his team could see and do something outside of special education. I had been reading disability studies in education perspectives on inclusion (Valle & Connor, 2011). I wanted to share these perspectives with educators and colleagues but felt that they were so entrenched in the special education discourse that talk of anything outside of it would be seen as a kind of treason or theoretical nonsense. I had also read Roger Slee's *The Irregular School* (2010) and wanted to share his notion of moving outside of what we called regular schooling altogether. I saw this early on in the year, but I strongly felt I could not tell Gary and his team this unless they were ready to hear it. At the same time I also thought that some students needed more than what Gary and his team could provide. It was difficult to maintain a balanced perspective amidst the crisis. As Wendell Berry (with Moyers, 2013) recently said, "the situation you're in is a situation that is going to call for a lot of patience, and to be patient in an emergency is a terrible trial."

What did Gary and his team see differently or anew? They saw the student's perpetual crises as the expression of their desire to live in a different or freer space, one where the dual gazing would be absent or, a place where they could be with other students as part of a school that is healthy and communal. They saw the students as saying they wanted to be together with other students in the school in a way that was inclusive, I suggest. As long as the segregated structure of a special education class existed, as well as the traditional normal class—thus representing the dual system of special and regular schooling—the dual gaze and its counterproductive consequences would continue to manifest. Gary and his team came to see that the students were expressing something like this all year long through their often violent acts of what I describe as an *expanding retreat*. James, the student who often fled the school and climbed trees in the school yard, used to say *"All I want to do is be in Mr. W's class. I don't wanna be in X (the specialized classroom)"* (Laura, personal communication, March 7, 2013).

Seeing the students as saying something akin to the desire to have an inclusive learning environment also made a claim upon special education. The traditional and often taken-for-granted aim of their specialized class to support the students so they could be successful in learning was disrupted. As Gadamer wrote, "Understanding becomes a special task only when natural life, this joint meaning of the meant where both intend a common subject matter, is disturbed" (2004, p. 181). Put differently, the demand Gary and his team faced, myself included, to understand why and how our expectations were thwarted had already begun by having to suffer through that year of ongoing crises. I had to wait it through, and I often resisted Gary's early calls to move certain students to specialized schools. I did not expect Gary to show me an opening through which I could share my new found ideas on inclusion. When it arrived, so did my mind on the matter. I shared with Gary possibilities for doing things differently the next year.

The suffering of all made their educational world interpretable. Gadamer (2004) claimed that any experience worthy of the name thwarts our expectations. Likewise, any true conversation plays us or, has us in ways we cannot control or predict up front. Anything else called conversation is nothing of the sort. It is a waiting to speak. Gary's "*like this*" was borne out of suffering and it revealed or broke forth towards other possibilities. "*Like this*" was a tear in and through the taken-for-granted fabric of special education practice; it is also a way of seeing that troubled, difficult pathway as necessary in order for understanding and therefore, a different way of being with the students, to arise. An opening towards possibility had been created by the year-long crises. We could see the year, the students, and our work differently. Such an opening could not have occurred without the structures of special education, Gary and his team, and the students and their families, and so on. Possibility arose co-dependently out of a complex ecology that is historically influenced—not on an essential notion of disability inherent to the children.

"Like this"

Thus, near the end of that school year Gary held his head in his hands and asked, "What do we do next year? This can't go on *like this*."

Thwarted *and* ready: Gary faced this forced opening after a years' worth of special education's strategies and techniques. The "*like this*" was spoken and understood broadly enough to suggest that Gary wanted to stop being a part of the special education apparatus or machinery which incessantly and repetitively demanded that the students needed to stop fighting, or running from the school, or to calm down: "*Like this*" was not the usual pattern of "like this and this and this and this."

Perhaps "*like this*" suggested that what was once seen as fixed and true was now interpretable or impermanent and thus, not necessarily all there was for helping children who suffered in school. The singular edifice of truth that special education had been venerated upon shifted, revealing that it was readable, finite, and possible. Gary's "*like this*" was sweeping, as if to say, "I see the whole of it as a particular family of approaches to children that has exacerbated their school lives, and so I am open to being something different with and for them." The realization that he was immersed in a seemingly rigid delusion of truth freed a space through which he and his team could see and be differently with those children. "*Like this*" was already on the way to an amelioration of a disproportionate and unnecessary suffering brought on by the taken for granted structures, policies, and practices inherent to special education and, as I have suggested, the very notion of self and normalcy in Western society.

Interpretively read, "*like this*" began to reveal a deeper and systematic logic at play in the typical ways we tend to address students with ongoing social and emotional suffering. Gary could be read as saying that special education as the seg-regation of like "kinds" of students into a special classroom within his community school and all that was entailed in that parallel yet separate structure was a "*this*" that made life for them all insufferable. "*Like this*" was expressed as the culmination of often futile "like this's" aimed at "*those kids.*" Gary's "*like this*" broke forth "as if from a centre" (Gadamer, 2004, p. 454), expanding outwards into interpretability.

That the instrumental measures of special education could be read as not measuring up to the demands of the students, and that those same measures ex-acerbated, even sometimes co-constituted their collective suffering in that school heralded the arrival of that event of understanding and the opening that ensued. The ongoing enactment of an idle knowledge intended to normalize the behaviour of what is typically seen as the inherently and essentially disabled was suddenly revealed to be inadequate for the children and their school team. We could see that understanding these particular children resulted from "what happen(ed) to us over and above our wanting and doing" (Gadamer, 2004, p. xxvi).

Maybe we were not doing special education right. Maybe we were doing it right but the strategies were not right for the students in all their complex par-ticularities. Maybe the logic inherent to the strategizing was part of the problem at play or, our collective clinging and attachment to that logic strangled the free space required to wisely decide what was best for each child in each situation that arose. For me, the year seemed like a perpetual roulette wheel of special education's reductionist strategies. It was often hard to see what to do through the onslaught of instrumental services and experts brought forward with each new crisis, myself included. There always seemed to be a sense of panic to the year.

Normalization

The "*like this*" of a largely medicalized and thus pathology-intense special edu-cation system within education, built upon the notion of healing and cure or the amelioration of suffering, was counterproductive to its aim in Gary's specialized class. On one hand, the desire and attempt to normalize via a highly structured and resourced system of marginalization, at the level of physical spaces, bodies and curriculum (math sheets and tri-folds, for example) seems the best thing going for children who have not thrived in "regular" schools. Through isolation and a focus on the symptoms of disability, students can properly learn to be like other students in regular classes. At the same time, normal children can feel safe to continue learning without having to suffer from the burden of having to learn alongside the problem children. This approach appears to be compassionate.

On the other hand, special education's move to retract suffering students from the norm seems absurd in the face of the desire to want students to be more like a bell-curved us. This bespeaks an educational practice that tells students what they should do upfront, and is also removed from the world of actually having to do learning together as inquiries into topics of concern in the world. Both students and curriculum face a dulling and dumbing down through preventative measures. As Jardine (2013) noted, this levelling action is seen by many educators as necessary so that "All hell doesn't break loose" under freer conditions of inquiry. Read in this light, special education's focus on mis-behaviour (*off* the norm) and its rectification as a ramp-way to general education learning (integration)—as if the high ground of the traditional ways we look at and teach curriculum is impervious to a questioning of its own dis-order of conduct—is a further step removed from an inclusive pedagogy. In this light, the above-said compassion is tainted with the dark hues of pity and victimization. The echo of a voice saying "poor little things" rings throughout this reading.

It is a strong claim to make however, the drive to fix conduct or teach children how to comply can often conceal our own historical amnesia and mis-conduct in education. After five years of consulting in hundreds of classrooms across a large Canadian city, I can attest to just how myopic that curing or fixing focus can be. It removes the ability to see how special education itself is often counter-productive to our shared goal of having students thrive and be successful in schools. In my consultative work it has been very difficult to talk about educator practices around teaching and learning but all too easy to talk about the problem child and how to fix those problems through new and novel behavioural strategies or specialized placement. This is not to say that all situations are one or the other, or even both. I am suggesting that a sense of measured and proportionate reflection on the complex circumstances we find ourselves in often seems lost to the discourse of normalization which is centred on a false sense of self-enclosed identity or ego-issuance. The self and other duality inherent to a logic of substance (Gilham, 2012; Jardine, 2012)—it is either in you or in me—is at play here. In other words, *it's that kid's problem* so there is no sense of need or urgency or even awareness for considering what we are doing that constitutes *that kid's problem*, for example. That our suffering and struggles dependently co-arise seems concealed in this modern world of individuals.

The discourse of normalization takes on special significance when one considers the history of the treatment of students with EBD, particularly in Alberta, Canada (Gilham, 2013; Dechant, 2006; Lupart, 2008). We have been entrenched in a system of normalization that has bifurcated students into "us" and "them" in the most concrete of ways: the province has segregated students since the official inception of schools in 1905. Alberta took a particularly dark route through eugenics along the way. The striving for social harmony or the alleviation of a communal suffering required the concealment and in some cases, elimination of future possibilities for abnormality (Gilham, 2013). Only the normal could be part of the happy utopia. The rest needed to stay on the margins, in the land of shadows (not fully concealed, but monstrously lurking as dark warnings for the normal) where their future could be controlled or even eliminated.

Perhaps today's continued marginalization of children deemed abnormal requires an unnecessary suffering so that "regular" education for typical or normal children is reinforced. "You see," it could be stated, "they needed that special education classroom. Just look at them." Vicious but unintentional circles have ensued reinforcing both the normal and the monstrous. The self-sustaining nature of the dual school system apparatus appears brilliantly effective. The dual gaze of that system as it lived in Gary's school is evidence of this. Through their collective suffering, Gary came to understand that the children needed something different, as did he and his team. "*Like this*" carried the suffered weight of a newly arrived at understanding about the complex fabric of our lives *together* with students in education: *pathei mathos*. Something more akin to compassion arose, perhaps.

Interpretation as Non-Attachment

I suggest it was not as if Gary believed that doing something different would cure or better manage the students rather it was that something different from traditional special education might just release them from the life-squeezing intensity and frequency of the crises in their school. Their attachment to the discourse of special education as Truth was part of an entrenched clinging to that played a part in their overall counter-productivity. As a school administrator Gary had a role to play in that grip, and he came to understand this differently from when the children first arrived. "*This can't go on like this*" is both human and worldly in its dense multiplicity. It gives a sense of readability to suffering and suffering's role in transforming how we see and understand the everydayness of the world. This is imbued with all the confusing richness of how we are in education with students and one another. Breaking forth as if from the world's centre "*like this*" is recognition that suffering is not "out there" (Jardine, 2012a, p. 73); rather it arises in the ways we *are in the world together*. No longer solely a question of amelioration through scientific progress along a developmental pathway, perhaps Gary was henceforth after a way (as being) of holding their suffering and challenges such that there would be more room for those students to find places of belonging in the school, and thrive even though they would all still face lives full of challenges. The deficit model had become finite, too.

Gary's understanding of "*like this*" was born out of misunderstanding, and resulted in his suffering. Some of this weight might just be unnecessary and some is inescapable, given our finiteness. That the students suffered is evident, too. I have tried to suggest that this gestalt of suffering co-dependently arose, and this is important to understand. I have even suggested that special education's practices—enlivened by coding structures and congregated classrooms in community schools—increases the cycle of co-dependent suffering. Yet these finite attempts and experiences are part of what it is to arrive at understanding.

Gadamer (2004) claimed that we only come to understand through a finite pathway, though the pathway can have its excesses of prejudices and things taken for granted, or forgotten, like the historical weight special education bears down upon students and educators. Gary's suffering led to understanding because of the opening it provided for seeing and doing things differently; because it converted special education into an interpretable or possible way of being with children, which then cleared the way for other possibilities to arise. Once Gary and his team could see that, they found a more generous space within which they could hear what the children were saying to them, and respond in kind. Perhaps through all this Gary and his team, me included, were reminded that all behaviour is language. If we listen carefully enough, we just might hear what is being said. The children spoke to us repeatedly, and we were finally able to hear them. As a result Gary and his team's work became free or non-attached and thus possible. The next year the "*like this*" of their previous year of suffering was largely absent. In its place were classrooms of students thriving in their learning, together. That story of inclusion, however, is for another time.

CHAPTER TWENTY-EIGHT

Morning Thoughts ON Application

DAVID W. JARDINE

> The text...if it is to be understood properly—i.e., according to the claim it makes— must be understood at every moment, in every concrete situation, in a new and differ- ent way. Understanding here is always application. (Gadamer, 1989, p. 309)

Below is an amazing passage in light of Gadamer's thoughts on application and how interpretation makes little sense "in general." Its character only starts to ap- pear once it is applied to a topic, a case, a locale, an instance. Only in the face of the specific resistances and demands that the case brings, is interpretation able to "work." The individual case is thus "fecund," not only in the sense that its new arrival demands that what has been previously established open itself up to the ar- riving sense of potency and possibility and demand that the new case brings (thus demonstrating the deep and unavoidable impermanence of such establishments). It is also fecund in the sense that facing and working through such moments of arrival, again and again, is how getting "good" at interpretation happens—it is fecund in relation to my ability to work interpretively. That is why it is always I, myself, who must take this venture. It is also why understanding a hermeneutic study requires precisely such a venture from readers.

Interpretation is, in this sense, an ongoing practice that takes practice to become practiced in. One's "general" ability in this regard is the product of some- thing specific being repeatedly practiced, and, therefore, it never becomes simply a method that can be handed over to someone unpracticed. It is always a practice whose practice can, and must be, cultivated in order to be understood. "Understanding here is always application," and this includes understanding a hermeneutic study and understanding how to "do" hermeneutic work. Hermeneutic work is thus always both about application and cultivated at the locales of application.

So, now, the amazing passage that parallels this hermeneutic arc. It is from Volume Two of Tsong-kha-pa's (2004), *The great treatise on the stages of the path to enlightenment*, originally composed in 1406 CE:

> It is an extremely important point. If you train in these attitudes of impartiality, love and compassion without distinguishing and taking up specific objects of meditation, but only using a general object from the outset, you will just seem to generate these attitudes. Then, when you try to apply them to specific individuals, you will not be able to actually generate these attitudes toward anyone. But once you have a transformative experience towards an individual in your meditation practice…you may then gradually increase the number of individuals you visualize within your meditation. (Tsong-kha-pa, 2004, p. 35).

This passage highlights why, earlier in this text, Tsong-kha-pa stated that we must avoid falling into the "problems of peace" (p. 24). Our professions—teaching, nursing, counseling, working with troubled students in schools, or any other locale of interpretive venture in the face of some face in the world—do not lead us to seek our own peace separate from the suffering of the world, but seek, rather, to "take on a life of suffering…in order to help all living beings" (p. 29). This is a life, shall we say, of enduring and undergoing, of venture, hidden as these images are in Gadamer's use of the term *Erfahrung* for the sort of "experience" from which we might learn (with its etymological root *Fahren*, to journey, venture, and its other derivative, *Vorfahren*, those who have ventured "before" [Vor-], i.e., ancestors). This is why Gadamer (1989, p. 356) cited in this regard an idea central to his hermeneutics that is inherited from the Greek tragedies of Aeschylus (c. 525 BCE): *pathei mathos*, "learning through suffering."

Hermeneutically understood, our professions are not seeking theories or explanations or models or interventions that promise to pacify or cure the life-world and its woes. We know precisely how often such promises have not only come to grief but unwittingly caused suffering. We know, too, from Alice Miller's (1989) work, how education in particular was once, and in many ways, still is, quite witting about such matters of inflicting suffering, as Miller's title announces, "for your own good." Still and all, and despite the understandable hesitancy that must surround our work, that work requires that we "remain in the realm in which beings dwell" (Tsong-kha-pa, 2004, p. 30). We turn toward suffering, again and again.

This is akin to hermeneutics persistently turning towards the life-world and not away from it to some Edenic world of essences cast in peaceful, finalized composure; this is how hermeneutics takes on part of the phenomenological lineages of a return to lived-experience whilst jettisoning Edmund Husserl's frightened desire to quell that life with the eidetic reduction. Hermeneutics interprets, not in order to thematize, essentialize, or placate, but in order to let our troubles be what they are, thus ameliorating our fraught "if onlys" and therefore making clear-sightedness and well-judged action possible. Letting it be what it is involves, in some sense, freeing ourselves from our attachment to it: "To rise above the pressure of what impinges on us from the world means to keep oneself so free from what one encounters of the world that one can present it to oneself as it is" (Gadamer, 1989, p. 444).

Tsong-kha-pa does say, earlier in the text, that "those who have developed the…spirit of enlightenment and [thus] aspire [to it], although they lack its application, still 'shine'" (2004, p. 16). I think, with student teachers for example, who sometimes desperately ask where to begin, of how taking on the spirit of interpretability is the key (Tsong-kha-pa calls this "aspiration"). It means, simply put, proceeding in light of an understanding of the interpretability of the world, seeking those dependent co-arisings that surround things, and resisting the logic of substance (Gadamer, 1989, p. 242) and the temptations of reification (Tsong-kha-pa, 2002, p. 120), both of which aim to suppress the uprisings of the world and seek false permanencies in this, the deeply human land of shadow. Even if you have not often practiced the application of such a spirit and have not therefore, built up the composures of practice, still, it is in this spirit that one proceeds in the repeated practice of application.

Again, however, the repeated practice of application is essential: "if you have only an intellectual understanding of this spirit, then you likewise have only an intellectually understanding of what it means to be a…practitioner" (p. 17). It is always this child's life, that parent's woes, this client's nightmare, that patient's desire to let go in the face of impending death, that is key. Interpretation always requires doing the work again in the face of the task we face. It is good to hear that:

> The more you practice these things, the more accustomed your mind will become to them, and the easier it will be to practice what you had initially found difficult to learn. (Tsong-kha-pa, 2000, pp. 185–186)

However, our proper relation to such matters must always and everywhere be re-won, here, and here. This is where is borne the deep hesitancy that is part of hermeneutic work and about such hesitancy, both hermeneutics and Buddhism are steadfast. Our composure must always be re-gained, re-dedicated to the work at hand. Our becoming experienced practitioners always involves venturing out all over again always having to suffer once again the exigencies of existence and their lessons. As I have found in my own work, the fellowship (Sangha) of such work is a great comfort. It is in this common fortitude or strength that the strength of hermeneutics lays, even though part of its demand is that I myself and no one else must take on this dedication and no one can take it on in my stead. It is with no irony at all, however, that Tsong-kha-pa (2004, pp. 182–207, emphasis added) names this "*joyous* perseverance." It is in this light that *pathei mathos* might shed something of its dour countenance.

CHAPTER TWENTY-NINE

In Praise OF Radiant Beings

DAVID W. JARDINE

We ought to be like elephants in the noontime sun in summer, when they are tormented by heat and thirst and catch sight of a cool lake. They throw themselves into the water with the greatest pleasure and without a moment's hesitation. In just the same way, for the sake of ourselves and others, we should give ourselves joyfully to the practice.
KUNZANG PELDEN (B. 1862, T), FROM THE NECTAR OF MANJUSHRI'S
SPEECH (2007, P. 255)

There is a great line from Lewis Hyde's beautiful book The Gift: Imagination and the Erotic Life of Property *(1983, p. xiii): "the way we treat a thing can sometimes change its nature." There is a joy to be had in the practice of turning towards suffering and letting it be what it is. It is not had in reveling in the pain of others or wallowing in their or one's own endurances. It is had because that practice, properly practiced, can change the nature of that suffering and our relation to it. My interest in this odd topic,* pathei mathos—*"learning through suffering"—rose up slowly through not only being with students and teachers in schools when wonderful, tough work was being done, but through also considering my own scholarly ventures over the years. Alan Block (see Chapter 22) is right: study may not precisely relieve the suffering we will inevitably face, but it can change its nature. We can experience our frailness and our momentary insights into the abundance of the world, and its dependent co-arising can flicker and glimmer and catch our breath. We can let go, even for a moment, of that panicky delusion of self-containedness that our animal body demands, so that all that trouble of a young child trying to learn to pronounce a word can be experienced in its real countenance. "A hitherto concealed experience" as Gadamer (1989, p. 100) called it. It is an experience of any fleeting thing ("even here") as residing in the midst of great nets of interdependence, radiantly full by being radiantly empty.*

Stepping out of the noontime sun in summer—the heat and exhaustion of "teaching kids to read"—and being able to experience the beautiful trouble that reading is for all of us, with all the lineages and ancestries that awaken in witness of this wee event, doesn't make the task of learning to read any less difficult an endurance contest that I myself, at this age, still experience. It does make that endurance an odd pleasure. It does make suffering such work sufferable. This chapter is, in part, about what happens when we treat pathei mathos *as something that is not an error but a gift.*

Concealed in what might seem to be a dour concession is a great relief, a cold plunge, something beautiful. Wisdom has it that this can be true even when suffering becomes bottomless. To this end, I've found it increasingly important to practice turning towards suffering when it is not quite so demanding.

The Dalai Lama was recently asked if all that meditation he'd been engaged in his whole life was doing any good. His reply: "We'll have to wait and see."

A Preambling Couplet

"To hold that the world is eternal" the Buddha declared, " …is the jungle of theorizing, the wilderness of theorizing, the tangle of theorizing, the bondage and the shackles of theorizing, attended by illness, distress, perturbation and fever." It is important to assimilate this passage in its entirety. It points to a reality that transcends ordinary thought but is nevertheless still knowable. To say that it is possible to know something that is beyond thought carries the important, indeed astonishing implication, that *there is in the mind a dimension that in the vast majority of living beings is wholly concealed, the existence of which is not even suspected.*

From the translator's introduction to
Introduction to the Middle Way: Chandrakirti's
[c. 7th Century CE] **Madhyamakavatara** *with Commentary by Jamgon Mipham*
[1846–1912] (2002, p. 9, emphasis added)

We will have to hold firmly to the standpoint of finiteness. [This] does not mean that [the human subjectivity] is radically temporal, so that it can no longer be considered as everlasting or eternal but is understandable only in relation to its own time and future. If this were its meaning, it would not be a critique and an overcoming of subjectivism, but an "existentialist" radicalization of it. The…question involved here…is directed precisely at this subjectivism itself. The latter is driven to its furthest point only in order to question it. In disclosing time as the ground hidden from [subjective] self-understanding it…opens itself *to a hitherto concealed experience that transcends thinking from the position of subjectivity.*

From H.G. Gadamer [1900–2002], *Truth and Method*
(1989, pp. 99–100, emphasis added)

"EVEN THERE"

Kai enthautha, "even here," at the stove, in that ordinary place where every thing and every condition, each deed and thought is intimate and commonplace, "even there" *einai theous*, "the gods themselves are present." (Heidegger, 1977b, p. 234)

Spending time in schools where good work is being done has become increasing hard for me to bear, not because of something negative (this, of course, has often taken its own toll) but because of something profoundly positive and nearly un-utterable. There is a practice at the heart of hermeneutic work (a practice shared in various and varying ways with ecological awareness and threads of Buddhist philosophy and practice) that results, mostly gradually, but sometimes sudden-ly and without warning, in the ability to intimately and immediately experience the dependently co-arising (Sanskrit: *pratitya-samutpada*) reality of things, ideas, word, selves, gestures, actions.

With deliberate practice, this ability, "hitherto concealed" by distraction and grasping at straws, builds, and as it builds, so too the build of the world and its ways (Dharma) flutters open and its interdependencies become more and more ex-perienceable (a process parallel to Hans-Georg Gadamer's work [1989, pp. 9–18] on the old German idea of *Bildung*, where "becoming experienced" leads to an *increasing* susceptibility and vulnerability in one's ability to experience the fabrics and textures of the world) more and more *loveable* "despite all my revulsions over its ugliness and injustice, and my bitterness over defeat at its hands" (Hillman, 2006a, p. 128).

"Even here," "not even suspected," the very tiniest and most meager of things, with experience and practice, can come to be experienced in beautiful repose.

AH! WABI SABI

What is of concern here in this chapter is something extremely simple, but it is a simplicity in which is concealed something miraculous which, when it appears, is often treated too casually, laughed off in ways that do not recognize the deep aesthetic truth that comes when the breath halts and the body leans over laughter.

Consider: When a young child tips forward into a word and finds herself struggling to sound it out, humming and murmuring over its sonority and the ancient, specific, detailed links lurking there with the look of its letters, its words, its spaces, tossing it around her tongue and breath, tripping unknowingly over all those old mongrel roots of English, all inbred and tangled together and pushing and pulling of attention this way and that, perhaps not yet sensing the haunting presence of such forgotten ancestors and ancestries that are ripe and ready to be known even though we can get along quite famously in sheer ignorance of their life and lives. This simple act of pronunciation is at once the most ordinary of classroom events and a great, roiling thing, a great nexus full of the "silence of a world turning" (Domanski, 2002, p. 245).

And then suddenly, yes!

Pronounced.

This word and *that* sit ready to be carried up out of the dust of written letters and outwards on the voice, held up on great pillars of breath, enspirited ("*aesthesis*, which means at root a breathing in…of the world, the gasp, 'aha,' the uh' of the breath in wonder…and aesthetic response" [Hillman, 2006, p. 36] and at once conspiratorial (Illich, 1998) because here I am, sit squat beside her in breathless anticipation of utterance.

"All writing is a kind of alienated speech, and its signs need to be transformed back into speech. This transformation is the real hermeneutical task" (Gadamer, 1989, p. 393).

Ah!

So *this* is what those words speak. *Wabi Sabi* (Reibstein & Young, 2008), that wandering cat off to find what her name means through the scrolling pages of this picture book. That young child's finger now pointing to the great, collaged images on the page, and then back to the cover, her hand rubbing its rough smoothness, and then, with the sound and the sight of this name now lodged in memory, safe for now in their keep, the story then continues to unfold, her smiling and pointing, me nodding in agreement, after all that tough and fruitful work along this book's path. And this young child's eye has ripened in its ability to scan the clusters of scrolling text for this cat's name's next appearance.

I have seen this so many times, such small events that have never happened before, here, now. "So that…sitting there, listening like that, becomes part of the story too," (Wallace, 1987, p. 47), me, a reader, having learned to read, having read countlessly about reading and its varying courses of ancient emergence, having been in hundreds of classrooms and felt this halt of breath over and over and over again, the life-breath of sounding out, as if the whole of the language itself depends for its very continuance, its very life, on this next moment's precarious venture. Again, and again, "where it seems impossible that one life even matters" (Wallace, 1987, p. 111), a small, simple, innocuous event that could easily be deemed perfectly trivial in the grand scheme of things becomes experienced as sitting in the center of worlds of relations, a residence, a "housing" (*ecos*). Right there in the very ordinariness and mundaneness of this event ("right now...*this*" [Wallace, 1987, p. 111]) we become huddled near the living origin of language itself, the very moment of its (oddly old-yet-brand-new, all at once) emergence, sustenance and survival. In this way, as a teacher, and in this smallest of examples, I get to be present as the world of language is being "set right anew" (Arendt, 1969, p. 197), right before my eyes and ears, revived, saved from its mortal lot just in the nick of time.

This sort of experience has become, for me, a simply *miraculous* thing to be around, something almost unbearable in its countenance. What is most deeply experienced here is the lovely, hearty frailness of these strange human ventures of reading, of speaking, of voice and utterance, and how the ancients in all human traditions have gathered around such ventures, most often unheralded and forgotten, and in myriad ways. They, too, are right "even here" in this act of breath, this pronunciation, holding their breath and ours in anticipation.

Hermeneutics and threads of the Gelug tradition of Tibetan Buddhism provide, in very different guises and for similar but still different motives, ways to articulate this kind of conspiratorial and deeply pedagogical experience of the world. Both detail how this way of experiencing the world can be cultivated through long and difficult practice ("one must learn how" [Gadamer, 2007b, p. 217]). They also share something of an *ontological theory* that attests to the reality of these experiences of dependent co-arising.

Both bespeak a "wisdom [which] thoroughly discerns *the ontological status of the object under analysis*" (Tsong-kha-pa, 2004, p. 211). The tough work of these scholarly traditions and practices helps keep at bay the commonplace trivializing of these experiences. The interlacing kinships between Gadamerian hermeneutics and the Gelug lineage of Tibetan Buddhism provide ways to elaborate what has become, for me, an elusive yet familiar experience in the haunts of schools, ways to remain with and true to these experiences.

"Protodoxa (Urdoxa)"

To realize the full import of dependent-arising, namely that all phenomena are empty of inherent existence, is an extremely forceful experience that reorients one in the very depths of one's being. (Lobsang, 2006, p. 51)

By virtue of repeated practice, you become free of your dysfunctional tendencies, undergoing a fundamental transformation. (Tsong-kha-pa, 2002, p. 36)

Indeed, this true mode must include…a conversion of the standpoint of Reason. (Nishitani, 1982, p. 117)

Perhaps it will become manifest that the total phenomenological attitude [is] destined in essence to effect, at first, a complete personal transformation, comparable in the beginning to a religious conversion. (Husserl, 1970, p. 137)

An *inner transformation*. (Husserl, 1970, p. 100)

One element of Hans-Georg Gadamer's philosophical hermeneutics is an *ontological insight* into how things, ideas, images, and selves *exist*, their manner of Being. This insight is in lineage back through the work of Martin Heidegger and is rooted in the work of their teacher, Edmund Husserl, the "father" of contemporary phenomenology.

This ontological insight involves a *critique of substance*—an age-old idea that runs back through the work of Descartes (1955, p. 255) in the 1600s and is rooted in Aristotelian ontology: "a substance is that which requires nothing except itself in order to exist." Under such an auspice, any thing, image, idea, concept, object, or self *is what it is independently of anything else. To be* something real is *to be* separate, substantive, and independent, a "permanent, unitary and autonomous entit[y]" (Yangsi, 2003, p. 241), something thus "inherently self-existing" (Tsong-kha-pa, 2002, p. 120). To understand anything in the world (like that young child's efforts at pronouncing that new name found in a new book) is to separate it off from everything else. We must adopt a "reifying view" (Tsong-kha-pa, 2002, p. 120) regarding the ontological status of the thing being experienced: whatever this thing is, *it is what it is*, and it is not something else. Simple. We may not know *what* it is, *why* it is thus or *how it came to be* thus, but we know, with this reifying view, *that* it is what it is. So if we have no specific knowledge of it at all and it is simply some unknown "X," we *do* know that, whatever this "X" turns out to be, "X=X."

To use the language of Edmund Husserl's phenomenology (1969, p. 106), we may have doubts about this thing but, despite all this trepidation, "the 'it' remains ever in the sense of a general thesis, a world that has its being 'out there.'" Husserl (p. 169) called this the "general thesis of the natural attitude." It is, as he suggested, not simply one belief among others, but *the* founding belief of the commonplace way in which, "in everyday life our minds apprehend [things] as existing" (Yangsi, 2003, p. 200). Husserl (1969, p. 300) named this "the *primary belief* (*Urglaube*) or *Protodoxa* (*Urdoxa*)" of the natural attitude. Note, however, that *in* the natural attitude, this Urdoxa is understood to be precisely *not* "a belief" but simply "the way things are." It is assumed and projected as an ontological "given" against which our everyday experience of the world is to be understood. This is the odd breakthrough of Husserlian phenomenology, unearthing this Urdoxa as a thesis *of* the natural attitude that does not appear *as* a thesis *in* our ordinary experience of the world. This thesis thus describes the founding yet concealed and unquestioned prejudice of everyday life.

Within this (as Buddhism would have it, false or delusional) *belief,* "the essence of truth is identity" (Heidegger, 1978, p. 39), and the formal consort of this presumption of identity is the mathematical and formal-logic principle of identity (X=X). This thus links up the possibility of *understanding* the substance/reality of things with logico-mathematically based, natural-scientific methodologies, concepts and categories. Since the thing itself is what it is (X=X), *knowledge of that thing* must itself have precisely such clarity and distinctness borne of one thing separated off from another.

"BREAK OPEN THE BEING OF THE OBJECT"

> Because this causes living beings to be confused in their view of the actual state of things, it is a delusion; ignorance mistakenly superimposes upon things an essence that they do not have. It is constituted so as to block perception of their nature. It is a concealer. (Tsong-kha-pa, 2002, p. 208)

The hermeneutic critique of the dominance of natural-scientific methodologies sits squarely here, on a critique of the idea of substance—this concealed Urdoxic belief in separate and inherent self-existence (Sanskrit *svabhava*) as a formulation for how things exist. Gadamer (1989, p. 242) states this directly: "the concept of substance is…inadequate for historical being and knowledge. [There is a] radical challenge to thought implicit in this inadequacy." Understood hermeneutically, interpretation and questioning are therefore not just a matter of "making connections" between two inherently separate things (we are not dealing here with the *epistemology* of constructivism, where a subject puts separate things together and thus "produces" connections). Rather, interpretation and questioning have an *ontological* force: they "break open the [falsely presumed to be self-existent and substantive] *being* of the object" (Gadamer, 1989, p. 362), making visible, experiencable and understandable the ontological inherence of one thing in the very being of another.

In Buddhism, this phenomenon of "cosmic interpenetration" (Loy, 1993, p. 481) is described in conjunction with another equally important ontological insight: emptiness (Sanskrit *shunya*). This insight is named and/or translated in various ways: things, ideas, images, selves, are considered to be "empty of self-existence (*svabhavasunya*)" (Tsong-kha-pa, 2000, p. 24), "empty of having an inherent self-nature" (Tsong-kha-pa, 2005, p. 183), having an "absence of self-nature" (Tsong-kha-pa, 2000, p. 20), possessing "not even an atom of…true existence" (Tsong-kha-pa, 2004, p. 215):

> The true mode of being of a thing as it is in itself, is selfless, for its self cannot be a self-identity in the sense of a substance. Indeed, this true mode must include a complete negation of such self-identity. (Nishitani, 1982, p. 117)

However, this "negation of self-identity [X=X]" does not lead to something null and void. "Empty of inherent existence" (Tsong-kha-pa, 2006, p. 33) is meant to point towards *how* things *do* exist—not as separate self-identical substances that need nothing except themselves to exist, but as, rather, "dependently co-arising" (Sanskrit: *pratitya-samutpada*): "the only way phenomena do exist is as interdependently related" (Lobsang, 2006, p. 51). Emptiness of substantive self-existence thus is identical to the fullness of dependently arising interrelatedness that defines things, words, objects, and selves. Things *are* thus—in the very being of every seemingly separate thing are nestled *worlds of relations* and our ordinary experience of this as simply a meager act of pronunciation leaves such worlds concealed. This is what is meant by the breaking open of the (falsely presumed to be self-enclosed) being of the object and thus releasing insight into the instead dependently co-arising being of the object. "Dependent-arising is the meaning of emptiness" (Tsong-kha-pa, 2002, p. 133). Emptiness (of separate self-existence) thus means fullness (of dependently arising existence).

"EVERY WORD BREAKS FORTH"

There is a passage I have always loved in Hans-Georg Gadamer's *Truth and Method* (1989, p. 458) where he portrays something of the experience that follows from this gathering sense of "break[ing] open the being of the object":

> Every word [has an] inner dimension of multiplication: every word breaks forth as if from a center and is related to a whole, through which alone it is a word. Every word causes the whole of the language to which it belongs to resonate and the whole worldview that underlies it to appear. Thus every word, as the event of a moment, carries with it the unsaid, to which it is related by responding and summoning.

This "*as if* from a center" is vitally important.

As if, because *"the center is everywhere.* Each and every thing ["every word"] becomes the center of all things and, in that sense, becomes an absolute center. This is the absolute uniqueness of things, their reality" (Nishitani, 1982, p. 146). "We should apply this [as if] to *every* phenomenon. Every phenomenon…is empty of having an inherent self-nature that exists from its own side" (Tsong-kha-pa, 2005, p. 182). So that at "the periphery" of experiencing that young child's slow and agonizing work of pronunciation resides, for example, the phenomenon of names and how we are called by them, how they "summon and respond," or the appearance of spaces between words into written English in the 11th century (see Carruthers, 2003; Illich, 1993; Illich & Sanders, 1988; Stock, 1983). There, too, is the example of a colleague (see Jardine & Naqvi, 2012) telling me of her daughter learning to read the Koran out loud, and how she often did this well-honed pronunciation without understanding what many of the words mean. I queried this and found that *uttering the very sound of the words themselves* was understood to be a mirroring of the very sound of God speaking to the prophet, so the very sonority itself was blessed and precious, independently of the meaning and message of the text. Yes, oral recitation, a commonplace of Canadian elementary school classrooms. Reading aloud, "even there." God uttering the world into existence over the face of the deep. And that silent reading didn't even enter Europe until around the 11th century and, in doing so, propagated a new understanding of ourselves and our "interiority" and individuality/privacy (see Illich, 1993; Illich & Sanders, 1998). And there, too, is the full cascade of cultures and tongues that have found their ways here into this classroom, and how each has suffered in their own way the great modern hegemony of the English tongue (even, of course, the native English speakers), even here, in efforts to pronounce this Japanese transliteration of a deeply culturally embedded Japanese name for a Japanese cat in this child's new book.

So that slow breath of pronunciation is thus experienced, not as an isolated object of consideration, but as existing in a broad and generous "residence" of possibilities, lineages, intergenerational bloodlines, and the like. Hermeneutically understood, every however-common event of language *is* a dependently co-arising, living inheritance, and therefore the contingent, localized, frail and fragile *taking up of that inheritance*—this girl's efforts, here, now—is (however small a) part of its being what it is. As is my own inhaled breath, here, in this classroom, witnessing all over again the arrival of this old, familiar, tough-minded companion: pronunciation.

This *seems* paradoxical, that the center is everywhere and that, therefore, "none is the fundamental entity" (Hahn, 1986, p. 70) while, at the same time, any thing can be experienced *as* ("if") the center of all things. This is only a "contradiction" against the presumed backdrop of the logic of substance. Nishitani Keiji (1982, p. 149) elaborates:

> To say that *a thing is not itself* means that, while continuing to be itself, it is in the home-ground of everything else. Figuratively speaking, its roots reach across into the ground of all other things and help to hold them up and keep them standing. It serves as a constitutive element of their being. *That a thing is itself* means that all other things, while continuing to be themselves, are in the home-ground of that thing. This way that everything has being on the home-ground of everything else, without ceasing to be on its own home-ground, means that the being of each thing is held up, kept standing, and made to be what it is by means of the being of all other things; or, put the other way around, that each being holds up the being of every other thing, keeps it standing and makes it what it is.

Our considerations can thus then shift to one of these constitutively surrounding things that constitute the peripheries of pronunciation. Such shifts would then make her efforts of pronunciation now peripheral to, but still constitutive of this new "as if" center of our attention. *As if*, because anything "at the center" *is* "itself" because it *is* the field of its residing.

Thus Gadamer's "*as if* from a center," because in looking "into" that center and focusing in with great care on that child's pronunciation, enjoying, praising, encouraging, waiting, laughing, demonstrating, we don't experience it like some sort of hard-shelled "core." In looking into that center, we are cast "outwards" into worlds of relations. We are drawn "into" this child's efforts and find that in being drawn into that center, it "draws us entirely outside of ourselves. Rather than meeting us in our world, it is much more a world into which we ourselves are drawn. *[T]he totality of a lived context has entered into and is present in the thing.* And we belong to it as well." (Gadamer, 1994, pp. (191–192), my emphasis). This is why, in nearing such events in a classroom, my own life as a teacher *necessarily* involves learning, because in properly taking up pronunciation as a teacher, I take up, inevitably, the implication of *my own being* in this phenomenon *and* my dependently co-arising responsibility for the well-being of this girl and this inheritance and our myriad places in this great residence.

This is why I am drawn to such events in the classroom, "responding" to this "summons," because, hermeneutically understood, I, too, am already "present in the thing." In interpretive work, then, we come to "recognize *[our]selves* in the mess of th[is] world" (Hillman, 1983, p. 49, emphasis added), by recognizing ourselves, not as some self-existent entity, but rather *as* the mess of the world. I myself, as with this young girl, as with her breath and mine—each of these is experienced as glancing through the reflected facets of the world, each being itself by being such glancing with no substance left over.

A metaphor for such cosmic interpenetration and lack of self-presence is found in the Avatamsaka Sutra of Mahayana Buddhism, Indra's Net:

> Far away in the heavenly abode of the great god Indra, there is a wonderful net that has been hung by some cunning artificer in such a manner that it stretches out infinitely in all directions. In accordance with the extravagant tastes of deities, the artificer has hung a single glittering jewel in each "eye" of the net, and since the net itself is infinite in all dimensions, the jewels are infinite in number. There hang the jewels, glittering like stars of the first magnitude, a wonderful sight to behold. If we now arbitrarily select one of these jewels for inspection and look closely at it, we will discover that in its polished surface there are reflected all the other jewels in the net, infinite in number. Not only that, but each of the jewels reflected in this one jewel is also reflecting all the other jewels, so that there is an infinite reflecting process occurring. (Loy, 1993, p. 481)

This not only means that we "are always open onto the horizons of others but also, more important, because [we] are *always already everywhere inhabited* by the Other in the context of the fully real." (Smith, 2006, p. xxiv). Oddly put, experiencing that young girl's efforts at pronunciation requires my experiencing that, in my fullest reality as dependently co-arising, *I am*, my very self, a dependently co-arising inhabitant of this very residence.

I am inhabited by her halting breath over that odd name. It is my very life being played out, here, in watching her paw that book's cover and loving its allure, just as surely as my life is played out in the grief I sometimes find in schools. Coming to understand, then, is "more a passion than an action" (Gadamer, 1989, p. 366), more an act of compassion for the suffering and impermanence that defines our deeply shared, often deeply concealed lot.

This is my own column of aging breath being summoned up in this event of pronunciation. In breaking open the being of the object, *my own being "myself" is broken open* and experienced as caught up and constitutively implicated in the very fabric of the object I meditate upon or study or happen upon in some local classroom. This great sentiment is so eloquently expressed by Rick Fields (cited in Ingram, 1990, p. xiv):

My heart is broken,
open.

This is why it is getting so tough to visit schools sometimes. That child's pronunciation venture is heartbreaking.

Therefore, in "[heart]breaking open the being" of this child's efforts at the pronunciation of a name, "we are not attempting to get rid of [it], only of the idea of [it] as self-existent" (Lobsang, 2006, p. 49). "Those objects that appear… do not stop appearing, but the concepts [e.g., "substance," or other reifications] that take them as having any true existence subside" (Patrul, 1998, p. 252). We still remain concerned after understanding pronunciation in the specificities of its appearance, here, with this child and this book and this name and all the oddities of its translations and transliterations. But, at the same time, "the object" of our consideration must also include "the emptiness of this [particular phenomenon], not just [the phenomenon]" (Yangsi, 2003, p. 433).

To use the language of Martin Heidegger (1962), our concern is not merely "ontic" ("What is this thing, pronunciation, and what are the threads of its dependent co-arising?") but "ontological" (our "ontic," interpretive concern for this particular entity is only authentically pursuable against the background of its *being* dependently co-arising). From Longchenpa (1308–1363):

> Knowledge is as infinite as the stars in the sky;
> There is no end to all the subjects one could study
> It is better to grasp straight away their very essence–
> The unchanging fortress of the dharmakaya. (cited in Patrul, 1998, p. 261)

("**Dharmakaya**– *chos sku*, lit. Dharma Body. The emptiness aspect of Buddhahood" [a glossary entry to Patrul, 1998, p. 410]). Thus "studying subjects" like pronunciation must be done against the ontological "backdrop" of a knowledge of emptiness (a knowledge, that is, that pronunciation is *interpretable*) and these two ways of proceeding support and cultivate each other. Careful attention to the great detail, specificity and particularity of *this* appearance of pronunciation ("distinguishing the exact particulars of an object" (Tsong-kha-pa, 2002, p. 17) is possible *because* pronunciation is treated, interpretively, as empty of self-existence, as breaking forth *as if* from a center. And likewise, in interpreting pronunciation, we can get a glimpse of, an experience of, emptiness.

"Accordingly there is the examination and analysis of *both* the real nature [emptiness—the 'ontological status of the object under analysis' [Tsong-kha-pa, 2004, p. 21] and the [ontic] diversity of phenomena" (Tsong-kha-pa, 2002, p. 17). Properly understood, between these "there is compatibility and a lack of contradiction" (Tsong-kha-pa, 2004, p. 215). (This helps unravel a bit why Martin Heidegger always insisted that the Being of beings is not a being, *and* he insisted that Being is always the Being of a being—I'll leave the tempt of this tangle for others to undo at their leisure).

"IT DRAWS YOU INTO ITS PATH"

> When [it] takes hold of us, it is not an object that stands opposite us which we look at in hope of seeing through it to an intended conceptual meaning. Just the reverse. The

work [e.g., of pronunciation] is an *Ereignis*—an event that 'appropriates us' into itself. It jolts us, it knocks us over, and sets up a world of its own, into which we are drawn, as it were. (Gadamer with Dutt, 2001, p. 71)

There is, of course, a danger here. The hermeneutic experience of the breaking open of the being of the object involves "the way you apprehend the object. By making the object extensive [you] expand your mind" (Tsong-kha-pa, 2002, p. 63). As "it" becomes more extensive we become, as St. Augustine put it, "roomier" (cited in Carruther, 2005, p. 199). My "self" expands as my apprehension of the dependent co-arising of the world—the "residence" of my self—expands: "making the object of meditation extensive so as to expand your mind" (Tsong-kha-pa, 2002, p. 63).

And as the object "breaks forth," "it draws you into its path" (Gadamer, 2007b, p. 198).

Hence arises the danger that many new to hermeneutics (and Buddhist meditative practices) often experience: *Everything* seems connected, *everything* is rampantly full, *everything* starts to beckon and summon. It expands and I expand and get caught up in an onrush that seems impossible to stop. This is sometimes named the "monkey mind" in Buddhist practice (and this breaching an ironic humiliation in the *Wabi Sabi* book, where Monkey is the teacher).

The more you practice these things, the more accustomed your mind will become to them, and the easier it will be to practice what you had initially found difficult to learn. You will have visions of the Buddha day and night. (Tsong-kha-pa, 2000, pp. 185–186)

One arises from formal meditation and goes about daily activities, seeing the manifestations of the world and living beings as mandala deities. This is the Samadhi that transforms the world and its living brings into a most extraordinary vision. *All* experiences ["even here"] are taken as manifestations of great ecstasy. (Tsong-kha-pa, 2005, p. 125, emphasis added)

Everything is connected to *everything*. And hence a common complaint for some students of hermeneutics: "How do I get it to stop?" or "*Now* what?"

This outward expansiveness can easily lead to a ravaging exhaustion of attention, a sort of cascading, post-modern "connectionism": "you [can easily become] like the leading edge of water running downhill—you go anywhere you are led, taking anything said to be true, wanting to cry when you see others crying, wanting to laugh when you see others laugh" (Tsong-kha-pa, 2004, p. 222). It is easy to become swamped by possibilities and simply outrun. This is why Gadamer (1989, p. 106) talks about how it is that the dependent co-arising of play of things (e.g., what is expandingly experienced as "at play" in that breath of pronunciation) can "outplay the players." In the face of that simple event in an elementary school classroom, in the face of that lovely book and its allure, one can become simply burdened by unseemly and unending cloys of "relatedness" which can weigh down attention and make me simply give up in overwhelmed frustration. Tsong-kha-pa (2002, p. 62 ff.) thus warns against the extremes of "laxity [which simply gives up, spent in the face of the rush] and excitement [which simply pursues the rush ever faster and with accelerating distraction]."

A key task of hermeneutics as a practice (as well as a task in Buddhist practice) is thus the practice of *composure* in the face of this ecstatic experience of breaking forth. Tsong-kha-pa insists that the insight into emptiness that comes from pursuing wisdom be coupled with the practice of meditation, of one-pointed stillness and composure. He uses the term "equanimity" (2002, p. 68) to describe a process of "relaxing the effort, but not sacrificing the intensity of the way you apprehend the object" (p. 68). What is called for, then, is facing the delusions of inherent self-existence and *interpreting* them, that is, breaking open these delusions so that the realities of dependent co-arising can be experienced and understood. But this must be taken on at the same time as *not* simply becoming caught up in mere pursuit of the ensuing cascades. "I compose this in order to condition my own mind" (Tsong-kha-pa, 2000, p. 111).

Moreover, I read these compositions of Gadamer and Tsong-kha-pa in the very same pursuit of conditioning my own mind. "Texts are instructions for [the] practice" (Tsong-kha-pa, 2000, p. 52) of precisely paying more proper attention to that girl's way through the sounds of words.

It is notable, then, that we are right back to the issue of proper pronunciation and of learning to read, and, right here, in the face of this ordinary classroom event, this is, of course, exactly where we should be. Admittedly, it is difficult to read many scholarly texts this way, as instructions for practice, and this, too, takes practice, just *exactly* as does learning to "read" that singular moment in the classroom as "breaking forth," that is, as an exuberant "event of appearing [*Vollzug*]." About such moments, we ask:

> [how does] it begin, end, how long [does] it last[?]; how [does] it remain in one's mind, and in the end how [does] it fade away, and yet somehow remain with us and [be] able to surface again[?]. (Gadamer, 2007b, p. 217)

And this faces us with the dilemma: what should I do now? What should I say or write or show or save? What should be highlighted and what forgotten? This takes time, but a certain kind of time that is itself meditatively proper to such composition:

Certainly one can call this process a "while" [*Weilen*], but this is something that no-body measures and that one does not find to be either boring or merely entertaining. The name I have for the way in which this event happens is "reading." With reading one does not imagine …that one can already do it. In reality, one must learn how …. Now the word *Lesen* ["read," a German kin to the English word "lesson"—I think, for example, of an old commonplace in Anglican church services, of saying "today's lesson is taken from Matthew," meaning both literally "a reading from Matthew" but also *reading* that reading for its "lesson"] carries within it a helpful multiplicity of harmonic words, such as gathering together [*Zusammenlesen*], picking up [*Auflesen*], picking out [*Auslesen*], or to sort out [*verlesen*]. All of these are associated with "harvest" (*Lese*), that is to say, the harvest of grapes, which persist in the harvest. The word *Lesen* also refers to something that begins with spelling out words, if one learns to write and read, and again we find numerous echo words. One can start to read a book [*anlesen*] or finish up reading it [*auslesen*], one can read further in it [*weiterlesen*], or just check into it [*nachlesen*], or one can read it aloud [*vorlesen*]. All of these point towards the harvest that is gathered in and from which one takes nourishment. (Gadamer, 2007b, pp. 217–218)

Harvest, gathering, nourishment. Lovely words to describe the yield that comes from the suffering undergone in learning to read. To pronounce.

This is why Gadamer follows his lovely exploration of the phenomenon of the play(s) of the world (1989, pp. 101–110)—like being drawn into what is "at play" in that girl's work with *Wabi Sabi*—with an imposingly titled section, "Transformation into Structure" (pp. 110–120). "Transformation into structure" is about creating, in the midst of the cascading and alluring play of the world that is experienced once it is broken open, a "play," a "work" or a "composition" which draws us into "what is at play" and makes possible a certain composure in the face of this insight. "Composition" thus "captures" something of the insight of breaking forth and, with practice ("one does not imagine…that one can already do it. In reality, one must learn how" [Gadamer, 2007b, p. 217]) a work can be shaped that can offer to others the possibility of engaging this insight. This is identical to the everyday work of a classroom that gathers students together to create beautiful things that will show others how their work is laced up in the dependent co-arising work of the world. In taking on the difficult work of composing such events of appearing, one offers an invitation into such arising worlds. They are thus things that allow me, invite me, into a "hitherto concealed experience that transcends thinking from the position of subjectivity" (Gadamer, 1989, p. 100), an experience of my own dependent co-arising in the face of such arisings.

This act of, shall we say, mutual composure, then, is not just a matter of achieving stillness in the face of the fray, but of cultivating a deep and well-studied knowledge of the topic of one's meditations and all the rich lineages and ancestries of thought that have handed this topic over to us and us over to it. It involves realizing that "you can't get anywhere without [also] reading a yak's load of books" (Tsong-kha-pa, 2004, p. 219). This study is a study *on behalf of* the practice of composure in the midst of every life. It is a matter of not simply slavishly following the heavy scholarly weight of "tradition" but of, odd to say, having "delighted those who have come before" (Dudom & Dorje, 2011, p. 16) as a way to thus oneself experience delight in this new arising. This is why Gadamer (see Grondin, 2003, p. 333) expressed soft and generous disappointment when he found certain works given in his honor at his 100th birthday celebration not very *lebensweltlich* (not very "life-worldly"). This accounts, also, for why, as a hermeneutic philosopher, I feel such an affinity to the Gelug stream of Buddhism that emphasizes the equanimity between study and practice. "Wisdom and the study that it causes are indispensable for proper practice" (Tsong-kha-pa, 2004, p. 220).

"Do not make study and practice into separate things" (Tsong-kha-pa, 2004, p. 221).

"Against fixity…" hermeneutic work, strangely akin to Buddhist thought, "makes the object and all its possibilities fluid" (Gadamer, 1989, p. 367). Therefore, the purpose of a "hermeneutic study"—the purpose of composure, of composition—is to create something that will draw others into this hermeneutic experience of fluidity—*into* an experience of the dependent co-arising of the world and *out of* the delusions of substance and the grasping-at-permanence syndrome that is its root. And all this has as its aim not simply philosophical erudition and the like. The aim of such meditations and work is the cultivation of the intimacy and immediacy of the experience of everyday life, here, as this next child draws breath over a text, here, where reading aloud and learning to pronounce can too often be treated as simply ordinary and commonplace. Not only is "wherever you are…a place of practice" (Tsong-kha-pa, 2004, p. 191). Tsong-kha-pa also insists (and this is a feature that distinguishes the Gelug tradition from other Buddhist lineages and makes its affinity to hermeneutic ripe), the purpose and object of scholarly study is *precisely* the deepening of practice itself. After all, "why would you determine one thing by means of study and reflection, and then, when you go to practice, practice something else?" (2000, p. 52). And this is why Gadamer insists that hermeneutics, with all its philosophical erudition and study, is "a practical philosophy" (2007c) with both theoretical and practical tasks (2007d). All those complex philosophical and historical twists and turns that typify his work are meant, in the end, to make us more susceptible to the beautiful abundance of things as we walk around in the world. "Even here," in this ordinary place.

"Present in the Thing"

> [In learning to experience events in this way], we experience an absolute opposition to [our] will-to-control ["the syndrome of grasping at a self-nature" (Tsong-kha-pa, 2005, p. 182)], not in the sense of a rigid resistance to the presumption of our will which is bent on utilizing things, but in the sense of [having come upon] the superior and intrusive power of a being reposing in itself. (Gadamer, 1977, 226–227)

All those complex lines of dependent co-arising that break forth from this event of pronunciation are experienced as being "present in the thing" (Gadamer, 1994, p. 192). This is not exactly a matter of attention "narrowing" back in on some separate thing, but rather of attention *intensifying* and this wee event becoming, one might say, "luminous," radiantly full of all its relations. This is akin to accounts of what is called "generation stage meditation" in the Gelug tradition of Buddhism:

> You develop the ability to see yourself as a…deity and your environment as the mandala or…abode of the deity. This is called *pure perception*: you perceive all objects of the physical senses and the mind the same way a meditational deity experiences them [as if sitting at the center of an open field of dependent co-arising, a mandala-like "residence"]. The opposite of this mode of perception is *impure perception*. This is ordinary appearance: seeing yourself as ordinary, seeing the world where you live as ordinary ["each deed and thought…intimate and commonplace"], and experiencing …objects…as ordinary ["familiar"]. This impure appearance is the main target to be removed by… practice. (Sopa, 2004, p. 30)

Tsong-kha-pa elaborates (2005, p. 182) that what is sought is the ability to see every phenomenon as such a radiant deity:

> We should apply this to *every* phenomenon. Every phenomenon…is empty of having an inherent self-nature that exists from its own side. One should understand exactly how strong the presence of the syndrome of grasping at a self-nature [X=X] is. On the basis of [applying this to every phenomenon] one transforms the…world and its inhabitants [from being experienced as separate, controllable, graspable substances] into the supporting and the supported mandala (i.e., residence and deities).

Picturing every phenomenon as a deity sitting in the middle of a mandala entails coming to experience every phenomenon as thus a *radiant being*, illuminatingly full of all its relations precisely by being empty of self-existence, a being in whose presence light is cast upon me, illuminating my own culpabilities. Such picturing, which arises as an often-agonizing of sustained practice:

> It is not merely one's "taking time" to linger over something, as in the slackening or slowing down to contemplate. [It is] not a function of lackadaisical, meandering contemplation, least of all passive in any way, but is a function of the fullness and *intensity* of attention and engrossment. (Ross, 2006, p. 109)

In cultivating this "hermeneutic experience," those radiating lines of dependently co-arising venture can be sensed shimmering all around "every phenomenon," akin to a "halo" of illumination. Jigme Lingpa (1729–1798): "concentration is to experience as deities all the appearances to which one clings" (cited in Patrul, 1998, p. 254), that is, as a footnote to this passage clarifies, "to meditate on appearances as deities…means as pure wisdom manifestations [pure manifestations of an emptiness of substantive self-existence] with no concrete reality" (Patrul, 1998, p. 389, fnt. 166). With repeated and intense practice, even an ordinary appearance like the breath of pronunciation, shall we say, "glows."

That is, this girl's pronunciation is *beautiful* and, through practice, my own life can become more open and illuminated in its presence:

> That which manifests itself [in this way] attracts the longing of love to it. The beautiful disposes people in its favor immediately. The beautiful…has its own radiance. For "beauty alone has this quality: that it is what is most radiant (*ekphanestaton*) and lovely" [*Phaedrus*, 250 d 7]. (Gadamer, 1989, p. 481)

That "every phenomenon" (Tsong-kha-pa, 2005, p. 182) ("every word") hides this lesson is the great and difficult pedagogical affinity between hermeneutics and this old lineage of Buddhist thought and practice. *This* is "hermeneutic experience," that "the more…the work opens itself, the more luminous becomes [its] uniqueness" (Heidegger, 1977a, pp. 182–183), just this, just here, just now, this lovely, simple, beautiful thing, right in the midst of all this frail and fraught suffering and endurance.

And so we look at each other, and the story continues, and she giggles as she sees the name again.

POST-AMBULATORY COUPLET

> Knowledge is not a projection in the sense of a plan, the extrapolation of the aims of the will, an ordering of things according to the wishes, prejudices, or promptings of the powerful; rather, it remains something adapted to the object, a *mensuratio ad rem*. Yet this thing is not a *factum brutum* [something "inherently existing"] but itself ultimately has the same mode of being as Dasein [human being]. [*Both are dependently co-arising*]. The important thing, however, is to understand this

oft-repeated statement correctly. It does not mean simply that there is a "homogeneity" between the knower and the known. The coordination of all knowing activity with what is known is not based on *the fact that* they have the same mode of being but draws it significance from the *particular nature* of the mode of being that is common to them. It consists in the fact that neither the knower nor the known is [substantively] "present-at-hand." (Gadamer, 1989, p. 261)

Because the ultimate mode of the existence of enlightened [radiant] beings and ordinary sentient beings is the same [even "enlightened beings" are dependently co-arising], we have the potential to be recipients of their divine activity. (Yangsi, 2003, p. 133)

Contributor Bios

Heesoon Bai is professor in philosophy of education at Simon Fraser University, Canada. Her co-edited and co-authored books include *Speaking of Teaching: Inclinations, Inspirations, and Innerworkings (2012); Speaking of Learning: Recollections, Revelations, and Realizations (forthcoming)* and *Contemplative Learning and Inquiry across Disciplines* (forthcoming).

Alan Block has been a professor of education at the University of Wisconsin-Stout for 25 years. Prior to that, for 18 years he taught high school English in the public high schools. He suffers.

Christopher B. Brown is a professor in the Departments of Medicine, Oncology, and Biochemistry & Molecular Biology. He is affiliated with the Southern Alberta Cancer Institute and a board member of the Kids Cancer Care Foundation of Alberta.

Avraham Cohen is the coordinator for the Full-Time Master's in Counseling Program at City University of Seattle in Vancouver BC, Canada. He is the lead author of *Attending to the Human Dimension in Education: Inner Life, Relationship, and Learning* (2014) and *Speaking of Learning: Recollections, Revelations, and Realizations* (forthcoming).

Alexander C. Cook is a professional petroleum engineer in Alberta, Canada. He has struggled with both his physical and mental health, and has learned how to reach his fullest potential through the use of mindfulness. In an effort to help fight stigma and discrimination regarding mental illness, Alexander speaks regularly to students and educators to share what he has learned.

Allan Donsky is a clinical assistant professor in the Department of Psychiatry at the University of Calgary and adjunct professor in the Department of Child and Youth Studies at Mount Royal University. He had a full-time clinical practice for 17 years and has been consulting psychiatrist with the Healthy Minds/Healthy Children program in Calgary, Alberta, Canada for the last decade. He currently spends most of his time working in mental health classrooms in Calgary using and teaching mindfulness practices to assist both staff and students toward greater mental health and well-being.

Gilbert Drapeau has practiced social work in the child intervention field for close to 20 years. He has worked with abused and/or disabled children and youth, their families, supports, and communities in a variety of settings. He currently supports caseworkers in their practice in Edmonton, Alberta, Canada.

Alexandra Fidyk is on faculty in the Department of Secondary Education, University of Alberta. Her work draws from process philosophy, depth psychology, Buddhism, curriculum theory, and poetic inquiry. She is completing a collection of essays entitled *Jung and the Classroom*. She is a certified Jungian psychotherapist in practice in Edmonton, Alberta.

Christopher Gilham is an assistant professor in the Faculty of Education at St. Francis Xavier University, Antigonish, Nova Scotia. He is a former junior high/elementary school teacher and consultant. His work is focused on helping cultivate spaces in school settings where typically marginalized and codified students and their educators can thrive together.

Jusdon Innes currently teaches grade five at Olympic Heights Elementary School, and has spent the last 15 years teaching, primarily at the elementary level. He is originally from the West Coast, and grew up only a few hundred feet from the shoreline of the Pacific Ocean.

David W. Jardine is a professor in the Werklund School of Education, Calgary, Alberta. He is the author of several books including, most recently, *Ecological Pedagogy, Buddhist Pedagogy, Hermeneutic Pedagogy: Experiments in a Curriculum for Miracles* (2014) with Jackie Seidel, and *Pedagogy Left in Peace: On the Cultivation of Free Spaces in Teaching and Learning* (2012).

Jodi Latremouille, from Merritt, BC, is a former high school social studies, English and French immersion teacher. She is a doctoral student at the University of Calgary, and her research interests include social and environmental justice, interpretive research, and ecological pedagogies.

Graham McCaffrey is an assistant professor in the Faculty of Nursing at the University of Calgary, Alberta. He worked in various capacities as a mental health nurse for many years before moving into academia. His doctoral work was about nurse-patient relationships in acute mental health units, using elements from Buddhist traditions as an interpretive frame.

Nancy J. Moules is a professor in the Faculty of Nursing at the University of Calgary. She also holds an Alberta Children's Hospital Foundation/Alberta Children's Hospital Research Institute Nursing professorship in child and family centred cancer care, and is the editor of the *Journal of Applied Hermeneutics*.

W. John Williamson is a PhD candidate in the Werklund School of Education, University of Calgary, and a diverse learning coordinating teacher for the Calgary Catholic School District. He is on an interpretive quest to find supportive, attentive, practical, and non-hierarchical ways of honoring student diversity.

References

Abram, D. (1996). *The spell of the sensuous: Language in a more-than-human world*. New York, NY: Pantheon.

Abram, D. (2011). *Becoming animal: An earthly cosmology*. New York, NY: Vintage Books.

Alberta Education. (2008). *Supporting positive behaviour in Alberta schools*. Edmonton, Canada: Author.

Alberta Education. (2009). *High school completion longitudinal study highlights*. Edmonton, Canada: Author.

Alberta Education. (2009). *Special education coding criteria 2009/2010: ECS to Grade 12 mild/moderate (including gifted and talented) severe*. Edmonton, Canada. Retrieved from http://education.alberta.ca/media/6606655/special%20education%20coding%20criteria%(202009-10).pdf

Alberta Education. (June 2009). *Setting the direction framework*. Retrieved from http://education.alberta.ca/media/1082136/sc_settingthedirection_framework.pdf

Alberta Education. (2011). *Severe disabilities profile review*. Retrieved from http://www.education.alberta.ca/admin/special/funding/profilereview.aspx

Allan, J. (2008). Foucault and the art of transgression. In J. Allan (Ed.), *Rethinking of inclusive education: The philosophers of difference in practice* (pp. 85–100). Dorecht, The Netherlands: Springer.

Allan, J. (2009). Disability arts and the performance of ideology. In S. Gabel (Ed.), *Disability studies in education: Readings in theory and method* (pp. 21–36). New York, NY: Peter Lang.

American Psychiatric Association. (2000). *Diagnostic and statistical manual of mental disorders* (4th ed., text revision). Arlington, VA: Author.

American Psychiatric Association. (2013). *Diagnostic and statistical manual of mental disorders* (5th ed.). Arlington, VA: Author.

Aoki, T. (2005). Teaching as indwelling between two curriculum worlds. In W. Pinar & R. Irwin (Eds.), *Curriculum in a new key: The collected works of Ted. T. Aoki* (pp. 159–165). New York, NY: Lawrence Erlbaum.

Arendt, H. (1969). *Between past and future: Eight exercises in political thought.* New York, NY: Penguin Books.

Armstrong, K. (2011). *Twelve steps to a compassionate life.* Toronto, ON: Vintage Canada.

Arndt, K., White, J. M., & Chervenak, A. (2009). "Gotta go now": Rethinking the use of *The Mighty* and *Simon Birch* in the middle school classroom. *Disability Studies Quarterly, 30*(1). Retrieved from http://dsq-sds.org/article/view/1014/1227

Bai, H. (1996). *Moral Perception in the nondual key: Towards an ethic of moral proprioception* (Unpublished doctoral dissertation). University of British Columbia, Vancouver, BC, Canada.

Barber, K. (Ed.). (1998). *Canadian Oxford dictionary.* Don Mills, Canada: Oxford University Press.

Barker, P. (2009). Psychiatric diagnosis. In P. Barker (Ed.), *Psychiatric and mental health nursing: The craft of caring* (pp. 123–132). London, England: Hodder Arnold.

Barker, P., & Buchanan-Barker, P. (2005). *The tidal model: A guide for mental health professionals.* New York, NY: Brunner-Routledge.

Batchelor, M. (2001). *Zen.* London, England: Thorsons.

Bayer, T. I. (2008). Vico's principle of sensus communis and forensic eloquence. *Chicago-Kent Law Review, 83*(3), 113–1155.

Becker, E. (1997). *The denial of death.* New York, NY: Free Press. (Original work published 1973)

Berry, C., Gerry, L., Hayward M., & Chandler, R. (2010). Expectations and illusions: A position paper on the relationship between mental health practitioners and social exclusion. *Journal of Psychiatric and Mental Health Nursing, 17*, 411–421. doi:10.1111/j.(1365–2850).2009.01538.x

Berry, W. (1983). *Standing by words.* San Francisco, CA: North Point Press.

Berry, W. (2012). *It all turns on affection: The Jefferson lecture and other essays.* New York, NY: Counterpoint.

Berry, W., & Moyers, B. (2013, October 11). Writer and farmer Wendell Berry on hope, direct action, and the "resettling" of the American countryside. *Yes Magazine.* Retrieved from http://www.yesmagazine.org/planet/mad-farmer-wendell-berry-gets-madder-in-defense-of-earth

Berube, M. (2003). Citizenship and disability. *Dissent*, Spring, 52–57.

Biesta, G., & Burbules, N. C. (2003). *Pragmatism and educational research.* Lanham, MD: Rowman & Littlefield.

Bob Simpson. (2012, May 23). *Mike Ervin explains why Stand Up Chicago is protesting at the Chicago mercantile exchange (CBOT)* [Video file]. Retrieved from http://www.youtube.com/watch?v=BXN5a9wW4sc

Bodhi, B. (Ed. & Trans.). (2005). *In the Buddha's words: An anthology of discourses from the Pali canon.* Boston, MA: Wisdom.

Boeree, G. (1997). *The four noble truths. An Introduction to Buddhism.* Retrieved from http://webspace.ship.edu/cgboer/buddhaintro.html

Bruford, W. H. (2010). *The German tradition of self-cultivation: "Bildung" from Humboldt to Thomas Mann.* Cambridge, MA: Cambridge University Press.

Buber, M. (1970). *I and thou.* New York, NY: Scribner.

Buckman, R. (2005). *Cancer is a word, not a sentence: A practical guide to help you through the first few weeks.* Toronto, Canada: Key Porter Books.

Burman, E. (2008). *Developments: Child, image, nation.* New York, NY: Taylor & Francis.

Canadian Down Syndrome Society. (2013). *Position statement on value-neutral language.* Retrieved from http://www.cdss.ca/blog/positioning/positioning/

Caputo, J. (1987). *Radical hermeneutics: Repetition, deconstruction, and the hermeneutic project.* Bloomington, IN: Indiana University Press.

Caputo, J. (1989) *Against ethics: Contributions to a poetics of obligation with constant reference to deconstruction.* Bloomington, IN: Indiana State University Press.

Carr, N. (2013, October 25). Frederick Taylor and the quantified self. *Rough Type.* Retrieved from http://www.roughtype.com/?p=3888

Chah, A. (2005). *Everything arises, everything falls away.* Boston, MA: Shambala.

Chambers, C., & Ryder, E. (2009). *Compassion and caring in nursing.* London, England: Radcliffe.

Charter for Compassion. (2009). *Charter for compassion.* Retrieved from http://charterforcompassion.org/the-charter/#charter-for-compassion

Chesterton, G. K. (1916). Introduction to the book of Job. In G. K. Chesterton, *The theologian.* Retrieved from http://www.chesterton.org/introduction-to-job/

Child and youth. Retrieved from Mental Health Commission website: http://www.mentalhealthcommission.ca/English/issues/child-and-youth?routetoken=5c00654cecf37123d220e35c5f9c2dea&terminitial=20

Clayton, M. P. (1959). Juvenile offenders and the law. *Exceptional Children, 38,* 95–105.

Cleary, T. (1989). *Zen lessons: The art of leadership.* Boston, MA: Shambhala.

Cleary, T. (2002). *Secrets of the Blue Cliff Record.* Boston, MA: Shambhala.

Climenhaga, D. J. (2013, June 2). Alberta Tories respond to protests by disabled citizens with instinctive diversionary attack [Blog post]. Retrieved from http://rabble.ca/blogs/bloggers/djclimenhaga/2013/06/alberta-tories-respond-to-protests-disabled-citizens-instinctive

Cohen, A. (2006). *Attending to the inner experience of an educator: The human dimension in education* (Doctoral dissertation). Retrieved from UBC DSpace website: https://circle.ubc.ca/handle/2429/18393

Cohen, A., & Porath, M. (2007, April). *Exceptional educators: Understanding the dimensions of their practice.* Paper presented at the AERA 2007 Annual Meeting/Self-Study SIG, Chicago.

Couture, J. C. (2012). Inclusion—Alberta's educational palimpsest. *ATA Magazine, 92*(3), 54–58.

Dallett, J. O. (1991). *Saturday's child: Encounters with the dark gods.* Toronto, Canada: Inner City.

Davis, L. (2002). *Bending over backwards.* New York, NY: New York University Press.

Dechant, G. M. (2006). *Winter's children: The emergence of children's mental health services in Alberta, 1905–2005.* Edmonton, Canada: Muttart Foundation. Retrieved from http://www.muttart.org/sites/default/files/Dechant_G_Winter's%20Children.pdf

Derrida, J., & Ferraris, M. (2001). *A taste for the secret.* Cambridge, England: Polity Press.

Descartes, R. (1988). Meditations on first philosophy. In J. S. Cottingham, R. Stoothoff, & D. Murdoch, Ed. & Trans.), *Descartes selected philosophical writings* (pp. 80–85). Cambridge, MA: Cambridge University Press. (Original work published 1637)

Domanski, D. (1998). *Parish of the physic moon.* Toronto, Canada: McClelland & Stewart.

Domanski, D. (2002). The wisdom of falling. In T. Bowling (Ed.), *Where the words come from Canadian poets in conversation* (pp. 244–255). Roberts Creek, Canada: Nightwood Editions.

Draper, H. J. (1900). *The lament for Icarus* [Painting]. Retrieved from http://www.tate.org.uk/art/artworks/draper-the-lament-for-icarus-n01679

Edinger, E. (1975). *Melville's Moby Dick: A Jungian commentary: An American Nekyia.* New York, NY: New Directions.

Ehrhard, F. K. (1991). *The Shambhala dictionary of Buddhism and Zen* (M. H. Kohn, Trans.). Boston, MA: Shambhala.

Eliade, M. (1968). *Myth and reality.* New York, NY: Harper & Row.

Eliot, G. (1900). *Middlemarch: A study of provincial life.* New York, NY: P.F. Collier & Son.

Eliot, T. S. (2014). *East Coker* [Poem]. Retrieved from http://oedipa.tripod.com/eliot-2.html

Eliot, T. S. (1943). *Four quartets.* New York, NY: Harcourt, Brace.

Ervin, M. (2002). There's no such thing as a mercy killing. *The Human Life Review, 28*(3). Retrieved from http://www.questia.com/library/1P(3-218540471)/there-s-no-such-thing-as-a-mercy-killing

Ervin, M. (2012, June 17). Will the reformers come for me, too? *The New York Times Opinion Pages.* Retrieved from http://www.nytimes.com/2012/06/18/opinion/vulnerable-to-reform.html

Ervin, M. (2013a, April 12). Obama's proposal hurts people with disabilities. *The Progressive.* Retrieved from http://progressive.org/obama-social-security-proposal-detrimental-to-people-with-disabilities

Ervin, M. (2013b, July 26). Why I celebrate the ADA at 23. *The Progressive.* Retrieved from http://progressive.org/celebrate-disabilities-act-at-23

Ferri, B. A. (2011). Undermining inclusion? A critical reading of response to intervention (RTI). *International Journal of Inclusive Education, 16*(8), 1–18.

Feyerabend, P. (1975). *Against method: Outline of an anarchistic theory of knowledge.* London, England; Atlantic Highlands, NJ: NLB; Humanities Press.

Fidyk, A. (2010). Hermaphrodite as healing image: Connecting a mythic imagination to education. *Jungian Journal of Scholarly Studies, 6*(2) Retrieved from http://jungiansociety.org/index.php/publications/journals/volume-(6-2010)

Fidyk, A. (2013). Conducting research in an animated world: A case for suffering. *International Journal of Multiple Research Approaches, Special Issue: Depth Psychological Research Approaches,*

7(3), 378–391. Retrieved from http://mra.e-contentmanagement.com/archives/vol/7/issue/3/article/5290/conducting-research-in-an-animated-world–a-case

Foucault, M., Marchetti, V., Salomoni, A., & Davidson, A. I. (2003). *Abnormal: Lectures at the Collège de France, 1974–1975*. New York, NY: Picador.

Gabel, S. (2005). An aesthetic of disability. In S. Gabel (Ed.), *Disability studies in education: Readings in theory and method* (pp. 21–36). New York, NY: Peter Lang.

Gadamer, H. G. (1977). *Philosophical hermeneutics*. Berkeley, CA: University of California Press.

Gadamer, H. G. (1983). *Reason in the age of science* (F. G. Lawrence, Trans.). Boston, MA: MIT Press.

Gadamer, H. G. (1986). The idea of the university—Yesterday, today, tomorrow. In D. Misgeld & G. Nicholson (Eds. & Trans.), *Hans-Georg Gadamer on education, poetry, and history: Applied hermeneutics* (pp. 47–62). Albany, NY: SUNY Press.

Gadamer, H. G. (1989). *Truth and method* (2nd rev. ed., J. Weinsheimer & D. G. Marshall, Trans.). New York, NY: Continuum.

Gadamer, H. G. (1994). *Heidegger's ways*. Boston, MA: MIT Press.

Gadamer, H. G. (1996). Hermeneutics and psychiatry. In H. G. Gadamer, *The enigma of health: The art of healing in a scientific age* (pp. 163–174). Stanford, CA: Stanford University Press.

Gadamer, H. G. (1996a). *The enigma of health: The art of healing in a scientific age*. Stanford, CA: Stanford University Press.

Gadamer, H. G. (2001). *Gadamer in conversation* (R. E. Palmer, Ed. & Trans.). New Haven, CT: Yale University Press.

Gadamer, H. G. (2007). Classical and philosophical hermeneutics. In R. E. Palmer (Ed. & Trans.), *The Gadamer reader: A bouquet of the later writings* (pp. 41–71). Evanston, IL: Northwestern University Press.

Gadamer, H. G. (2007a). From word to concept: The task of hermeneutics as philosophy. In R. E. Palmer (Ed. & Trans.), *The Gadamer reader: A bouquet of the later writings* (pp. 108–122). Evanston, IL: Northwestern University Press.

Gadamer, H. G. (2007b). The artwork in word and image: "So true, so full of being!" In R. E. Palmer (Ed. & Trans.), *The Gadamer reader: A bouquet of later writings* (pp. 192–224). Evanston IL: Northwestern University Press.

Gadamer, H. G. (2007c). Hermeneutics as practical philosophy. In R. E. Palmer (Ed. & Trans.), *The Gadamer reader: A bouquet of the later writings* (pp. 227–245). Evanston IL: Northwestern University Press.

Gilham, C. (2010). *Trauma anew: An interpretive study* (master's thesis). Retrieved from http://www.academia.edu/1003203/Trauma_anew_An_interpretive_study

Gilham, C. (2013). *The hermeneutics of inclusion* (doctoral dissertation). Retrieved from http://theses.ucalgary.ca/handle/11023/828

Gilham, C., & Williamson, W. J. (2013). Inclusion's confusion in Alberta. *International Journal of Inclusive Education*. doi:10.1080/13603116.2013.802025

Goggin, G., & Newell, C. (2004). Fame and disability: Christopher Reeve, super crips, and infamous celebrity. *M/C Journal*, 7(5). Retrieved from http://journal.media culture.org.au/0411/02-goggin.php

Gottlieb, P. (2011). Aristotle on non-contradiction. Retrieved from http://plato.stanford.edu/archives/sum2011/entries/aristotle-noncontradiction

Gouthro, T. J. (2009). Recognizing and addressing the stigma associated with mental health nursing: A critical perspective. *Issues in Mental Health Nursing*, *30*, 669–676. doi:10.3109/01612840903040274

Graham, L., & Slee, R. (2008). An illusory interiority: Interrogating the discourse/s of inclusion. *Educational Philosophy and Theory*, *40*(2), (277–293). doi: 10.1111/j.(1469-5812).2007.00331.x

Greenberg, G. (2010). *Manufacturing depression: The secret history of a modern disease*. New York, NY: Simon & Schuster.

Grondin, J. (1995). *Introduction to philosophical hermeneutics*. New Haven, CT: Yale University Press.

Hacking, I. (1995). *Rewriting the soul: Multiple personality and the sciences of memory*. Princeton, NJ: Princeton University Press.

Hacking, I. (2004). *Historical ontology*. New York, NY: Harvard University Press.

Hahn, T. N. (2001). *Thich Nhat Hahn: Essential writings*. Maryknoll, NY: Orbis Books.

Harrison, J., & Gill, A. (2010). The experience and consequences of people with mental health problems, the impact of stigma upon people with schizophrenia: A way forward. *Journal of Psychiatric and Mental Health Nursing*, *17*, 242–250. doi:10.1111/j.(1365-2850).2009.01506.x

Hass, R. (Ed.). (1994). *The essential haiku: Versions of Basho, Buson, & Issa*. Hopewell, NJ: Ecco.

Hatfield, G. (2011). René Descartes. Retrieved from http://plato.stanford.edu/archives/sum2011/entries/descartes/

Hayward, S. (2009). The Canadian legal system, the Robert Latimer case, and the rhetorical construction of (dis)ability: "Bodies that matter?" *Developmental Disabilities Bulletin*, 37(1 & 2), 187–201. Retrieved from http://files.eric.ed.gov/fulltext/EJ920696.pdf

Heidegger, M. (1962). *Being and time*. (J. Macquarrie & E. Robinson, Trans.) New York, NY: Harper Collins.

Heraclitus. (2001). *Fragments. The collected wisdom of Heraclitus* (B. Haxton, Trans.). New York, NY: Penguin.

Heschel, A. J. (1959). *Between God and Man: An Interpretation of Judaism*. (F. A. Rothschild, Ed.) New York: The Free Press.

Hillman, J. (n.d.). Alchemical blue and the Unio Mentalis. Retrieved from http://www.panthe atre.com/pdf/6-reading-list-JH-blue.pdf

Hillman, J. (1975). *Revisioning psychology*. New York, NY: Harper Colophon Books.

Hillman, J. (1979). *The dream and the underworld*. New York, NY: Avon.

Hillman, J. (1991). *Inter/views*. Dallas, TX: Spring.

Hillman, J. (1997). The seduction of black. In S. Marlan (Ed.), *Fire in the stone: The alchemy of desire* (pp. 42–53). Wilmette, IL: Chiron.

Hillman, J. (2006). Anima Mundi: Returning the soul to the world. In J. Hillman (Ed.), *City and soul* (pp. 27–49). Putnam, CT: Spring.

Hillman, J., & Shamdasani, S. (2013). *Lament of the dead: Psychology after Jung's Red Book*. New York, NY: W.W. Norton.

Hirsch, E. D. (1967). *Validity in interpretation*. New Haven, CT: Yale University Press.

Hoover, S. (2007). Transformation of children's mental health services: The role of school mental health. *Psychiatric services, 58*(10), doi: 10.1176/appi.ps.58.10.1330

Hopper, S. R. (1989). Once more: The cavern beneath the cave. In D. R. Griffin (Ed.), *Archetypal process: Self and divine in Whitehead, Jung, and Hillman* (pp. 107–124). Chicago, IL: Northwestern University Press.

Horsfall, J., Cleary, M., & Hunt, G. E. (2010). Stigma in mental health: Clients and professionals. *Issues in Mental Health Nursing, 31*, 450–455. doi:10.3109/01612840903537167

Hume, D. (2005). *On suicide*. London, England: Penguin.

Husserl, E. (1964). Edmund Husserl: A letter to Arnold Metzger. *Philosophical Forum, 21*, 48–68.

Husserl, E. (1965). Philosophy as a rigorous science. In *Phenomenology and the crisis of philosophy* (pp. 71–148). New York, NY: Harper & Row.

Husserl, E. (1969). *Formal and transcendental logic*. The Hague, The Netherlands: Martinus Nijhoff.

Husserl, E. (1969a). *Ideas toward a pure phenomenology*. New York, NY: Humanities Press.

Husserl, E. (1970). *The crisis of European science and transcendental phenomenology*. Evanston, IL: Northwestern University Press.

Husserl, E. (1970a). *The idea of phenomenology*. The Hague, The Netherlands: Martinus Nijhoff.

Husserl, E. (1970b). *Cartesian meditations*. The Hague, The Netherlands: Martinus Nijhoff.

Hyde, L. (1983). *The gift: Imagination and the erotic life of property*. New York, NY: Vintage Books.

Hyde, L. (1998). *Trickster makes this world: Mischief, myth, and art*. New York, NY: North Point Press.

Illich, I. (1975). *Limits to medicine. Medical nemesis: The expropriation of health*. London, England: Marion Boyars.

Illich, I. (1993). *In the vineyard of the text: A commentary on Hugh's Didascalicon*. Chicago, IL: University of Chicago Press.

Jardine, D. (1976). *The question of phenomenological immanence* (Master's thesis). Retrieved from www.digitalcommons.mcmaster.ca/opendissertations/4567/

Jardine, D. (1998). *"To dwell with a boundless heart": On curriculum theory, hermeneutics and the ecological imagination*. New York, NY: Peter Lang.

Jardine, D. (2008). Because it shows us the way at night: On animism, writing, and the re-animation of Piagetian theory. In D. Jardine, S. Friesen, & P. Clifford (Eds.), *Back to the basics of teaching and learning: Thinking the world together* (2nd ed., pp. 105–116). New York, NY: Routledge.

Jardine, D. (2012). *Pedagogy left in peace: Cultivating free spaces in teaching and learning*. New York, NY: Continuum.

Jardine, D. W. (2012a). The Descartes lecture. *Journal of Applied Hermeneutics*. Retrieved from http://hdl.handle.net/10515/sy5pr7n88

Jardine, D. (2013). Guest editorial: Morning thoughts on application. *Journal of Applied Hermeneutics*. Retrieved from http://jah.synergiesprairies.ca/jah/index.php/jah/article/view/52

Jardine, D. (2013, July). How to prevent all hell from breaking loose. Keynote speech at the *Eighth International Imagination in Education Conference*, Vancouver, BC, Canada.

Jardine, D. (in press). In appreciation of modern hunting traditions and a grouse's life unwasted. *One World in Dialogue*.

Jardine, D., Bastock. M., George, J., & Martin, J. (2008). Cleaving with affection: On grain elevators and the cultivation of memory. In D. Jardine, S. Friesen, & P. Clifford (Eds.), *Back to the basics of teaching and learning: Thinking the world together* (2nd ed., pp. 31–58). New York, NY: Routledge.

Jardine, D., Clifford, P., & Friesen, S. (2008). *Back to the basics of teaching and learning: Thinking the world together*. New York, NY: Routledge.

Jardine, D., Friesen, S., & Clifford, P. (2006). *Curriculum in abundance*. New Jersey, NJ: Lawrence Erlbaum.

Jardine, D., Naqvi, R., Jardine, E., & Zaidi, A. (2010). "A zone of deep shadow": Pedagogical and familial reflections on "The Clash of Civilizations." *Interchange*, *41*(3), 209–232.

Jeary, J., Couture, J.-C., & Alberta Teachers Association. (2009). *Success for all: The teaching profession's views on the future of special education in Alberta*. Edmonton, Canada: Alberta Teachers' Association.

Johnson, M. (1992). A test of wills: Jerry Lewis, Jerry's orphans, and the telethon. *The Disability Rag*. Retrieved from http://www.ragged-edge-mag.com/archive/jerry92.htm

Jordan, A., & Stanovich, P. (2003). Teachers' personal epistemological beliefs about students with disabilities as indicators of effective teaching practices. *Journal of Research in Special Educational Needs*, *3*(1).

Jordan, A., & Stanovich, P. (2004). The beliefs and practices of Canadian teachers about including students with special needs in their regular Elementary classrooms. *Exceptionality Education Canada*, *14*(2–3), 25–46.

Jung, C. G. (1953). *Psychology and alchemy* (R. F. C. Hull, Trans.). Princeton, NJ: Princeton University Press.

Jung, C. G. (1963/1989). The personification of the opposites. In R. F. C. Hull (Ed., Trans.), *Mysterium coniunctionis. The collected works of C. G. Jung* (Bollingen ed., Vol. 14, pp. 89–257). Princeton, NJ: Princeton University Press.

Jung, C. G. (1966/1978). Picasso. In the spirit in man, art, and literature. In R. F. C. Hull (Ed., Trans.), *Mysterium coniunctionis. The collected works of C. G. Jung* (Bollingen ed., Vol. 15, pp. 135–141). Princeton, NJ: Princeton University Press.

Jung, C. G. (1977). In W. McGuire & R. F. C. Hull (Eds.), *C. G. Jung speaking: Interviews and encounters*. Princeton, NJ: Princeton University Press.

Kabat-Zinn, J., & University of Massachusetts Medical Center/Worcester. (1990). *Full catastrophe living: Using the wisdom of your body and mind to face stress, pain, and illness*. New York, NY: Delacorte Press.

Kant, I. (2009). *The critique of judgment*. London, England: Oxford University Press.

Kant, I., & Paton, H. J. (1964). *Groundwork of the metaphysics of morals.* New York, NY: Harper & Row.

Kearney, R. (2003). *Strangers, gods, and monsters: Interpreting otherness.* New York, NY: Psychology Press.

Kearney, R. (2011). What is diacritical hermeneutics? *Journal of Applied Hermeneutics.* Retrieved from http://jah.journalhosting.ucalgary.ca/jah/index.php/jah/article/view/6

Keown, D. (2004). *Oxford dictionary of Buddhism.* New York, NY: Oxford University Press.

Kornfield, J. (2008). *The wise heart: A guide to the universal teachings of Buddhist psychology.* New York, NY: Bantam.

Kuhn, T. S. (1970). *The structure of scientific revolutions.* Chicago, IL: University of Chicago Press.

Laing, R. D. (1965). *The divided self.* Baltimore, MD: Pelican.

Lao Tzu. (1972). *The way of life according to Lao Tzu* (W. Bynner, Trans.). London, England: Lyrebird.

Latremouille, J. (in press). A modern hunting tradition. *One World in Dialogue.*

Laurence, J., & McCallum, D. (2009). *Inside the child's head: Histories of childhood behavioural disorders.* Rotterdam, The Netherlands; Boston, MA: Sense.

Layton, B. (1987). *The Gnostic scriptures.* London, England: SCM Press.

Leighton, T. D. (2003). *Faces of compassion: Classic bodhisattva archetypes and their modern expression.* Boston, MA: Wisdom.

Loy, D. (1996). *Lack and transcendence: The problem of death and life in psychotherapy, existentialism, and transcendence.* Atlantic Highlands, NJ: Humanities Press International.

Loy, D. (1999). *Nonduality: A study in comparative philosophy.* Atlantic Highlands, NJ: Humanity Books.

Loy, D. (2003). *The great awakening: A Buddhist social theory.* Boston, MA: Wisdom.

Lupart, J. L. (2008). Achieving excellence and equity in Canadian schools: Can inclusion bridge the gap? *Proceedings of the International Inclusive Education Research Professorial Series, Monash University, Victoria, Australia.*

Madison, G. B. (1978). Eine Kritik an Hirschs Begriff der "Richtigkeit." In H. G. Gadamer & G. Boehm (Eds.), *Die Hermeneutik und die Wissenschaften* (pp. 393–400). Frankfurt, Germany: Suhrkamp Verlag.

Madison, G. B. (1988). *The hermeneutics of postmodernism.* Bloomington, IN: Indiana University Press.

Marlan, S. (2005). *The black sun.* College Station, TX: Texas A&M University Press.

Marx, G. (1959: 1995). *Groucho and me.* New York, NY: First Da Capo.

Maslow, A. (1962/2011). *Toward a psychology of being-reprint of 1962 edition first edition.* Eastford CT: Martino Fine Books.

Maxwell, N. (2009). Ideas [Radio series episode]. In *How to think about science.* Retrieved from http://www.cbc.ca/ideas/episodes/2009/01/02/how-to-think-about-science-part-1---24-listen/#episode24

McCourt, F. (1996). *Angela's ashes.* New York, NY: Scribner.

McMurtry, J. (2009). Rationality and scientific method: Paradigm shift in an age of collapse. *Interchange, 40*(1), 69–91.

Mental Health Commission of Canada (2014). Topics: Child and youth. Retrieved from http://www.mentalhealthcommission.ca/English/issues/child-and-youth?terminitial=20.

Miller, A. (1989). *For your own good: Hidden cruelty in child-rearing and the roots of violence*. Toronto, Canada: Collins.

Miller, A. (2005). *The drama of being a child: The search for the true self*. New York, NY: Harper & Row.

Mills, C. B., & Erzikova, E. (2012). Prenatal testing, disability, and termination: An examination of newspaper framing. *Disability Studies Quarterly, 32*(3). Retrieved from http://dsq-sds.org/article/view/1767/3096

Mindell, A. (1982). *Dreambody: The body's role in revealing itself*. Boston, MA: Sigo.

Mindell, A. (2000). *Working on yourself alone: Inner dreambody work*. Portland, OR: Lao Tse.

Moules, N. J. (1999). Guest Editorial. Suffering together: Whose words were they? *Journal of Family Nursing, 5*(3), 251–258.

Moules, N. J. (2002). Hermeneutic inquiry: Paying heed to the history and Hermes. An ancestral, substantive, and methodological tale. *International Journal of Qualitative Methods, 1*(3), 1–21.

Munson, C. E. (2001). *The mental health diagnostic desk reference*. New York, NY: Haworth.

Murphy, A. (2013, March 11). A tribute to the greats—Charlie and Edie seashore. Retrieved from http://www.beaconassociates.net/node/279

Muscular Dystrophy Association. (2011). Jerry Lewis completes run as MDA national chairman [Press release]. http://static.mda.org/news/110803.html

Nagarjuna. (1995). *The fundamental wisdom of the middle way: Nāgārjuna's mūlamadhyamakakārikā* (J. L. Garfield, Trans.). Oxford, England: Oxford University Press.

Niwa, C., & Wilson, W. S. (2012). *The demon's sermon on the martial arts: And other tales*. Boston, MA: Shambhala.

Orange, D. (2011). *The suffering stranger: Hermeneutics for everyday clinical practice*. New York, NY: Routledge.

Oxford English Dictionary (1971). Oxford, England: Oxford University Press.

Packer, M. J. (2011). *The science of qualitative research*. New York, NY: Cambridge University Press.

Pelden, K. (2007). *The nectar of Manjushri's speech*. Boston, MA: Shambala Books.

Perera, S. B. (1981). *Descent to the goddess: A way of initiation for women*. Toronto, Canada: Inner City Books.

Perry, B., & Rosenfelt, J. (2013). *A child's loss: Helping children exposed to traumatic death*. Houston, TX: The Child Trauma Academy Press.

Phelan, A. M. (1996). "Strange pilgrims" disillusionment and nostalgia in teacher education reform. *Interchange, 27*(3), 331–348. doi: 10.1007/bf01807411

Phillips, D. C., & Burbules, N. C. (2000). *Postpositivism and educational research*. Lanham, MD: Rowman & Littlefield.

Pinar, W. (1995). *Understanding curriculum: An introduction to the study of historical and contemporary curriculum discourses*. New York, NY: Peter Lang.

Pinar, W. (2011). *The character of curriculum studies: Bildung, currere, and the recurring question of the subject*. New York, NY: Palgrave MacMillan.

Postel, D., & Drury, S. (2003, October 18). Noble lies and perpetual war: Leo Strauss, the Neo-Cons, and Iraq. Danny Postel interviews Shadia Drury. Retrieved from http://www.informationclearinghouse.info/article5010.htm

Privilege. (2012). Retrieved from http://www.oxforddictionaries.com/definition/english/privilege

Reeves, G. (2008). *The lotus sutra*. Boston, MA: Wisdom.

Reich, W. (1972). *Character analysis* (V. R. Carfagno, Trans.). New York, NY: Farrar, Strauss, and Giroux.

RenegadeEconomist. (2011, July 8). *Noam Chomsky—on Darwinism* [Video file]. Retrieved from http://www.youtube.com/watch?v=RjermDZ1qfI

Richardson, K. (Producer & Director). (2005). *The kids are alright* [Motion picture]. USA: The Paul Robeson Fund for Independent Media.

Ricoeur, P. (2007). *Reflections on the just*. Chicago, IL: University of Chicago Press.

Robinson, D. (Producer). (2011, June 25). *Just what is Kant's project?* [Audio podcast]. Retrieved from http://podcasts.ox.ac.uk/people/dan-robinson

Rogers, C. R. (1961). *On becoming a person: A therapist's view of psychotherapy*. Boston, MA: Houghton Mifflin.

Ross, S. (2006). The temporality of tarrying in Gadamer. *Theory Culture Society*, *23*(1), 101–123.

Ross, S., & Jardine, D. (2009, February). Won by a certain labour: A conversation on the while of things. *Journal of the American Association for the Advancement of Curriculum Studies*, *5*. Retrieved from http://www2.uwstout.edu/content/jaaacs/Vol5/Ross_Jardine.htm

Rousseau, J. J. (1953). *The confessions*. (J. Cohen, Trans.) New York, NY: Penguin.

Saint Jerome (1964). Homily 40: On Psalm 115 (116B). In *The fathers of the church # 48. The homilies of Saint Jerome, volume I (1–59 on the psalms)* (M. Liguori, S. Ewald, Trans., pp. 293–299). Washington, DC: The Catholic University of America Press.

Santoka, T. (2009). *Mountain tasting: Haiku and journals of Santoka Teneda* (J. Stevens, Trans.). Buffalo, NY: White Pine Press.

Sartre, J. P. (1970). Intentionality: A fundamental idea in Husserl's phenomenology. *Journal for the British Society for Phenomenology*, *1*(2), 3–5.

Schellenbaum, P. (1990). *The wound of the unloved: Releasing the life energy* (T. Nevill, Trans.). Dorset, England: Element Books. (Original work published 1988)

Scherman, N. R. (Ed.). (1996). *Tanach*. Brooklyn, NY: Mesorah.

Schneider, K. (2004). *Rediscovery of awe: Splendor, mystery, and the fluid center of life*. St. Paul, MN: Paragon House.

Schrift, A. (1997). *The logic of the gift: Toward an ethic of generosity*. New York, NY: Routledge.

Seidel, J. (2014). Losing wonder: Thoughts on nature, mortality, education. In J. Seidel & D. Jardine, *Ecological pedagogy, Buddhist pedagogy, hermeneutic pedagogy: Experiments in a curriculum for miracles*. New York, NY: Peter Lang.

Seidel, J., & Jardine, D. (2014). *Ecological pedagogy, Buddhist pedagogy, hermeneutic pedagogy: Experiments in a curriculum for miracles*. New York, NY: Peter Lang.

Shakespeare, T. (2002). The social model of disability: An outdated ideology? *Research in Social Science and Disability*, *2*, 9–28.

Simms, K. (2003). *Paul Ricoeur*. London, England; New York, NY: Routledge.

Simms, L. (2000). Crossing into the invisible—How the storyteller guides us into an unseen realm. *Parabola, 25*(1), 62–68.

Simon, M. (Ed.). (1990). *Hebrew-English edition of the Babylonian Talmud* (M. Simon, Trans.). London, England: Soncino Press.

Simpson, B. (May 23, 2012). Mike Ervin explains why Stand Up Chicago is protesting at the Chicago mercantile exchange (cbot). Retrieved from http://www.youtube.com/watch?v=BXN5a9wW4sc

Slee, R. (1995). *Changing theories and practices of discipline*. London, England; Washington, DC: Falmer Press.

Slee, R. (2010). *Irregular schooling: Special education, regular education and inclusive education*. London, England: Routledge.

Slee, R. (2011). *The irregular school: Exclusion, schooling, and inclusive education*. London, England; New York, NY: Routledge.

Slee, R. (2013). How do we make inclusive education happen when exclusion is a political predisposition? *International Journal of Inclusive Education*, *17*(8), 895–907. doi:10.1080/13603116.2011.602534

Slee, R., & Allan, J. (2001). Excluding the included: A recognition of inclusive education. *International Studies in Sociology of Education*, *11*(2), 173–191.

Smart Ass Cripple. (n.d). Smart Ass Cripple [Blog side panel]. Retrieved from http://smartasscripple.blogspot.ca/

Smart Ass Cripple. (2010, October 27). The Washington rancid spuds [Blog post]. Retrieved from http://smartasscripple.blogspot.ca/2010/10/washington-rancid-spuds.html

Smart Ass Cripple. (2010, November 17). Gorilla suit [Blog post]. Retrieved from http://smartasscripple.blogspot.ca/2010/11/gorilla-suit.html

Smart Ass Cripple. (2011, January 21). Oprah's death squads [Blog post]. Retrieved from http://smartasscripple.blogspot.ca/2011_01_21_archive.html

Smart Ass Cripple. (2012, June 11). Ain't nobody takin' my cripple away [Blog post]. Retrieved from http://smartasscripple.blogspot.ca/2012_06_11_archive.html

Smart Ass Cripple. (2012, June 20). Four out of five cripples prefer a kick in the crotch [Blog post]. Retrieved from http://smartasscripple.blogspot.ca/2012/06/four-out-of-five-cripples-prefer-kick.html

Smart Ass Cripple. (2012, July 2). Coulda beena borted [Blog post]. Retrieved from http://smartasscripple.blogspot.ca/2012/07/coulda-beena-borted.html

Smart Ass Cripple. (2012, September 14). Where's the keeper? [Blog post]. Retrieved from http://smartasscripple.blogspot.ca/2012/09/wheres-keeper.html

Smart Ass Cripple. (2012, October 2). The legend of crippled Clint Eastwood [Blog post]. Retrieved from http://smartasscripple.blogspot.ca/2012_10_02_archive.html

Smart Ass Cripple. (2013, January 3). Pit crew [Blog post]. Retrieved from http://smartasscripple.blogspot.co.uk/2013/01/pit-crew.html

Smart Ass Cripple. (2013, February 17). The day I quit walking day [Blog post]. Retrieved from http://smartasscripple.blogspot.ca/2013/02/the-day-i-quit-walking-day.html

Smart Ass Cripple. (2013, February 22). One last laugh [Blog post]. Retrieved from http://smartasscripple.blogspot.co.uk/2013/02/one-last-laugh.html

Smart Ass Cripple. (2013, May 26). A perfect People Magazine death [Blog post]. Retrieved from http://smartasscripple.blogspot.ca/2013_05_26_archive.html

Smart Ass Cripple. (2013, May 31). Life lessons learned at SHIT [Blog post]. Retrieved from http://smartasscripple.blogspot.ca/2013_05_31_archive.html

Smart Ass Cripple. (2013, June 17,) Branded. [Blog post] Retrieved from http://smartasscripple.blogspot.ca/2013_06_17_archive.html

Smart Ass Cripple. (2013, July 28). Pit crew members say the darndest cute things [Blog post]. Retrieved from http://smartasscripple.blogspot.ca/2013/07/pit-crew-members-say-darndest-cute.html

Smart Ass Cripple. (2013, September 2). Smart Ass Cripple as a role model [Blog post]. Retrieved from http://smartasscripple.blogspot.ca/2013/09/smart-ass-cripple-as-role-model.html

Smart Ass Cripple. (2013, September 7). Amazing and astounding [Blog post]. Retrieved from http://smartasscripple.blogspot.ca/2013/09/amazing-and-astounding.html

Smart Ass Cripple. (2013, October 21). I was a college Marxist [Blog post]. Retrieved from http://smartasscripple.blogspot.ca/2013/10/i-was-college-marxist.html

Smith, D. G. (1999). *Pedagon: Interdisciplinary essays in the human sciences, pedagogy and culture.* New York, NY: Peter Lang.

Smith, D. G. (2006). *Trying to teach in a season of great untruth: Globalization, empire and the crises of pedagogy.* Boston, MA; Rotterdam, The Netherlands: Sense.

Smith, D. G. (2006). The specific challenges of globalization for teaching and vice versa. In D. G. Smith, *Trying to teach in a season of great untruth: Globalization, empire and the crises of pedagogy* (pp. 15–34). Rotterdam, The Netherlands: Sense.

Smith, D. G. (2014). *Teaching as the practice of wisdom.* New York, NY: Bloomsbury Press.

Smith, P. (2006). Split——ting the ROCK of {speci[ES]al} e.ducat.tion: FLOWers of lang[ue] age in >DIS<ability studies. In S. Danforth & S. L. Gabel (Eds.), *Vital questions facing disability studies in education* (pp. 33–61). New York, NY: Peter Lang.

Snow, K. (2009). *People first language national inclusion project.* Retrieved from http://inclusionproject.org/nip_userfiles/file/People%20First%20In%20Depth.pdf

Snyder, G. (1990). Survival and sacrament. In G. Snyder, *The practice of the wild* (pp. 175–185). Berkley, CA: Counterpoint Books.

Spiegelman, J. M., & Miyuki, M. (1994). *Buddhism and Jungian psychology.* Tempe, AZ: New Falcon.

Springer Publishing Company. (2013, October 4). *Disenfranchised grief: Dr. Ken Doka* [Video file]. Retrieved from http://www.youtube.com/watch?v=BhfxzY65SmI

Suffer. (2001). Retrieved from http://www.etymonline.com/index.php?search=suffer&searchmode=term

Tait, G. (2010). *Philosophy, behaviour disorders, and the school*. Boston, MA; Rotterdam, The Netherlands: Sense.

Taylor, F. W. (1911). *The principles of scientific management*. New York, NY: Harper & Brothers.

Thompson, W. I. (1998). *Coming into being: Artifacts and texts in the evolution of consciousness*. New York, NY: St. Martin's.

Titchkosky, T. (2001). Disability: A rose by any other name? "People-first" language in Canadian society. *Canadian Review of Sociology*, 125–140. doi: 10.1111/j.1755-618X.2001. tb00967.x

Titchkosky, T. (2008). "To pee or not to pee?" Ordinary talk about extraordinary exclusions in a university environment. *Canadian Journal of Sociology*, *33*(1), 37–60. Retrieved from http:// ejournals.library.ualberta.ca/index.php/CJS/article/view/1526/1058

Trungpa, C. (1991). *The heart of the Buddha: Entering the Tibetan Buddhist path*. Boston, MA: Shambhala.

Trungpa, C. (2003). The myth of freedom and the way of meditation. In C. Gimian (Ed.), *The collected works of Chogyam Trungpa, volume three*. Boston, MA: Shambhala Press.

Tsong-kha-pa. (2000). *The great treatise on the stages of the path to enlightenment* (Vol. 1). Ithaca, NY: Snow Lion.

Tsong-kha-pa. (2002). *The great treatise on the stages of the path to enlightenment* (Vol. 3). Ithaca, NY: Snow Lion.

Tsong-kha-pa. (2004). *The great treatise on the stages of the path to enlightenment* (Vol. 2). Ithaca, NY: Snow Lion.

Valle, J. W., & Connor, D. J. (2011). *Rethinking disability: A disability studies approach to inclusive practices*. New York, NY: McGraw-Hill.

Von Humbolt, W. (2000 [1793–1794]). Theory of Bildung. In I. Westbury, S. Hopmann, & K. Riquarts (Eds.), *Teaching as a reflective practice: The German Didaktik tradition* (G. Horton-Krüger, Trans., pp. 57–61). Mahwah, NJ: Lawrence Erlbaum.

Wallace, B. (1987). *The stubborn particulars of grace*. Toronto, Canada: McClelland & Stewart.

Wallis, G. (2007). *Basic teachings of the Buddha*. New York, NY: Modern Library.

Weiner, J. (2011). The end of the Jerry Lewis telethon—it's about time. Retrieved from http:// www.thenation.com/blog/163119/end-jerry-lewis-telethon-its-about-time

Weinsheimer, J. (1985). *Gadamer's hermeneutics*. New Haven, CT: Yale University.

Weinsheimer, J. (1991). Gadamer's metaphorical hermeneutics. In H. G. Gadamer & H. J. Silverman (Eds.), *Gadamer and hermeneutics* (pp. 181–201). New York, NY: London.

Weis, C. T. (2010). People with disabilities and human exploitation. *Disabled World*. Retrieved from http://www.disabled-world.com/editorials/human-exploitation.php

Wente, M. (2012). Is anybody normal anymore? *The Globe and Mail*. Retrieved from http:// www.theglobeandmail.com/news/opinions/margaret-wente/is-anybody-normal-anymore/article2423352/

Wheatley, M. (2009). Beyond fear and hope. *Shambhala Sun*, 79–83.

Williams, P. (2009). *Mahayana Buddhism: The doctrinal foundations* (2nd ed.). New York, NY: Routledge.

Williamson, W. J., & Paul, W. J. (2012). The level playing field: Unconcealing diploma exam accommodation policy. *Journal of Applied Hermeneutics*. Retrieved from http://hdl.handle.net/10515/sy5f766p2

Winzer, M. A. (2009). *From integration to inclusion: A history of special education in the 20th century.* Washington, DC: Gallaudet University Press.

Wittgenstein, L. (1968). *Philosophical investigations* (G. E. M. Anscombe, Trans.). Oxford, England: Basil Blackwell. (Original work published 1953)

Wright, D. (2011). *Downs: The history of a disability.* New York, NY: Oxford University Press.

Yates, F. (1974). *The art of memory.* Chicago, IL: University of Chicago Press.

Young, A. (1995). *The harmony of illusions: Inventing post traumatic stress disorder.* New Jersey, NJ: Princeton University Press.

Zabel, R. H., Kaff, M. S., & Teagarden, J. M. (2011). An oral history of first-generation leaders in education of children with emotional/behavioral disorders, Part 2: Important events, developments, and people. *Journal of Emotional and Behavioral Disorders, 19*(3), 131–142.

Zheleznova, I. L. (1966). *Vasilisa the beautiful: Russian fairy tales.* Moscow, Russia: Progress.

Index

II Chronicles 36:16, 154

A

ableism, 124–25, 128–29, 131, 135, 137, 139
abnormality. *See also* exclusion
    as behaviour problems in children,
        29–46, 213–25
    as mental illness, 92–93, 200–202, 204–5
    as physical disability, 46, 125, 218–19,
        224
Abram, David, 9, 109–10
abuse, 141–43
activism, 125–26, 129, 137
ADHD. *See* Attention Deficit Hyperactivity
    Disorder
adversity, 26, 148–51
Aeschylus, 3, 16, 177, 220
    pathei mathos and, 118, 228
aesthetic, 34, 88, 127–28, 133, 135, 138–39,
    233–34
affinities, 3, 89, 111, 246, 248

alethia, 22, 51
Allan, Julie, 127–29, 134, 136
anger
    in children, 30–31, 72–73, 77
    compassion and, 51
    grief and, 116–20, 158–65
    physical disabilities and, 30–31 (*See also*
        Smart Ass Cripple)
    suffering and, 22–23, 27, 100, 130, 187,
        190, 219
anxiety, 23, 97, 100, 119, 188–90, 214, 218
Anxiety Disorder, 40, 55
Aoki, Ted, 8, 146
Aquinas, Thomas, 162
Arendt, Hannah, 121, 158, 160, 235
Aristotle
    logic of non-contradiction, 32–33, 236
    mensuratio ad rem, 32–33, 85
    phronesis, 160, 176
Armstrong, Karen, 20–22
attachment, 14, 50–52, 71, 103–4, 112, 194.
    See also letting go
        Buddhism and, 7, 124, 168

interpretation as non-attachment, 112, 222, 224–25, 229

Attention Deficit Hyperactivity Disorder (ADHD), 35, 40, 73

authenticity, 3, 13, 57–59, 65, 193, 242. *See also* inauthenticity

B

Baba Yaga, 101

back to the basics, 9

Barker, Phillip, 91

Bava Metzia, 83b, 85a, 151, 153, 156

Bayer, Thora Ilin, 162

behaviour problems. *See* Emotional and Behavioural Disabilities

Behaviourism, 33–35, 223

Being
as becoming someone, 3, 101–6, 147–48, 159, 180–81, 233, 241

hermeneutics and, 50, 163–65, 177–78, 236, 240–41

phenomenology and, 11, 100, 236–37, 242

radiant being and, 247–49

towards death, 38, 136–38, 145–46, 175, 192, 196

belonging, 11, 134, 218, 225, 240. *See also* exclusion; isolation
Maslow's Pyramid and, 199–201, 203, 211

Berakoth, 5b, 150

Berry, Wendell, 112, 114–15, 118–19, 121–22, 158, 162–63, 220

Bildung, 3, 159, 180, 233. *See also* soul making

binaries, 35–36, 39, 219. *See also* duality

bipolar disorder, 201–5

body, 205–11

Borderline Personality Disorder, 55, 201–5, 207

Buber, Martin, 55

Buckman, Robert, 174–75, 178, 181–82

Buddhism
compassion and, 19–27, 58–65

First Noble Truth of, 89, 99, 190

four modes of consciousness and, 58

Gelug tradition of, 228–30, 233, 235–38, 240–49

impermanence and, 115, 124, 187

key insights of, 3, 19, 172

mindfulness in education and, 168, 172, 188–97

practice and, 228–30, 232–49

resources for counselling relationships and, 19–26, 51, 53–62, 73, 183–97

resources for mental health nursing and, 89–98

sati (mindfulness), about, 58, 188–90

on suffering, 3, 19–26, 89, 96–100

witness consciousness and, 58–62

Buddhism, Mahayana, 19, 23–24, 26
Avalokitesvara (The Cry Regarder), 26–27

Buddhism, Vajrayana, 19
Zen, 19, 27, 53, 146, 172

C

Camus, Albert, 172

Canadian Mental Health Association, 95

cancer, 38, 75–81, 83–85, 87, 141, 145, 173–81. *See also* oncology

Cancer Is a Word, Not a Sentence (Buckman), 175

Caputo, John D., 114, 124, 126–27, 131, 138

caring, 16, 112, 134, 172. *See also* compassion

character, cultivation of, 3, 148, 159, 164

Charter for Compassion, The, 20–22

Chesterton, G.K., 124

classroom practice
hermeneutics and, 2, 10–12, 110, 234–48

special education and, 29–46, 213–17

youth counselling and, 183–97

Clinical Depression, 55
co-arising, 229–30, 233, 235, 238–49.
 See also co-generative spaces
Codes (Williamson), 67–69
codification
 program funding and, 41, 213–14
 students and, 31–33, 36–38, 41–47,
  67–69, 219, 225
co-generative spaces, 183–90, 195, 197, 224
community, 230
 common sense and, 159–65
compassion. *See also* Buddhism; nursing
 Buddhism and, 2–3, 14, 19–27, 58–65,
  171–72
 in counselling relationships, 51, 53–65,
  183–97
 definition of, 58
 essentialism and, 22–24
 in healthcare, 22, 97–98, 211
 as hermeneutic endeavour, 112, 164,
  168, 171–72, 177, 228, 241
 as idiot compassion, 19–27
 in schools, 72, 156, 171–72, 190, 195,
  223–24
composition/composure, 111, 229, 244–49
Comte, Auguste, 33, 38
Confessions, The (Rousseau), 147, 149
conflict, 3, 21, 32, 186–88, 217
consciousness. *See also* Buddhism; Daoism
 education and, 44, 116, 148, 172
 enlightenment, 58, 60, 62, 65, 228–29,
  247–49
 human states of, 20, 44, 55, 58–59
 market, 10, 40, 114–18, 134, 164
 mindfulness and, 189–91
 suffering and, 60, 84, 103–4, 138,
  209
 transcendental, 8, 11–12, 14–15, 21, 50,
  54, 124
constructivism, 49, 237
consumer culture, 22, 39–40, 115, 119
contingence, 3, 10–11, 42, 178, 182, 239
conviviality, 34, 46
counselling relationships, 53–67, 183–97

counter-productivity, 44–45, 186, 217–19,
 223–24
Craighead, Peter, 174
*Crisis of European Science and Transcendental
 Phenomenology, The* (Husserl), 8
curriculum-as-lived, 8, 223, 241
cycles of suffering, 50–51, 71–73, 115–17,
 146, 216, 225
 bi-polar disorder and, 202–5
 iatrogenic loops and, 163–65

D

Dalai Lama, 232
Daoism, 54, 62–65
Dasein, 248
Davis, Leonard J., 125
death-trance, 63
delusion
 anger and, 50–51, 73
 Buddhism on, 7, 25, 115, 236–37, 244
 ego and, 60, 70, 190
 ignorance and, 237
 love and, 92–93, 200, 204
 mental illness and, 90–92, 96–98,
  199–201
demeaning, 123–25, 130, 132, 138
Derrida, Jacques, 111
Descartes, Rene, 9, 33, 45, 125, 236
Descent into the Womb Sutra, 1
destabilization, 142–43
Dewey, John, 127, 148
Dharma, 23, 172, 233, 242
*Diagnostic and Statistical Manual of Mental
 Disorders* (DSM), 32, 35, 37–38, 90–92,
 97–98, 213
Dialectical Behavioural Therapy, 202, 207
Dilthey, Wilhelm, 9
disability. *See also* Emotional and
 Behavioural Disabilities
 aesthetic of, 127–29
 as difference, 39, 42–43, 46, 128
 language of, 124–39

two mindsets regarding, 127, 131
disability studies, 123–39, 230
distancing, strategies of, 58, 94–95
Dong-Shan, 146
Down Syndrome people, 123, 134–35
DSM. *See Diagnostic and Statistical Manual of Mental Disorders*
DSM IV,V, 90–91
duality, 54, 60, 103, 218–20, 223–24

E

EBD. *See* Emotional and Behavioural Disabilities
ecology, 3, 21, 114–15, 216, 221
education. *See also pathei mathos*
    as becoming someone, 3, 159, 180, 233
    dual system of, 213–25
    EBD, Special Education and, 31–47, 212–17
    hermeneutics and, 4, 49, 111–18, 161–65, 183–97, 231–49
    mindfulness in, 188–91
    as moving towards suffering, 231–49
    punishment "for your own good" and, 167–68, 219, 228
    as relief from suffering, 151–56, 231–49
    rules and, 160–65
    study of Torah and, 152–56
    as suffering transformation, 149
educational psychology, 37–39, 41–46, 212–17
ego, 34, 36, 60, 72, 131, 190, 219, 223. *See also* delusion; letting go
    flight response and, 195
    release of, 26, 101, 103–5
eidetic phenomenology, 10–13, 15, 229. *See also* reductionism
eidos (essence), 11–13, 16
Elazar ben Azariah, Rabbi, 151–53, 155
Eliot, T.S., 101, 104, 183, 196
emergence, 10, 25, 59, 114, 234–35
Emotional and Behavioural Disabilities (EBD), 29–46, 213–25

codification of, 31–33, 36–38, 41–47, 213–14, 219
    diagnosis and, 38–41, 44
empathy, 58–59, 98, 104–5, 134, 142. *See also* compassion
emptiness, 23, 73, 237–38, 242–44, 248
enlightenment, 58, 60, 62, 65, 228–29, 247–49
Enlightenment rationality, 10, 34–35
Epstein Barr virus, 105
Erfahrung, 100, 161, 228
Ervin, Mike (aka Smart Ass Cripple), 129–39
essentialism, 11–13, 15–16, 20–24, 32–33, 228–29. *See also* eidos
esteem, 45–46, 121, 199, 201, 203, 211
exclusion, 41, 43, 69, 125–26, 134. *See also* isolation
experience. *See also* life-world
    hermeneutic, 3, 50, 92, 123, 161–65, 175–82, 231–48
    phenomenology and, 9–12, 15–16, 100, 233, 236–37, 242

F

facticity, 11–13
failure. *See* school failure
Faust (Goethe), 101
fear
    hermeneutical inquiry and, 115–22, 197
    illness and, 23, 61–63, 77–81, 83, 85–86, 174–82
    as panicky retreats, 3, 50–51, 71, 120–21, 158, 165, 168
    process of change and, 101, 106, 141–43
    teaching and, 35, 111, 115–16, 222
    troubled youth and, 187, 189–91, 195–96
fellowship, 230. *See also* community
Fields, Rick, 241
finitiude, 12–13, 50, 100, 123, 125, 138, 232–33. *See also* impermanence; permanence

First Noble Truth, 89, 99–100, 190
fixity, 13, 164, 246
forgetting (elision), 44, 91–96
    as formative process, 167–68
Foucault, Michel, 218–19
Frances, Allen, 37
Freire, Paulo, 88
Freud, Sigmund, 189
Full Catastrophe Living (Kabat-Zinn), 189
F[ull] T[ime] E[quivalent], 163–65
funding, 41, 114–22, 126, 129–31

G

Gabel, Susan L., 125, 127–28
Gadamer, Hans-Georg
    about, 8, 15–17, 34–35
    Being and Time, 16
    hermeneutic practice and, 44, 87–88,
        110–13, 164, 173–82, 215–21,
        238–47
    Hermeneutics and Psychiatry, 176
    interpretive inquiry and, 29–44, 50,
        83–86, 227–29, 234–35, 238, 245
    limits of rationality and, 35–37
    pathei mathos and, 100–111, 118,
        177–78, 238–47
    pathways of understanding and, 83–86,
        121, 178, 225, 231–33
    phenomenology and, 13, 22, 51, 235–37
    scholarship and, 158–65, 245
    Truth and Method, 15–16, 49, 88,
        157–59, 161, 177, 233, 238
Gelug tradition (of Tibetan Buddhism), 235,
    246–47
gender and identity issues, 185
generosity, 2, 84
Gift: Imagination and the Erotic Life of Prop-
    erty, The (Hyde), 231–32
Golden Age, 21
Great Treatise on the Stages of the Path to En-
    lightenment, The (Tsong-kha-pa), 228
Greenberg, Gary, 35, 37–38, 40
grief, 3, 14–15, 27, 91, 157, 228, 241

Guanyin, 26

H

Hades, 101–2
Hahn, Thich Nat, 54, 239
haiku, 27, 146
Havel, Vaclav, 197
healthcare, 22, 27, 105
healthcare reform, 20, 131
Heidegger, Martin, 8, 13–16, 51, 100, 112,
    136
    hermeneutic experience and, 233,
        236–37, 242, 248
Heraclitus, 13, 102
hermeneutic philosophy. *See also* Gadamer,
    Kearney, Ricoeur
    in depth psychology, 102–6
    in education, 49, 111–18, 183–97,
        215–17, 220–21
    as emancipatory philosophy, 29–46,
        49–50
    as emptiness, 237–38, 241, 243–45
    as interpretive writing, 75–81, 85–88,
        107–22, 157–65, 235
    in mental health, 89–107, 199–211
    in oncology, 75–81, 173–83
    as openness, 16, 50, 72, 162, 207, 223,
        227
    as repeated practice, 10, 111, 158, 161,
        168, 229–49
    in scholarship, 71–73, 107–22, 155,
        162–65, 168, 171–72
    in teaching, 10, 160–62, 228–29,
        231–32, 234–35, 240
    as a way of being, 164–65
hermeneutic writing, 75–81, 85–88, 107–22,
    157–65, 244–49
Hermeneutics of Postmodernity: Figures and
    Themes, The (Madison), 15
Hierarchy of needs. *See* Maslow's Pyramid
Hillman, James, 88, 102–6, 110, 112,
    233–34, 240
Hirsch, E.D., 15

hopelessness, 189, 196

hubris, 10, 24

Hughes, Donna, 205

Humanist tradition, 3, 54, 159–62, 180

humility, 105, 176

humour. *See* Ervin, Mike (aka Smart Ass
    Cripple)

Husserl, Edmund, 8–16, 22, 51, 88, 236–37
    eidos and, 11–13, 229
    Protodoxa (Urdoxa) and, 235–37

Hyde, Lewis, 2, 106, 231–32

I

iatrogenic illness (doctor-made), 29, 37,
    115–17. *See also* Illich

iatrogenic looping, 163–65

idealization, 19, 23

Ideas Towards a Pure Phenomenology
    (Husserl), 13

identity, 25, 45, 62, 94, 172, 185, 187
    difference and, 13, 31, 34–35, 223
    scholarship and, 157–65
    substance and, 33–34, 223, 237–38

ignorance, 7, 73, 151, 189–90
    of ableist thinking, 134–35, 139
    delusion and, 237–38
    as welcome guest, 190–91

Illich, Ivan, 30, 33, 35–40, 44, 158, 218, 234,
    239

impermanence
    fear and, 50–51
    hermeneutics and, 14–16, 84, 100, 227
    the *life-world* and, 11, 91
    mortality and, 3, 12, 15, 177, 194, 241
    as slender sadness, 145–46

In the Vineyard of the Text (Illich), 158

Inanna and Ereshkigal, myth, 101

inauthenticity, 125, 127, 136

in-between, 73, 179, 216
    as borderline, 92, 95
    as co-generative space, 183–90, 195,
        197, 224

inclusion, 57, 69, 124–25, 129, 220–21, 225.
    See also exclusion

individuation, 102–4

insufferability, 22, 50, 164

interdependence, 232, 238. *See also* co-
    arising; co-generative spaces

inter/intra-subjectivity, 54–55. *See also*
    subjectivism; substance

interpretive tradition
    composition, composure and, 229,
        244–49
    Descartes and, 33
    in education, 183–84, 213–26
    emptiness as particular to, 237–40
    in field of mental health, 96–98, 185–97
    hermeneutic inquiry and, 15, 34, 44,
        71–73, 161, 227–29, 237
    in oncology, 83–86, 173–81
    rabbinical study and, 149–56
    in school psychology, 71–73, 184,
        213–26
    in Special Education, 29–46
    Wittgenstein and, 55

interpretive writing, 75–81, 109–22, 157–65,
    229, 234–35, 244–49

Irregular School, The (Slee), 220

isolation, 62, 75, 77, 93, 105, 132, 218–19

It All Turns on Affection (Berry), 162

J

Jardine, David
    the fecundity of the individual case and,
        12, 174, 179
    Gadamer and, 14–17, 215, 223

Jeremiah 6:11, 154

Jeremiah 9:11, 153

Jeremiah 9:12, 153

Jerome, Saint, 7, 9, 50

Jerry Lewis telethon, 129–31

Jerry's Orphans, 129–31

Job, Book of, 101, 124, 150–51

Johanan bar Nappaha, Rabbi, 149–50

Journal of Applied Hermeneutics, 87
joy, 2, 51, 58, 111–12, 114, 231
    impermanence and, 146, 195, 208
Judah ben Hiyya, Rabbi, 149–50
Jung, Carl, 101–4, 189
Juvenal, 162

K

Kabat-Zinn, Jon, 188
Kannon, 26
Kant, Immanuel, 88, 159
Kasparian, Benjamin, 157, 162–63
Kearney, Richard, 32, 34–36, 71
Kids Are All Right, The (Richardson), 129
knowledge
    good judgement and, 26, 112, 149,
        159–63, 179–81
    health professionals and, 94, 174–82,
        184–86
    as hermeneutic practice, 16, 85, 116,
        118, 222, 236–37, 242–49
    interpretability of the world and, 29–46,
        227–30, 242–46
    as knowing differently, 44, 49–50, 176,
        232, 237–38
    not-knowing and, 189–91, 195–96
    phenomenology and, 10, 13
    prejudice and, 44–45, 135, 237
    wisdom and practice of, 3, 102–4,
        159–62
Kore-Persephone, myth, 101
Kornfield, Jack, 97
Kraepelin, Emil, 38
Kunzang Pelden, 1, 231
Kynicism, 128–29, 132–33

L

Laing, R.D., 54
language
    of behaviour, 225, 239

of Buddhism, 183, 193
of disability, 124, 128, 131, 135, 138–39,
    187
of the heart, 194–95, 234–35, 238
hermeneutics and, 83–86, 164–65,
    234–35, 238–39
of suffering, 34–35, 43, 71, 76, 88,
    101–6, 115
learning and well-being, 154–56, 162–63,
    172
learning through suffering *(pathei mathos)*, 3,
    16, 224–25, 228, 230–32
    Gadamer and, 100–111, 118, 177–78
    hermeneutics and, 177, 180
Lethe, 51. *See also* alethia
letting go, 26, 62, 189, 191, 196–97, 209,
    231
life-world
    Gadamer and, 16, 42–45, 88, 246
    hermeneutics and, 16, 84, 88, 174,
        228–29, 246
    Husserl and, 8, 10–14, 88
    sufferability of, 14, 50, 164, 168, 174
    teaching and, 10, 228
Lingpa, Jigme, 248
Lobsang, Tulku, 235, 238, 241
locales (places of practice)
    of in-between, 73, 179, 184–85, 197,
        216
    of interpretive venture, 2, 75–81, 85,
        111, 161, 190–91, 227–30
    of pedagogy, 111, 161, 215–16
    of scholarship, 110–22, 164–65, 231–49
    of shadows, 91, 101–6
    of staying put, 158–65, 184–85
    of suffering, 3, 22–26, 60–62, 75–81,
        90–95, 101–6, 194–97
    of time, 107, 115–17
    of where you are, 120–22
logos, 34, 42–43, 102
Longchenpa, 242
loss, 2, 39, 45, 56, 90, 93, 174
love
    hermeneutics and, 111–18, 233, 248

interpretive writing and, 75–81
scholarship and, 155, 162–63, 168, 171–72
suffering and, 2, 25, 51–65, 75, 81, 126–27
Loy, David, 57, 60, 237, 241
Lyme Borreliosis, 105

M

Madison, Gary, 8, 15
Mahayana Buddhism, 19, 23–24, 26
Manichaeism, 21–22. *See also* binaries
Manufacturing Depression (Greenberg), 37
marginalization, 137, 161, 222, 224
Maslow, Abraham, 201–8
Maslow's Pyramid, 199–207, 209, 211.
 See also self-actualization
MDA. *See* Muscular Dystrophy Association
meaning. *See also* demeaning
 disability and, 41, 46, 127–28
 hermeneutics and, 178, 220, 242–43
 loss of, 55, 104–5, 197 (*See also* trauma)
 meaning-making, 34–35, 57, 59, 102, 138, 158, 167–69
 phenomenology and, 8, 11, 13–14
 subjectivism and, 229–30, 232–33
 suffering and, 25, 147–57, 167–69
medicine, 3, 33, 38, 42, 104, 175–76
meditation, 3, 54, 58, 188, 228, 232, 243–44, 247. *See also* mindfulness
Melville, Herman, 101
memory, 44, 91–96, 162–65, 167–68
mental illness, 23–25, 53–65, 89–98
Metzger, Arnold, 8
Miller, Alice, 3, 57, 120, 228
mind, 199–205, 232, 244
mindfulness
 body/mind connection and, 202, 205–11
 definitions of, 189, 202
 Dialectical Behavioural Therapy and, 202–5
 as enlightenment, 58–65, 228–29, 247–49

as opening, 191–92, 207–8, 221, 225
pain management and, 208–11
practice in education and, 188–91, 231–49
Vipassana meditation and, 58
Moby Dick (Melville), 101
mortality, 44, 117, 119, 121, 145–46, 150, 177
 suicide and, 192–97
mortificatio, 105
Moules, Nancy, 87, 102, 177
Munson, Carleton E., 90–91
Muscular dystrophy, 129–31
Muscular Dystrophy Association (MDA), 129–31

N

narration-sickness, 88
natural sciences, 9–10, 173–74, 182
 hermeneutical inquiry and, 176–79
neuroscience, 21
 'brain people' and, 72–73
Nishitani Keiji, 236, 238–40
normality, 69, 92, 97, 124, 203, 218, 220–22.
 See also abnormality; stigmatization
normalization, 128, 131, 222–24
norms, 8, 10, 33, 37, 39–43, 46, 136
 exclusion and, 41–44
numbering, 11–12, 30, 174
nursing, 19–27, 89–98, 203–5, 208–10

O

Obsessive Compulsive Disorder (OCD), 73
oncology, 167, 173–81
ontology, 23, 43, 54–55, 110, 164
 emptiness and, 235–37, 242
oppression, Jewish history and, 152–56
Orme, Katy, 2
Orpheus and Eurydice, 91, 94
otherness, 36, 50, 58–62, 64–65, 184–85, 241

stigmatization and, 43, 45–46, 90,
   95–96, 98, 217–19

P

pain. *See also* oncology; suffering
   breaks from, 152, 207–8
   chronic, 203, 205–11
   in counselling relationships, 53–54,
      56–57, 59–64, 183–97
   hermeneutic practices and, 171–72,
      174–81
   mindfulness and, 206, 208–11
pain killers, 206–7
particularities, 88, 179, 222, 242, 248–49
   hermeneutics as science of, 11, 86,
      174–75, 182
pathei mathos, 3, 16, 224–25, 228, 230–32.
   See also learning through suffering
pathology, 33, 42–43, 179, 188, 222
patience, 16, 84, 99, 158–65, 167–68,
   220
   suffering patience and, 109–22
patients, 22–23, 53–54, 178–82
patriarchal-adversary-scapegoating, 104
Patrul, 241–42, 248
Pavlov, Ivan, 34
pedagogy of suffering, 1–4, 17, 19, 101,
   148–56, 219–21. *See also* hermeneutic
   philosophy; interpretive tradition; locales;
   pathei mathos
Pelden, Kunzang, 1, 231
people first, 124, 138–39
Perera, S.B., 101, 104
permanence, 9–12, 14, 50, 196, 229, 236,
   246. *See also* delusion; impermanence
Perry, Bruce, 142
personhood, 138
phenomenology, 8–15, 22, 100, 236–37. *See*
   also Husserl
   eidetic, 10–13
   reductionism and, 11, 51, 222, 229
Picasso, Pablo, 2
Pilgrim's Progress (Bunyan), 101

pity, 127, 129–31, 135, 138, 223
Plato, 15
Pocket of Darkness, A (Innes), 47
positivism, 33–34, 38
Post-Traumatic Stress Disorder, 55
practice. *See also* locales
   application of repeated, 10, 111, 158,
      161, 168, 227–49
   classroom as, 2, 10–11, 30–31, 35, 116,
      172, 183–90
   community as, 160–65
   counselling as, 53–65, 183–97
   of hermeneutic inquiry, 117–22, 159–63,
      227–30, 238–49
   medical, 4, 19–26, 89–98, 173–82
   of mindfulness, 58, 71–73, 171–72,
      188–90, 238–49
   relief of suffering in, 151–56, 168–69,
      171–72
   rules and, 160–65
   of scholarship, 109–22, 149–56, 159–65,
      231–33, 244–46
prejudice, 125, 135, 161, 225, 237, 248
presence, 247–49
problems of living, 90–92, 96
pronunciation, 234–35, 239–44, 247–48
Protodoxa (Urdoxa), 235–37
psychiatry, 3, 31, 38, 42, 104, 176, 187. *See*
   also educational psychology
public education, 29, 40, 115, 213
purity, 11–13

Q

Qi Gong, 63
Question of Phenomenological Immanence, The
   (Jardine), 15
quickening, 109–22

R

rabbinical tradition of inquiry, 149–56
reductionism, 11, 51, 222, 229

Reibstein, Mark, 234
Reich, Wilhelm, 57
reification, 35, 49–50, 72–73, 229, 241
relations, world of, 75–81, 85–88, 229–30, 237–49
religious experience, 32, 56, 126–27, 131, 153
    compassion and, 20–22, 27, 123–24
    Husserl and, 9, 11, 236
Richardson, Kerry, 129–30
Ricoeur, Paul, 34, 38, 41–43, 45–46
right conduct, 3, 13, 26, 114–22, 143, 159–65, 244–45
rights, 39–41
disability, 125, 128, 131, 134, 139
Rogers, Carl, 58–59
Romance, 9, 85
Ross, Sheila, 163–64
Rousseau, Jean-Jacques, 21, 147–49
rules, 160–65, 178–79

S

Sam Houston Institute of Technology (SHIT), 132–33, 136. See also Ervin, Mike
Sanhedrin, 98b, 153
Sante, Luc, 57
Santoka, 27
Schellenbaum, Peter, 56–57
scholarship
    pathei mathos and, 157–65, 231–32
    rabbinical tradition and, 154–56, 167–69
    as relief of suffering, 151–56, 168–69, 231–32
    under surveillance, 114–22
school failure, 187–88
school psychology. See educational psychology
Seashore, Charlie, 189–90
self-actualization, 199–201, 205–7, 211
self-esteem, as relational, 45–46, 121. See also esteem

self-formation. See esteem; identity
sensus communis (common sense). See community
Shabbat, 119b, 154–55
shadows, land of, 7–10, 13–14, 17, 189, 224, 229
    Jung and, 102–3
    as locale of healing, 101–6
    as locale of suffering, 91, 101–6
    suicide and, 194–97
SHIT. See Sam Houston Institute of Technology
Sisyphus, 172, 187
Skinner, B.F., 34–35
Slee, Roger, 34, 40, 42, 126, 134, 220
Smart Ass Cripple, 123–39
Smith, David G., 88, 110, 114–15, 121, 160
Smith, P., 125
Snyder, Gary, 146
Social work, 141–43
Socrates, 15
songlines, 109–22
    singing and, 110–14, 120
Sorge (care), 16, 112
soul making, 101–6, 148–49.
    See also Bildung
spaciousness beyond thought, 88, 191, 232
Special Education, 67, 69, 72, 213–25
    Alberta, Canada and, 224
    EBD and, 29–46, 213–15
    school-to-prison pipeline and, 217
Spell of the Sensuous, The (Abram), 109
stigmatization
    of disability, 95–96
    of mental illness, 90, 95–98, 202–4
    of specialized classroom, 43, 217–19
subjectivism, 12, 34, 49–50, 232–33, 245
    interpretability and, 229–30
    as worlds of relations, 237–49
substance, 14, 33–34, 148, 223, 229, 236–41, 248–49
    no truth in our substance, 7, 9–10, 50
suffering
    as becoming someone, 95–107, 158–65

Buddhism and, 3, 19–26, 89, 96–100, 190
comfort of, 141–43
compassion and, 19–27, 156
in counselling relationships, 53–67, 183–97
definitions of, 53, 91, 99–100, 148
in education, 88, 151–56, 167–69, 171–72, 186–97, 213–25
as form of love, 2, 25, 38, 51–65, 75, 81, 126–27
hermeneutics and, 100–111, 118, 124, 173–81
as isolation, 62, 75, 77, 93, 105, 132, 218–19
in nursing, 19–27, 89–98
pedagogy of, 1–4, 17, 101, 148, 171–72, 219–21
rewards of, 147–49
scholarship as relief from, 151–56, 168–69
suffering from, 123–27. *See also* ableism
suffering is, 150–56
suffering patience, 110, 112, 118, 120–21
suffering with, 12, 24, 53–65, 71–73
suicide. *See* youth suicide
Szasz, Thomas, 91

T

Tai Chi, 63
taxonomy, 89, 91, 97
teaching
    hermeneutics and, 10, 160–62, 177, 228–29, 231–32, 234–35, 240
    patience and, 112–13, 116, 121, 186
    special education and, 30–46, 67, 73, 213–25
    as suffering practice, 81, 88, 147, 151–56, 158–65, 167–69, 194–96
teen years, 186–88, 191–97
theorizing *vs.* application, 232–33
Time (Innes), 107

Titchkosky, Tanya, 123–26, 138
Tom Baker Cancer Centre, 174
transcendence, 15, 21, 59, 124, 232–33, 245
    consciousness and, 8, 11–12, 14–15, 20–21, 50
trauma, 3, 8, 58, 72, 111, 177
treatment, 22–23, 41, 53–55, 76–77, 105, 126, 224
    choice and, 136, 180–82
    mindfulness as, 202–7
    pharmacological, 91, 201–2, 204–5
Trungpa, Chogyam, 20, 25–26
truth
    Correspondence Theory of Truth, 34
    First Noble Truth, 89, 99–100, 190
    natural sciences and, 10, 42
    Noble Truths, 13–14, 23, 73, 96, 103, 112, 172
    personality disorders and, 201–5
    phenomenology and, 8–13, 236–37
Truth and Method (Gadamer), 15–16, 49, 88, 157, 159, 161, 177, 233, 238
Tsong-kha-pa, 51, 73, 228–30, 235–39, 242–44, 246–48
    quotes from, 1, 7, 99, 110, 228–29, 236–37, 247

U

unconscious, 62, 103–4, 189
undergoing
    becoming someone, 3, 101–6, 121, 147–49, 228, 236
    compassion as, 172, 177, 179–80
    as suffering under, 2–3, 53, 91–92, 167–68, 172–73, 245
understanding
    as application, 227–30
    hermeneutics and, 174–81, 220–21, 239–40
    as interpretability of the world, 29–46, 113, 227–30
    as knowing differently, 44, 50, 176, 227

pathways of, 83–86, 121, 178, 225, 231–33, 242–46
"suffering from," 124–25
wisdom and, 168–69, 244, 246
underworld, 91–92, 94, 101–2, 104
universality, 13, 40–41, 83–86, 160, 162, 178–79
  of ignorance, 190
  meaning and, 197
  of suffering, 96, 125, 150–56, 190
  truth and, 34

V

Vico's Principle of Sensus Communis and Forensic Eloquence (Bayer), 161–62
Vipassana (insight) meditation, 58

W

Wabi Sabi (Reibstein and Young), 233–35, 243, 245
Wade, Cheryl Marie, 128
Waste Land, The (Eliot), 101

wisdom, 25–26, 103, 154, 158–65, 168–69, 244, 246
Wittgenstein, Ludwig, 31, 55, 215
worthwhileness, 19, 90, 114, 118, 164–65
  whiling and, 245, 248
wu-wei (no effort), 64

X

X = X, 15, 236–38, 247

Y

Yangsi, 236, 242, 249
Yehudah HaNasi, Rabbi, 156
Young, Ed, 234
youth counselling, 183–97
youth suicide, 191–97

Z

Zen Buddhism, 19, 27, 53, 146, 172

Studies in the Postmodern Theory of Education

General Editor
Shirley R. Steinberg

Counterpoints publishes the most compelling and imaginative books being written in education today. Grounded on the theoretical advances in criticalism, feminism, and postmodernism in the last two decades of the twentieth century, Counterpoints engages the meaning of these innovations in various forms of educational expression. Committed to the proposition that theoretical literature should be accessible to a variety of audiences, the series insists that its authors avoid esoteric and jargonistic languages that transform educational scholarship into an elite discourse for the initiated. Scholarly work matters only to the degree it affects consciousness and practice at multiple sites. Counterpoints' editorial policy is based on these principles and the ability of scholars to break new ground, to open new conversations, to go where educators have never gone before.

For additional information about this series or for the submission of manuscripts, please contact:

Shirley R. Steinberg
c/o Peter Lang Publishing, Inc.
29 Broadway, 18th floor
New York, New York 10006

To order other books in this series, please contact our Customer Service Department:
(800) 770-LANG (within the U.S.)
(212) 647-7706 (outside the U.S.)
(212) 647-7707 FAX

Or browse online by series:
www.peterlang.com